Java Gently

Judy M. Bishop

Department of Computer Science
University of Pretoria

 Addison-Wesley

Harlow, England • Reading, Massachusetts • Menlo Park, California • New York
Don Mills, Ontario • Amsterdam • Bonn • Sydney • Singapore Tokyo • Madrid San
Juan • Milan • Mexico City • Seoul • Taipei

Addison Wesley Longman Limited
Edinburgh Gate
Harlow
Essex CM20 2JE
England

and Associated Companies throughout the World.

Cover designed by odB Design & Communication, Reading
and printed by The Riverside Printing Co. (Reading) Ltd.
Text design by Sally Grover Castle
Illustrations by Pantek Arts, Maidstone
Typeset by 42
Typeset in 10/12pt Times
Printed and bound in Great Britain by Biddles Ltd., Guildford & King's Lynn

First printed 1997

ISBN 0-201-59399-8

British Library Cataloguing-in-Publication Data

A catalogue record for this book is available from the British Library

Library of Congress Cataloging-in-Publication Data
Bishop, J. M. (Judith Mary), 1951-
    Java gentley/Judy M. Bishop.
       p. cm. -- (International computer science series)
    Includes index.
    ISBN 0-201-59399-8 (alk. paper)
    1. Java (Computer program language) I. Title. II. Series.
QA76.73.J38B58   1997
005.13'3--dc21   97-14391
                                                                    CIP

To my dear sons, William and Michael,
who are growing up in the world of the Web.
May they enjoy Java and this book.

Contents

List of examples

Preface

Java Gently is a first programming text. It aims to teach students, as well as those fascinated by the possibilities of their desktop computers, how to program, and how to do it in the best possible style in the Java programming language. In the process, *Java Gently* covers all of the Java language, most of its standard libraries and utilities and the prospects it offers for the future. In terms of programming, it covers object-orientation, software design, structured programming, graphical user interfacing, networking and an introduction to data structures.

A philosophy of teaching Java

When this book began in 1996, the way to teach Java as a first programming language was still uncharted. Those of us who have gone through a change of first programming language more than once know that the one guiding beacon is not to assume that the pattern of teaching a new language will follow that of the old. Java is no exception to this rule.

Two possible approaches

Java is different from its predecessor first languages (Pascal, C++, Ada) in the following ways:

1. It is small, yet object-oriented.

2. It has no built-in data structure types other than the array, but gives access directly to classes that implement a rich variety of data structures.

3. It provides for full graphical user interface (GUI) and multimedia (sound, image and animation) facilities, and promotes GUI programs as applets associated with web browsers.

4.   It provides built-in concurrency features and facilitates programming on the network.

Given this list there seem to be two possible approaches to presenting Java as a first teaching language. The first is immediately attractive: start at point 3; go straight into GUI, multimedia, applets and the whole network environment, thereby catching the students' interest and showing them how modern and different Java really is. The second approach is to start at the beginning, laying a sound foundation of basic concepts, and then moving on to the newer aspects.

Java Gently does **some of both**, as they both have advantages. Starting with applets and GUI is exciting, but requires so much underlying knowledge of objects that even if students learn the outer shell of programs parrot-fashion, they may never fully understand what they are doing. On the other hand, proceeding at a steady pace through all the background first is a sound policy, but can be both boring and overwhelming.

Java Gently's approach

The approach we have devised is a middle ground, which hinges on Java's two main selling points: it is network-enabled but it is small. So we start off with programs that show how the web is used, but then move straight into covering the basic concepts. Because Java has a smaller number of constructs than Pascal or C++, we can spend *less time* here, and therefore can *get back* to the GUI and network aspects sooner, certainly within the first half of a course. Then applets, multimedia, graphics and so on can be introduced properly, to students who have already encountered classes, objects, instantiation and inheritance, and know how to handle them.

Approach is not everything, however, and *Java Gently* uses three other tried and tested teaching techniques:

- diagrams everywhere,
- explanation by example,
- self-check quizzes and problems after every chapter.

There are also three kinds of diagrams used throughout the book:

- **algorithm** diagrams, which show the flow of small programs, and also serve to illustrate new concepts such as exceptions and multi-threading;
- **class** diagrams, which show the structure of the program at the class level, while still revealing the basic components such as methods and variables and the interaction between them;
- **form** diagrams, which show the syntax of each new Java construct in a way that mirrors its usage in practice.

There are over 50 complete fully worked examples, together with test data and output. Each example has been carefully chosen so that it both illustrates the feature that has just been introduced, and also solves a real problem in the best possible Java style. Many of the examples have a 'real world' flavour, which reinforces the need for a programmer to understand the user's problem, and to write programs in a user-friendly way. As soon as a new feature is introduced, it becomes part of the repertoire of the programmer, and will re-emerge in subsequent examples when needed. As the book progresses, the examples get longer and more challenging.

The book subscribes to the belief that Java is, and will be for many years in the future, an excellent first teaching language, and that it is in a different class from its competitors, C++, Pascal and Ada. For that reason, we teach Java properly, with the web, objects and exceptions coming in right at the beginning.

Teaching programming *vs* teaching Java

For a first-year course, it is no longer sufficient to just teach a language. The expectation of today's computer users is that the whole computing milieu will assist in the solution of day-to-day problems. In addition to explaining syntax and the construction of a well-formed program, a programming textbook of the 1990s has to include techniques for problem solving.

Java Gently is indeed such a modern textbook. Each worked problem – and there are over 50 of them – is introduced with a typically inexact statement. This is then refined in the process of devising a solution. Where applicable, the appropriate technique is selected from those previously discussed, and then we proceed to algorithm development. As an additional aid, algorithms are illustrated with structured diagrams, and important techniques are discussed, highlighted and identified for reuse later on. The important programming paradigms of:

- structured programming,

- object-oriented programming,

- class design,

- abstraction,

- software reuse, and

- generality

all receive attention, and examples are carefully chosen to show how these techniques can encourage correctness and efficiency. For example, there are discussions on guidelines for class design, on the relationship between arrays and classes, on the interplay between loops and exceptions, and on the different ways of implementing data structures, to mention just a few.

Order of topics

The topics are grouped into chapters to enable an easy introduction to programming right at the beginning. The order of statements as covered is: output, assignment, for, input, if, while, do, switch. This grouping does not follow that of the Java reference manual, nor of a book intended for someone who already knows programming. It is a pedagogically tried and tested order, which gets the student through the fundamentals of Java, gently, but without undue delay and fuss.

Most of the chapters contain an even mix of program, control and data structure issues, plus some Java specialities. Our experience has shown that this integrated approach to the order of topics has tremendous benefits for motivation and understanding, and that students are able to get ahead and accomplish more in a shorter time, without compromising their assimilation of the principles of Java and programming. The key points of the order of all the material are:

- rapid entry to genuine programming problems;

- the power of object-oriented programming presented with realistic examples from the start;

- exceptions introduced early on and explained as a natural way to control flow between classes;

- 'no fuss' discussion of features that are simple in Java (such as class structure) but in-depth treatment of potentially difficult topics (such as casting and cloning);

- hash tables grouped with arrays to show their efficacy in providing for non-integer indices;

- a custom-made input package, which is used from Chapter 4, and explained in full in Chapter 6 once strings tokenizers have been covered;

- introduction to object references and their implications through the development of a linked list class;

- almost full coverage of the awt (Abstract Windowing Toolkit) facilities, but geared towards examples;

- applets presented through a viewer and a browser, and the differences between applets and applications explained once the student can genuinely appreciate the issues;

- multi-threading done before socket programming, so that the socket programs can illustrate multiple client–server operations.

Full coverage

In terms of full coverage, *Java Gently* ensures that the reader is presented with **all** of the language. Applets and graphics are covered, as are threads. Some of the finer points of

Java's packages are relegated to the description of Java's libraries kept on the web site, but there are pointers to them in the text.

Java Gently aims to excite students and to keep them interested in programming, so the Web aspects of Java are covered, but they are not allowed to overshadow the primary purpose of the book, which is to teach good principles of programming. So much of programming-in-the-web is knowing the correct library method to call, and there is a great deal of repetitive setting of fonts and so on, the details of which can be easily left to a second course.

Because object-oriented programming lends itself to presenting data structures, Part II has a thorough treatment of classical data structures, with mention of sorting and searching algorithms. There is discussion of the standard Java data structures as well as several written especially for the book. *Java Gently* gives its readers a direct entry into a second course syllabus.

Teaching aids

Java Gently contains:

- over 50 fully worked examples and case studies;
- summaries after each chapter;
- ten-point quizzes at the end of each chapter, with solutions;
- over 100 exercises;
- a web site;
- special Text class for augmenting Java's input from the keyboard;
- notations for algorithms and classes resulting in over 50 diagrams;
- a unique way of presenting Java syntax to the novice programmer.

All examples have been tested and run and are available on a web site which will be actively maintained and updated. The web site also contains:

- web pages which introduce the book,
- the multimedia applets,
- a list of the Java libraries used in this edition, and
- solutions to selected exercises.

Who the book is for

The book is intended for students learning to program for the first time in Java, and who have access to the Java Development Kit from Sun, running on PCs, Macs or Unix. There is no reliance in the book on any of the myriad of development environments that are becoming available. Students would normally be in their first year at a university or college, and could be in the science, engineering, commerce or liberal arts faculties: the examples are sufficiently wide-ranging to cater for all. The book does not require mathematical experience, and would certainly be accessible for school pupils taking computer science in senior years. Because there is an emphasis on facts and examples, rather than long discussions, the book would also be suitable for experienced programmers or hobbyists who wish to pick up Java quickly.

The book is based on courses given in Java since 1996, and on courses in other languages presented to science and engineering students at first year university level since 1980. Included are many of the class-tested examples and exercises from these courses. All examples have been tested on JDK 1.0.1 on a Sun (Unix) and PC (Windows 95) as well as via Microsoft's Visual J++. The browser used was Netscape Gold 3.0, as well as earlier versions.

Because technology, and especially Java, is advancing at a rapid rate, it may be that a new version of the Java library is available simultaneously with this book. Consult our web site for the latest information, i.e. www.cs.up.ac.za/javagently.

Acknowledgements

This book was greatly influenced and improved by the reviewers, and I thank them for their time, energy and expertise, given willingly over the festive season. I am grateful to the technical staff and research students in the department who helped solve numerous problems of multimedia networking on multiple platforms: John Botha, Louis Botha, Charl Brits, Henri-John Kock and Alwyn Moolman. The members of the University's Java Interest Group spurred my interest in Java right from the beginning, and we drank many happy cups of coffee together on Monday evenings. Addison-Wesley have surpassed themselves in professional service in getting this book to print on time: my gratitude to Emma Mitchell, Elaine Richardson and their team. Finally, as always, my thanks to Nigel, William and Michael for being so understanding over the summer holiday while I was busy with the book.

Judy Bishop
Pretoria, South Africa
March 1997

Chapter summary

The book is divided into two parts – Part I introduces Java and covers the fundamentals of object-oriented programming (OOP) and programming-in-the-small. The chapters are:

Chapter 1   **Introduction**

All about Java on the web using a multimedia presentation on nature conservation with images and applets. A description of how Java software is developed via the software components of a typical computer (editor, compiler, and so on) plus an introduction to the diagrammatic notations used in the book.

Chapter 2   **Simple programs**

Introduction to Java via two starter programs; fundamentals of classes and objects; all about printing and assignment. Examples involving output and the use of some Java classes such as `Date`.

Chater 3   **Structuring**

The objective of this chapter is to reach a point where programs can be written which do more than a human would be prepared to do! The three areas covered are: Java primitive types, counting loops and methods. Either side of these, there are sections on how to design good programs, and an introduction to the class diagram notation which is used extensively hereafter. A case study which uses multiple classes and objects is used to bring all these points together and to illustrate the class notation in action.

Chapter 4   **Changing the state**

Following naturally on from Chapters 2 and 3, we add facilities to read data, and to make decisions which change the path of a program, either by means of selection statements or by means of exceptions. Exceptions have to be done at this point, because they are intimately bound up with the way input is handled in Java.

Chapter 5   **Controlling the flow**

The last two control structures are discussed – conditional loops and switching. Conditional looping is one of the areas of programming which can be profitably studied at length, and two sections are devoted to loop design. The chapter ends with an interactive game case study which illustrates most of which has gone before.

Chapter 6   **Arrays and tables**

To complete Java's programming-in-the-small capabilities, we consider arrays and their applications. The two array-like classes – `String` and `Hashtable` – are also discussed in detail and there is an explanation of sorting.

At this point, the student can write complete Java applications consisting of several classes interacting via data and method accesses. Part II builds on this foundation by extending the coverage of objects and introducing GUI, applets, networks and data structures.

Chapter 7   **Objects at work**

This chapter centres around a case study of an inventory program, looking at dynamically created objects, linked lists and the rules about objects which Java's strict classing enforces.

Chapter 8   **Inheritance and abstraction**

Java's approach to inheritance is covered with genuine working examples. The chapter discusses interfaces as a really useful alternative to multiple inheritance, and shows how abstract classes are used. Potentially difficult subjects of references and cloning are covered in detail, with diagrams.

Chapter 9   **Graphical user interfaces**

We assume that the student has not encountered GUI programming before and therefore needs to be introduced gently to the different components such as buttons, text fields, frames and canvases. Each new feature is introduced with an example. Event-driven programming is treated seriously as a separate topic, and the chapter winds up with a case study of a supermarket till.

Chapter 10   **Applets in action**

The transition from applications to applets can now be smoothly achieved. The steps for converting applications are given, as well as guidelines for developing applets from scratch. How to add multimedia excitement of sound and images is covered, and the nature conservation system shown in Chapter 1 can now be dissected and explained.

Chapter 11   **Networking**

Java's networking facilities are extensive and novel, so this is one of the longest chapters in the book. It starts by looking at URL (Universal Resource Locator) connections, moves on to threads and synchronization, and ends up with socket programming. There are seven different examples as well as a case study of a chat system.

Chapter 12   **Algorithms and data structures**

Looks at two searching and two sorting algorithms (including Quicksort) and gives an introduction to performance estimation. Classes for stacks (from Java), queues, linked lists and bit sets (from Java again) are then presented with in-depth examples.

Review board

Alan Dearle   University of Stirling
Priscilla Griscom   University of New Haven, Connecticut
Mark Harman   University of North London
Brendan Hodgson   University of Durham
Steven Jenkins   Iowa State University
Mike Joy   University of Warwick
Andrew McGettrick   University of Strathclyde
Narayan Murthy   Pace University, New York
Andy Ormsby   University of Sussex
Sagar Pidaparthi   De Montfort University
Jon Rowson   Queen Mary and Westfield College, University of London
Steve Webster   Bournemouth University

PART I

Fundamentals

CHAPTER 1

Introduction

1.1   Welcome to Java

Java is unlike any other language that has gone before. It is designed to work easily within the World Wide Web of computers through commonly available, user-friendly software called **browsers**. All computers these days have a browser – be it Netscape, Explorer or Mosaic – and all browsers are now **Java-enabled**. This means that you can scan through documents stored all around the world, and at the click of a link, activate a Java program that will come across the network and run on your own computer. You do not even have to know that it is a Java program that is running.

The key advantage of being Java-enabled is that instead of just passive text and images appearing on your screen, calculations and interaction can take place as well. You can send back information to the **host** site, get more Java programs, more documents, and generally perform in a very effective way. Figure 1.1 sums up the circle of activity that takes place with a Java-enabled browser. Java programs that run on the web are actually called **applets** (short for 'little applications'), and we shall use this term from now on

Another important property of Java is that it is **platform-independent**. This means that it is independent of the kind of computer you are using. You may have a Macintosh, or a Pentium, a Silicon Graphics or a Sun JavaStation. Java applets do not mind. They are stored on a **host site** in such a way that they can run on any computer that has a Java-enabled browser.

3

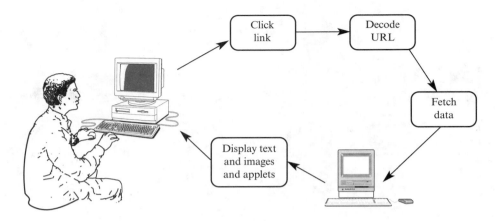

Figure 1.1 *Browsing the World Wide Web with Java applets (URL = Universal Resource Locator).*

So what does Java-enabled mean? It means that inside the browser there is a program known as a **Java Virtual Machine** (JVM) which can run Java for that particular computer. The Java that comes over the net is in a standard form known as **Bytecode**. Your JVM can understand the applet in Bytecode and make it work properly on your particular computer. That is why if you get an applet when running under Windows, it will have a Windows 'look and feel' to its buttons and layout. If you pull the same applet down onto a Macintosh, it will look like a typical Mac program. Figure 1.2 sums up this process.

Figure 1.2 *A Java applet going to two different computer types X and Y.*

Enough of theory. What are applets actually good for, and what would one really look like? Let us now consider an example especially set up on *Java Gently's* web site. This site can be found at the URL[1] http://www.cs.up.ac.za /javagently.

The Nature Conservation project

As part of its international outreach programme, the country of Savanna (situated on the grasslands of Africa) is funding a project to make information about nature available on the web. Rather than just finding an electronic book, visitors to the web site will be able to make enquiries about animals, birds or trees that they have spotted, and even to contribute interactively to the information on the site. Consider the web pages from the first version of the site, shown in Figures 1.3 to 1.5. It all looks pretty interesting, and even impressive, but where is the Java?

Figure 1.3 *The first page of the web site, showing two links to animals and trees.*

---

[1]The term URL, also referred to in Figure 1.1, stands for Universal Resource Locator. It is a unique reference to a document on the web, usually consisting of a protocol such as http and the name of the site or computer where the item is stored, followed by some subdirectory information.

Figure 1.4   *The second web page, showing images and text.*

The fact that it is not obvious is a tribute to Java's usefulness and power. The first web page (Figure 1.3) announces the project and gives the links to the three proposed sections. The birds section is not yet ready, so the link is not enabled. If we click on the animals link, we get Figure 1.4. The animal section is just pictures at the moment, but the section on trees (Figure 1.5) has a table showing how to codify a tree according to its leaf appearance. You are then invited to enter in three values related to your tree. This is the applet at work, running quietly on your machine should you want it. Once it has three values, it calculates a tree code and then asks the browser to bring down from the web site information about that specific tree. For the information as entered, the web page could contain a picture of a Milkplum tree, plus information about its seeds, flowers and habitat. There is more about this applet in Section 10.4.

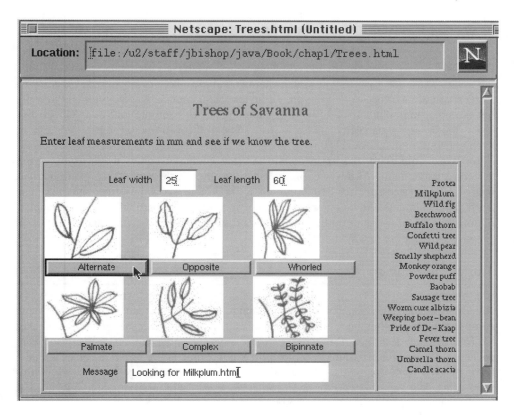

Figure 1.5   *The Trees web page with an applet at the bottom.*

Should the applet not recognize the combination of leaf appearance and size that you entered, it will give you the opportunity of entering these as a problem for the resident botanists, who will come back to you via e-mail in a few days with whatever information they can glean.

Of course, Java is not just a means for moving information around on the web: it is a real programming language, of the stature of C++, Pascal, Ada and Modula-3. Learning to use Java is what this book is all about, but it also serves as a general introduction to the principles of programming. By the end of the book, you will be able to program Java applications and applets to perform such diverse tasks as inventory control, averaging and sorting marks, computer games and competitions and of course web 'surfing'.

1.2 Software development

Computers consist of hardware and software. When one buys a computer, or uses it in the laboratory, the tendency is to focus on the hardware: how much memory does it have, what is the speed of the processor and so on. These are factors in using a computer, but they are not the most important. It is, of course, annoying if, for example, one runs out of disk space, but at least a plan can be made to store some of the information somewhere else, or even delete it, to make room.

We would claim that the software that the computer comes with is what really determines its quality. In this section, we shall briefly run through the software components that are necessary for programming in Java, and show how they interact. The description is intended to be a general one, not specific to any particular make or supplier of software. Then we shall outline the stages of software development. The next section shows how these are tackled in this book.

The programming process

The programming process is the activity whereby programs are written in order to be stored and made ready for execution or running. The programs can be run on the same computer on which they were written, or they can be fetched over the web in the manner we have already described. Programming these days needs the support of many software packages, themselves programs developed by others. Some of the software comes with the computer you buy, some you can purchase later, and some you can get as freeware, shareware or applets over the web. In order to develop your own programs, you will need at least an operating system, an editor and a compiler.

Operating systems

The core software loaded on a computer is its **operating system**. Some operating systems are specific to certain types of computers – for example Windows runs on Intel processors – and others are designed to run on a variety of different designs. Unix and its derivative, Linux, are examples here. The operating system provides the necessary interfaces to the hardware: reading from disk, writing to the screen, swapping between tasks and so on. It also looks after files and provides commands for the user to move files, change their names, etc. Through the operating system, we activate the next level of software.

Editors and compilers

The programming process involves creating a sequence of instructions to the computer, which are written down in the particular programming language. The creative process is expressed through an **editor**, of which there are many on the market. Once ready, the program is submitted to a **compiler**. The function of the compiler is two-fold. In the first instance, it makes a thorough check on the validity of what has been written. If there are any errors (called compilation or syntax errors) then these must be corrected and the program resubmitted for compilation. Activating the Java compiler can be done at a simple level by typing in the following to the operating system, where Trees.java is the file we created through the editor:

```
javac Trees.java
```

Once the program is free from compilation errors, the compiler enters a second phase and translates the program into a form that can run on a computer. For compilers for most other languages this form will be the native machine instructions of the particular computer's processor. For Java, though, it is the Java virtual machine that is the target of compilation, no matter what the computer is that will ultimately run the translated program.

Although the compiler checks the grammar of the program and can look for quite a range of potential errors, it cannot detect errors in the logic. For example, in the applet shown in action in Figure 1.5, it would be quite possible for a careless programmer to read the width value as the length and the length as the width by mistake. These are known as **logic** errors (also known as **execution** errors).

Logic errors can be avoided by

- carefully structuring the program in the first place,
- following good programming guidelines, and
- actually reusing existing pieces of program instead of rewriting everything from scratch each time.

However, sometimes the only way to detect a logic error is to run the program and see what happens. This is the second last stage of the software development process. The program is **executed** or **run** by activating it through the operating system. In Java we would activate an ordinary program by a command such as

```
java Trees
```

Some logic errors can be detected by carefully testing the program with well-chosen test data. After finding and correcting an error, the test should be re-run because it is very easy to introduce some other error while fixing the first. All of these topics are covered in this book. The programming process is summed up in Figure 1.6.

Development environments

Because the edit–compile cycle repeats itself over and over again in the programming process, software exists which combines editing and compiling, and enables one to switch between them at the touch of a button. Examples of such Java systems are Java Workshop,

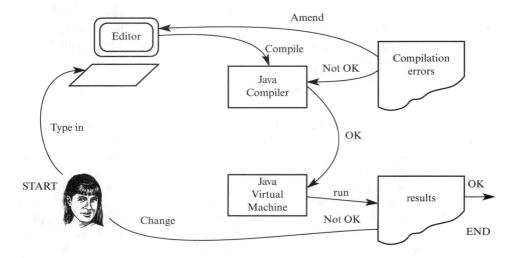

Figure 1.6   *The programming process in Java.*

Visual J++ and Symantec Café. An integrated development environment (IDE) also includes facilities for managing large projects, perhaps involving several programmers. Another feature is an enhanced editor for creating user interfaces by designing them on the screen.

An advantage of some Java IDEs is that, like Java itself, they are platform-independent, so that you can continue working in the same environment even if you change computers. A disadvantage of IDEs is that they are not always intuitive and sometimes take a while to learn to operate effectively.

Maintenance

It is suprising, but true, that Figure 1.6 represents in industry terms only about 30% of the programming process. The real hard programming starts after the product has been delivered and it begins its useful life. Then it has to be **maintained**, an activity which is similar to the maintenance on an airplane: essential and sometimes costly. Maintenance for software includes fixing errors, making user-required changes and adding enhancements. A primary aim of a programmer even when learning to program should be to make maintenance as easy as possible. Throughout the book we shall mention ways of achieving this goal.

1.3   The approach of this book

Java Gently teaches programming by example. There is a tried and tested progression of examples which leads you from first principles through to the more complex constructs in the language. Each example is carefully chosen so as to use only those features that have been covered, and each example uses the features correctly. Achieving this balance means that the order of topics covered has to be precise. While it is possible to dip into the later chapters of the book, the first five should be covered sequentially. They form the core and are closely interlinked.

Each example follows a sequence of steps which is usually:

- problem
- solution
- algorithm
- class design
- example
- program
- testing

The problem is a short statement in the user's terms of what needs to be done. The solution starts to give an idea as to what approach should be followed to solve the problem, including what software can be reused from elsewhere. The algorithm forms the nub of the problem-solving process. The program is a complete, running Java program and each of them can be found on our web site given on page 5. The example and testing help to make the programs realistic.

Algorithms

An **algorithm** is a precise, unambiguous statement of steps to follow to solve a problem. Algorithms can be expressed in a variety of ways and we shall use a mixture of English and lines and arrows to express the concepts of decision making and repetition. The resulting diagrams are formal enough to show the structure of the program yet informal enough to be written down with the minimum of fuss. For example, in the trees applet, there are three values to be entered. The algorithm for getting all three in, in any order, before proceeding, would be represented as in Figure 1.7.

In general the flow of the algorithm is downwards. Sideways arrows indicate action to be taken if the condition is true. Often, the algorithm will need to be repeated, and the line from the bottom and up the left joins around the top again to show that this should happen.

Class design

Java is an object-oriented language, which means that a program in Java is composed of interrelated objects. *Java Gently* describes programs in terms of their objects and the relationships between them using a simple set of blocks and lines. The notation used is based on OMT (object modelling technique), with additions to make it more suitable for the level

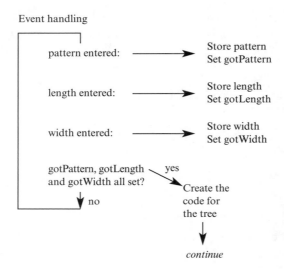

Figure 1.7 *A sample algorithm.*

of programming that we are tackling, and to make visible all of Java's interesting features. For example, there are symbols for simple methods and variables, as well as for interfaces and abstract classes. An example of a class diagram related to the Nature project would be as in Figure 1.8.

Nature is a class with a name and a means of displaying it. Animals, Birds and Trees are all derived from Nature. Herbivore is a class which, among other things, records the amount of grass needed by such an animal. All of these classes are shown as dotted

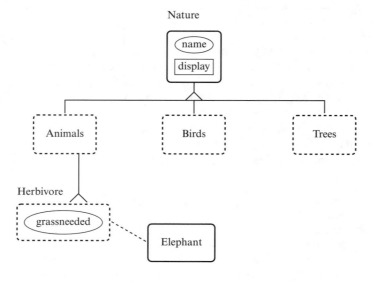

Figure 1.8 *A sample class diagram.*

oblongs because they are only descriptions of what could exist. Elephant is our only real object, and it is instantiated from Herbivore. There is much more about this notation in Section 3.5.

Programs

Programs are written in programming languages. There are many such languages, but relatively few are available on all kinds of computers. Those that have achieved more or less universal use include Pascal, Ada, FORTRAN, COBOL, BASIC, C++, LISP, PROLOG, Modula and now, of course, Java. Java was developed in 1993 under the name of Oak, and achieved popularity in 1996 when Sun Microsystems launched their Java compilers free on the web.

Java programs look like stylized English, and examples can be found on any page of this book. The form of a program is important: any mistakes will cause the compiler to reject your efforts. It is therefore necessary to learn the syntax of the language precisely. To assist you in this endeavour, *Java Gently* has a unique approach. When a new construct is introduced, its syntax is shown precisely in a **form** that not only explains how a feature is constructed, but also gives an indication of how it should be laid out in a regular way. An example of a simple form is:

if-statement
```if``` (condition) then-part; ***else*** else-part;

The meaning of the bold face and italics will become clear as we start introducing Java statements.

SUMMARY

It is often said that programming is fun. It certainly can be, and *Java Gently* tries to make it so. However, no matter how much you enjoy learning to program – and I sincerely hope you do – I hope that you will also remember the following, adapted from the immortal words of Rudyard Kipling:

> 'If you can keep your head when all about you
> Are losing theirs and blaming it on you,
> If you can trust yourself when all men doubt you,
> But make allowance for their doubting too;
> If you can wait and not be tired by waiting, …
> If you can fill the unforgiving minute
> With sixty seconds' worth of Java run,
> Yours is the Web and everything that's in it,
> And – which is more – you'll be a Programmer, thank SUN!'

QUIZ: TO GET YOU STARTED

1.1   What does a compiler do?

1.2   What is the difference between a compilation error and a logic error?

1.3   What is the clock speed of the computer you are using?

1.4   How much memory does your computer have?

1.5   What is the capacity of the disks you are using?

1.6   Would this textbook (including all the spaces) fit on your disk, assuming one printed character per byte of memory?

1.7   List all the computer applications that you come into contact with in the course of an ordinary week.

1.8   Have you ever been on the wrong end of a computer error? If so, could you tell whether the mistake was in the program or was caused by the data that was read in?

1.9   Find out the name, version and creation date of the computer, operating system and compiler that you will be using.

1.10   Get into *Java Gently's* web site and try out the Nature system. The address is http://www.cs.up.ac.za/javagently.

CHAPTER 2

Simple programs

2.1   Two starter programs

To start this chapter we shall look at two small programs. The first is a simple text-based program, and the second uses drawing and colours. We shall not go into the details of the programs, but just use them as a starting point for introducing programming in Java, and for enabling you to start using the computer straight away. There are several amendments you can make to the programs, which will give you a reason to get to grips with your programming environment.

A first program – Welcome

The aim of the first program is to display the message 'Welcome to Java!'. The program is given in Figure 2.1, and it does indeed, if run, display the required message on the screen as follows:

```
Welcome to Java!
```

```
1.      class Welcome  {

2.      /* Welcome to Java!  Program          by J M Bishop Dec 96
3.          Illustrates a simple program displaying a message.   */

4.       public static void main (String [ ] args)  {
5.          System.out.println("Welcome to Java");
6.          }
7.       }
```

Figure 2.1   *Welcome to Java! program (the line numbers are for reference only).*

At this stage we shall note only a few points about the program. Firstly, the text between /* and */ (lines 2 and 3) is called a **comment** and is there to help explain to the reader what the program does. It is not **executed** (or **run**) by the computer. Secondly the text in quotes (line 5) is known as a **string** and is what is actually displayed. The rest of the lines (1 and 4) and the closing braces are part of the outline which always accompanies a Java program. We shall learn more about them soon.

Exercise: Run the Welcome program. Change it so that it includes your name in the message, e.g. Welcome to Java, Peter! Change it again so that it prints out more than one line of greeting, or underlines the greeting using hyphens. Experiment and use the opportunity to become familiar with your programming environment.

A second program – Olympic Rings

One of the advantages of Java is its built-in facilities for graphics, colour, animation, sound and so on. Figure 2.2 gives a very simple program to display the five Olympic Rings in a window. The output produced by the program is shown (not in colour, unfortunately) in Figure 2.3.
      This is a much longer program, but if you look carefully, you will see that the real substance of the program – drawing the rings – occurs on lines 17–28. Each of the lines such as

```
g.drawOval (35,30,30,30);
```

draws one of the circles. The numbers in brackets are measurements in pixels (screens can have 600 or more pixels across). In order, the numbers represent:

●   *x*-coordinate of the top left of the oval,

●   *y*-coordinate of the top left of the oval,

●   width of the oval,

●   height of the oval.

Of course, circles are a special case of ovals, with the width and height the same. We can therefore see that the instructions to draw the circles progress across in the *x* direction, but keep the *y* values the same.

```
1.      import java.awt.*;

2.      class Rings extends Frame  {

3.      /* Ring drawing program
4.                              J M Bishop Dec 1996
5.         illustrates colour and simple graphic output  */

6.       public static void main  (String [ ] args)  {
7.           // Create a graphics frame of the
8.           // given size and show the drawing
9.           // outlined in the paint method.
10.          Frame f = new Rings ();
11.          f.resize (300, 200);
12.          f.show ();
13.      }

14.      public void paint (Graphics g) {
15.         // Draw five interlocking rings
16.         // of different colours.
17.         g.setColor (Color.red);
18.         g.drawOval (10,30,30,30);
19.         g.setColor (Color.blue);
20.         g.drawOval (35,30,30,30);
21.         g.setColor (Color.green);
22.         g.drawOval (60,30,30,30);
23.         g.setColor (Color.yellow);
24.         g.drawOval (85,30,30,30);
25.         g.setColor (Color.black);
26.         g.DrawOval (110,30,30,30);

27.         // Label the drawing
28.         g.drawString("Olympic Rings",40,100);
29.      }

30.      public Rings ( ) {
31.         setTitle ("Program 2.2: Rings");
32.      }

33.      public boolean handleEvent (Event e) {
34.         // Enable the program to react to
35.         // the user clicking on the close
36.         // window box.
37.         if (e.id == Event.WINDOW_DESTROY)
38.           System.exit(0);
39.         return super.handleEvent (e);
40.      }

41.  }
```

Figure 2.2 *A simple program using graphics to display coloured, interlocking rings (the line numbers are for reference only).*

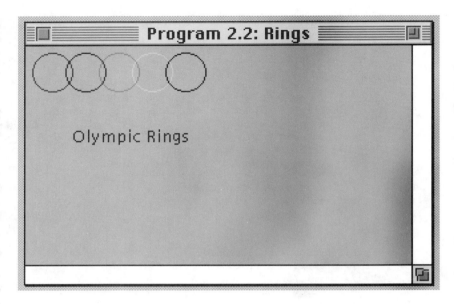

Figure 2.3   *Graphical output from the Rings program in Figure 2.2 (rendered in black and white – the original is in colour).*

The rest of the program can be described as 'baggage': necessary Java instructions which give us access to the graphics facilities, but which are not particular to our problem. In brief, these are:

- creating a graphics window of a particular size (lines 6–13),

- giving the window a name (lines 30–32),

- enabling the window to be closed (lines 33–40).

This program also illustrates the use of Java's second type of comment: the one-liner, introduced by //.

Being able to program in a graphics environment is an essential skill for today's programmers, but there is a lot of detail to learn, much of which is repetitive and can be looked up when needed. We therefore leave graphics to Part II and will concentrate on text programs while we learn the fundamentals of programming, and of how to do this well in Java.

Exercises: Run the Rings program and check that the rings come out in the right colour and in the right order for the Olympic emblem. In fact, the emblem does not have the rings in a straight line as in Figure 2.3, but the second and fourth are set lower down. Change the program to fix this. Also experiment with making the rings bigger and positioning them in the centre of the screen.

Fundamentals of object-oriented programming **19**

2.2   Fundamentals of object-oriented programming

In this section we give a broad overview of the different parts of a Java program and how they fit together. The rest of the chapter will concentrate on a few of the essential components so that by the end, we shall be able to create and run simple programs that have tangible results. These results will be in text form rather than diagrams and pictures as producing the latter requires specialized programming techniques which are best left to Part II.

A Java **program** consists of a set of one or more inter-dependent classes as shown in Figure 2.4. **Classes** are a means for describing the properties and capabilities of the objects in real life that the program has to deal with. For example, the Nature Conservation program described in Chapter 1 could well have classes for trees, animals and birds. Once we have a class, we can create many objects of that same class. Not every class is related to every other, and the kinds of relationships vary, as we shall see later. The notation used to illustrate object-oriented programs shows the different relationships with arrows, diamonds and triangles. Their significance will become clear as early as Section 3.2.

An **object** is a concrete realization of a class description. It is usually associated with a noun, such as a tree or a book, a student or a map. The process of generating new objects for a program is referred to as creating an **instance** of a class. For example, suppose we have defined a `Trees` class:[1] then we could create three instances of the class as follows:

```
Trees acacia  = new Trees ();
Trees willow  = new Trees ();
Trees palm    = new Trees ();
```

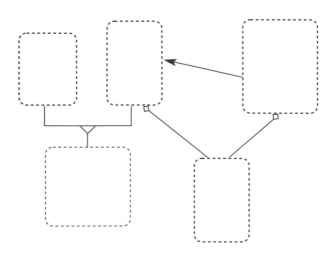

Figure 2.4   *A diagram of a program consisting of interrelated classes.*

[1]From now on, Java programs, and parts of them, are shown in Courier font.

50017490

The first occurrence of the class name `Trees` indicates that the object is of this class. Then the '= new' is the signal to create a new instance of the class and we once again say that we want the storage to be for items of the size of the `Trees` class, as shown in Figure 2.5. The class is once again a dotted oblong and the objects are solid, or concrete.

Each of the new objects will have all the properties and capabilities of the `Trees` class. Although in most cases the class used for declaring the object is the same as the one for creating the instance, there are occasions when they need not be, and these will be explained in Section 2.2.

The properties and capabilities of a class are called **declarations** and **methods**, respectively, in Java. Thus following on from Figure 2.4, the next level of decomposition is shown in Figure 2.6. There are several kinds of declarations and methods, and we shall touch on some of them here. The topic is revisited in later chapters.

Notice that although the diagram in Figure 2.6 might indicate that there is a section of declarations which precedes a section of methods, this is not the case: individual declarations and methods can be interleaved as required to make the class easier to read.

Declarations

The properties of a class are given by means of **declarations** of data items that its objects can use to store information. An example of such a data item would be the number of times people enquire about a particular tree. Declarations in Java indicate both the name of the data item and its **type**. The simplest is an integer number. In Java terms, we refer to an integer as `int`. Therefore, as part of the `Trees` class, we would have the declaration:

```
int noOfEnquiries;
```

Names in computer languages are called identifiers. An **identifier** in Java consists of letters and digits, but must start with a letter. Spaces are not allowed, and capital and small letters are considered to be different so that `noOfEnquiries` is not the same as

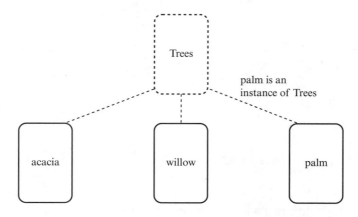

Figure 2.5   *An example of creating objects as instances of a class.*

class name

declarations

methods

Figure 2.6 *The structure of a class.*

noofenquiries. Unlike Trees, this identifier consists of more than one word, so to make it easier to read, we use capitals for the inner words.

The declaration sets aside storage in the computer's memory for this item, and the amount of storage will depend on the type. An integer, for example, occupies four bytes.

The correct Java term for the data item we have defined is a **variable**. When making declarations, we can also declare other objects. 'Data item' would be the correct term to use to encompass both, but it is clumsy, so we shall start to refer to the variables of a class, but bearing in mind all along that the term encompasses objects as well.

We shall now look at methods, and come back to declarations again before the end of this section.

Methods

The capabilities of a class are expressed in one or more methods. A **method** is a named sequence of instructions to the computer, written out in the language we are using, in this case Java. The instructions are properly called **statements,** and fall into the following categories:

- **invocation** – causing a method to be performed;

- **assignment** – changing the state of a variable by using another value of the same type;

- **repetition** – performing certain statements over and over again;

- **selection** – deciding whether to perform certain statements or not;

- **exception** – detecting and reacting to unusual circumstances.

Most languages have a similar set of options.

In addition, a method can also declare its own variables which are said to be **local** to it, and therefore not accessible to other methods, even those in the same class. On the other hand, the declarations which are made in the class itself (see Figure 2.6) are accessible to all the methods in that class.

Finally, a method can declare at its start a set of **parameters** which enable it to be customized when it is invoked. Figure 2.7 follows Figures 2.4 and 2.6 with the third level

```
                           method name
                        ┌─────────────────┐
                        │ (parameters)    │
                        │                 │
                        │ declarations    │
                        │                 │
                        │ statements      │
                        └─────────────────┘
```

Figure 2.7   *The structure of a method.*

of decomposition – from a program to a class to a method. For example, in the `Trees` class, a likely method would be one to increase the count of the number of enquiries by one. In Java, such a method would be written as:

```
void enquiry () {
  noOfEnquiries ++;
}
```

The term `void` indicates that in this method all its activity takes place within its statements, and that is the end of it. It does not return anything when it is finished. Methods which are not void, but have a type instead, can return values as well.

The name of the method is `enquiry`, and it does not have any parameters, as indicated by the pair of brackets. The curly brackets, or braces as we shall call them, indicate the start and end of the statements in the method. In this case there is only one statement. It is of the assignment type, and adds one to our data item, `noOfEnquiries`, by using the special operator ++.

Invoking a method

At this point, we wish to examine how we cause the method to perform its statements. In simple terms, when we mention the name of a method, control within the program is transferred to that method, which then progresses through its statements until it reaches the end. The method then passes control back to where it was called from. This process is called method invocation, and we talk about **invoking** a method.[2] In object-oriented parlance, calling a method is also sometimes referred to as passing a message; this is not usual in Java.

The methods in a class define its capabilities, which are then available for every object created from that class. However, there has to be a way of indicating **which** object we want a method to act on. Therefore, when we refer to a method, we prefix it with the name of the object whose variables we wish to access. Recalling that `willow` is an object, if we invoke

```
willow.enquiry ();
```

[2] *Invoke* is the formal, correct term for causing the statements of a method to be performed. It is a rather unusual word, and since its derivation is from the Latin *vocare* 'to call', we shall sometimes adopt (as many other books do) the more gentle English word *call*.

the `enquiry` method gains access to the `noOfEnquiries` variable in the `willow` object, not the one in either of the other trees.

Constructors

An object is created when its declaration is reached in the program. Upon creation, a special kind of method, a **constructor**, is automatically called by the Java system. The programmer writing the class can set up one or more constructors which have different numbers of parameters, and will be matched against those supplied at creation. Constructors have the name of the class itself. Thus we could have the following two constructors in the `Trees` class:

```
Trees () {
  noOfEnquiries = 0;
}

Trees (int n) {
  noOfEnquiries = n;
}
```

In the first constructor, there is no parameter, and so we initialize the variable to zero. In the second, we take the value given at creation as the number of enquiries so far. Thus the following are both valid object creations:

```
Trees willow = new Trees ( );
Trees acacia = new Trees (55);
```

The first creates `willow` as a tree with zero enquiries. The second creates `acacia` as a tree with 55 enquiries already.

Class variables

We explained above that each time an object is created as an instance of a class, a completely new instance of all variables that the class declared is created for this object. This is not always desirable.

We may not always want a new copy of every variable for each object: we may want to have some which are common to all objects of the class. For example, the variable `noOfEnquiries` will tally the enquiries for each tree object, i.e. there will be a separate tally kept for acacias, willows and palms. Suppose we also want to keep track of the total enquiries for all trees (as opposed to animals and birds, which have their own classes). What we need here is a **class variable**, as opposed to an **instance variable**. To distinguish such variables, Java uses a **modifier** before the type name. There is a whole selection of modifiers that we shall introduce as they are required, but the one we need here is called **static**. Using the modifier `static` indicates that storage for the variable is to be created once only for the class, and not each time a new object is created. So for example, the counter for the total number of enquiries would be declared as:

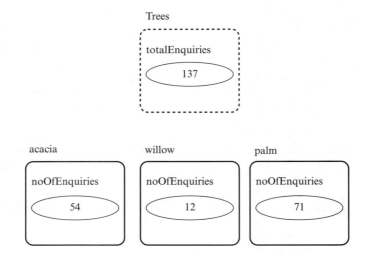

Figure 2.8   *The tree objects after a number of enquiries.*

```
static int totalEnquiries;
```

Now the method to increment the original variable will be expanded to:

```
void enquiry () {
  noOfEnquiries ++;
  totalEnquiries ++;
}
```

To illustrate the difference between the type of variables, Figure 2.8 shows how the three sample tree objects will look once some queries have come in. In earlier figures, we used a rounded rectangle for a class and a squared off rectangle for a method. Here an oval represents a variable. From the diagram in Figure 2.8 we can see clearly that each of the objects has its own version of the instance variable noOfEnquiries, even though the variables all have the same name.

Suppose now that we would like to get a record of the number of enquiries to date. How would we refer to these variables? The rule is simple:

- Within their class, variables can be referred to by their names alone.

- When used from another class or object, preface the variable with the name of its class (for class variables) or its object (for instance variables).

So, at the point where these objects were created, we could refer to the following variables:

```
acacia.noOfEnquiries
willow.noOfEnquiries
palm.noOfEnquiries
Trees.totalEnquiries
```

Class and instance methods

The `enquiry` method is an **instance method**. It relies on being told which particular object it must access. In the same way as there may be variables common to all objects in a class, so there may be methods which do not depend on a particular object for their operation.

An example within the `Trees` class might be a method to issue a report after every 100 enquiries. This method would not be called by user's object, but would be activated from with the `enquiries` method, say. Class methods will be further discussed in the last section of this chapter. What we do note here, for completeness, is that a class method is defined with the modifier `static` and is called with the class name as a prefix.

The form of a program

Before leaving this section, we note precisely how to write down the instructions that introduce a Java program. The following pattern gives the format we must use for a simple program. Java is a language and as such has a syntax. In this book, Java's syntax is explained by means of **forms** and examples.

Simple program

```
class classname {
  public static void main (String [] argname) {
    declarations and statements
  }
}
```

There are three kinds of words in a form, with the following meanings:

- bold text – Java keywords that must be there, e.g. **class**;

- italics – identifiers and other parts that we fill in, e.g. *classname*;

- plain words – identifiers that have to be there but are not keywords, e.g. `main` and `String`.

Keywords are those identifiers that are reserved for Java's use and may not be used by the programmer for anything else. Thus we cannot call a variable 'static'. The braces must match for each class and method. In the form, the outer set refers to the class and the inner set refers to `main`. The words in italics describe parts of the program that must be supplied by the programmer. The class name is compulsory, but the declarations and statements are optional. Thus the following is a valid Java program which does nothing:

```
class DoNothing {
  public static void main (String [] args) {
  }
}
```

When there are statements, each ends with a semicolon. In this way, there can be several statements to a line, but most of the time Java programmers stick to one statement per line.

Following on from the discussion in this section, we can interpret what is meant by each of the lines of the program. The introduction of the class name is clear. Thereafter, we have a single method called `main`. It is a `void` method, and also has a `static` modifier, indicating that it is a class method and will be called by the outside world as `DoNothing.main`. Who calls it? When the Java virtual machine is activated, as described in Chapter 1, it must be given the name of a class. It then looks for a method called `main` in the class of that name, and starts running it from there.

Because the method has to be accessed by the virtual machine, it must have an additional modifier, `public`. The rest of our methods for the moment do not need this modifier, nor its opposite, `private`, and we shall discuss the need for them in more detail in Part II.

Finally, the parameter in the form is there so that information can be transmitted to the program when it starts up. The square brackets indicate that the parameter is going to be an array – a computer term used for several variables, all with the same name and indexed by numbers. Arrays are fully covered in Chapter 6. In general we do not use the main method's parameter, but it is still necessary to include it when the method is defined.

2.3 Beginning with output

Having covered the fundamental structure of a Java program in terms of its most important constituents – classes and objects – we can now consider how to write a simple program that displays something on the screen. In programming parlance, what goes to the screen is called **output**, but programmers often use the terms write, print, output and display interchangeably. If we refer to the previous section, we shall see that there is no special statement group for output in Java. All input and output is handled by methods in classes supplied by the language. Thus in order to print, we have to know *which* methods to call: we already know *how* to call them from Section 2.2.

The methods we are looking for are called `println` and `print`. They are found in a class called `PrintStream`. They are instance methods, so there must be an object through which we call them. Within the special, universally available class called `System`, there is already such an object defined, called `out`. The object `out` is connected by Java to the screen of your computer. Therefore from these three components:

- the class `System`

- the object `out`, and

- the methods `print` and `println`

we can construct the correct method call statements for output. Because these method calls will be used so often, we refer to them as output statements as a shorthand. The simple form of Java statements to display a piece of text is:

Output statements

```
System.out.println (items);
System.out.println ();
System.out.print (items);
```

The first kind of items we consider for printing are strings. A **string** is any sequence of characters enclosed in quotes, for example

```
"London"
"USA"
"$5.95 per lot"
```

If a quote itself is needed in the string then a backslash \ precedes it. The backslash is called an **escape character**: it does not form part of the string, but enables the next character to do so. An example is:

```
"He said \"No\""
```

which is the string *He said "No"*. Calling the println method displays the string given as a parameter and ends the line of printing. (The '-ln' in `println` is short for 'line'). Thus, the statements

```
System.out.println("$5.95 per lot");
System.out.println("He said \"No\"");
```

will cause the following to be displayed:

$5.95 per lot
He said "No"

(In examples from now on, Java statements are given in plain type, and the corresponding output is shown in bold.)

The `print` method works in a similar way except that it does not end the line, so that a subsequent `print` or `println` will continue on the same line from the last point reached.

The string is optional for the `println` method. If `println` is called on its own, then it will finish off the current line. This facility can also be used to obtain a blank line, as in:

```
System.out.println ("$5.95 per lot");
System.out.println ();
System.out.println ("He said \"No\"");
```

which would give as output:

$5.95 per lot

He said "No"

Note that any Java method call that does not provide parameters (the items in brackets) must still have the brackets. To obtain several blank lines, we can use several `println` calls in a row, as in:

```
System.out.println();
System.out.println();
System.out.println();
```

Alternatively, we can make use of another escape character, \n, standing for 'new line', as in:

```
System.out.println ("\n\n\n");
```

One final point about strings and printing. What happens should a string be too long to fit on a single line of a screen when we are writing a program? We cannot go onto the next line. We have to end the string and start a new one, joining the two together with a plus operator. This is known formally as **concatenation**. An example of concatenation would be:

```
System.out.println ("Your tree is not known to us. Would "+
    "you like to submit details of it by WWW or " +
    "courier?");
```

There are many more examples of long strings in the programs that follow.

EXAMPLE 2.1 Displaying a warning

Problem Display a warning message on the screen that the computer might have a virus.[3]

Program This program is very simple, and similar to that in Figure 2.1. It has a class and a main method, followed by several output statements which when executed will display the box shown below.

```
class DisplayWarning {

/* Displaying a warning program by J M Bishop Aug 1996

    illustrates the form of a program and
    the use of println. */

public static void main (String [] args) {
```

---

[3] A virus is a program that can infect your computer and cause damage to files on the disk and so on. This program does not in itself detect the virus: it just prints out the warning message.

```
System.out.println ("--------------------------");
System.out.println ("|                          |");
System.out.println ("|      W A R N I N G        |");
System.out.println ("| Possible virus detected  |");
System.out.println ("|   Reboot and run virus   |");
System.out.println ("|     remover software     |");
System.out.println ("|                          |");
System.out.println ("--------------------------");
    }
}
```

Testing   The output produced by this program would be:

```
--------------------------
|                        |
|      W A R N I N G     |
| Possible virus detected |
|  Reboot and run virus  |
|    remover software    |
|                        |
--------------------------
```

Here we use dashes and bars for effect, but in Part II we shall see how to make use of the graphics facilities of a computer screen to obtain smarter looking output.

Layout

How the program is written down, in terms of lines and spaces, does not have an effect on how the output appears. Only what is inside the quotes is actually displayed when the program executes.When the output statements display strings, there is no gap in the output if the string in the program had to be split into different pieces joined by +. In the same way, blank lines or comments in the program do not have any effect on the output. Therefore, the following statements will cause the same output to be displayed as before:

```
System.out.println("$5.95 " + "per lot");

                System.out.println;
    System.out.println("He " +
"said \"No\"");
```

The point is that the instructions given to the computer do not *have* to be in any special layout. We usually write them neatly one underneath each other, and we also use **indenting** to make groups of statements stand out, but there is no formal rule that says this should be so. Other points about the layout of the program which we can make right now are:

● more than one statement can be written on a line;

● statements can be split over several lines (but strings cannot);

● statements are ended by semicolons.

2.4   All about assignment

Assignment is the first real statement that we shall consider from the five groups mentioned in Section 2.2. An assignment statement is used to give a value to a variable or object. There is quite a lot involved in getting ready for an assignment, and we shall tackle it in the following steps:

- explaining what a type is;
- how to declare a variable and a constant;
- how to compute values from expressions;
- assignment itself;
- how to print variables and expressions;
- an example.

Types

Java, like most modern languages, is what is known as **strictly typed** and also **strictly classed**. This means that every variable, expression and object has a type or a class, and only those of the same types or classes can be used together. Put in simple terms, this means that we cannot mix strings and numbers, nor could we mix trees and birds. Java has eight built-in types, known as the **primitive types**, but the three that are commonly used in calculations are:

- int for ordinary positive and negative integer numbers in a range extending over two thousand million;
- long for even longer integer numbers or for the results of integer calculations;
- double for numbers with fractional parts (i.e. real numbers) or for the results of calculations that could give a fraction, as in division.

The other types are boolean, byte, char, float and short, and we shall introduce them as they are needed in the next chapters.

A type governs how much storage is made available for the values that are stored in variables of that type. Thus an int uses 32 bits (4 bytes), and long and double each 64 bits (8 bytes).

Declarations

We have already mentioned in Section 2.2 that objects store their data in variables. Variables may be declared anywhere in a Java class or method, but usually most of them are grouped at the start or end. The form of a declaration is one of the following:

Variable declaration

```
type name;
type name1, name2, name3;
type name = value;
```

The declaration introduces one or more variables of the given type. The last form can be used to initialize a variable at the same time as declaring it. Examples of declarations of variables are:

```
int      temperature;          // in degrees Celsius
int      oldWeight, newWeight  // in kilograms
double   salary;
double   tax;
long     k, m, n;              // integer unknowns
double   x, y, z;              // real unknowns
```

It is worth while keeping declarations neat and tidy, with the identifiers and types lined up. It is also a useful habit to indicate what the variables are to be used for, if this is not immediately obvious from their identifiers, as well as to give some supporting information regarding the units that are intended, as shown in the first two examples.

In the real world, many values acquire names. For example, 3.141592 is known as *pi*, and a *decade* is 10. Giving names to quantities makes them easier to remember and use. In Java, named entities whose values are not going to change are known as **constants**. They are declared in declarations of the form:

Constant declaration

```
static final Type name = value;
```

Examples of constant declarations are:

```
static final int speedLimit = 120;
static final int retirementAge = 65;
static final double kmperMile = 1.609;
```

We have already seen that the declaration modifier `static` makes the item into a class item. Thus constant declarations can occur only at the class level, and not inside methods, even inside `main`. The second modifier, `final`, indicates that the contents of the item cannot be changed during the program: in other words, it is constant.

When variables are declared we have the option of specifying an initial value or of receiving a **default initialization**. For the numeric types, the default is zero. For this reason, initialization is seldom used in Java programs. The third form of declaration is more common when we are declaring constant values. How does such an initialization differ from a constant declaration? The fundamental difference is that once constants are set, they cannot be changed again. With variables, the values can change through assignment.

Expressions

Expression is the term given to formulae in programming languages. The way in which expressions are written in programming languages is somewhat different from the normal way of writing them. The main differences are that:

- multiplication is indicated by an asterisk *;
- division is indicated by a slash /;
- denominators follow numerators on the same line.

For example, consider some simple formulae and their Java equivalents:

$$\frac{1}{2} \quad \rightarrow \quad 1/2$$

$$6\,(7-3) \quad \rightarrow \quad 6*(7-3)$$

The implication of the last point – writing on one line – is that we use more parentheses in Java expressions than we would in ordinary arithmetic or mathematics. Division that would usually be written as a fraction has to be split into two parenthesized parts separated by a slash. For example, consider the following:

$$\frac{100-9.99}{15+0.1} \quad \rightarrow \quad (100-9.99)\,/\,(15+0.1)$$

As another example, to print 15 °C converted to Fahrenheit, using the formula

$$\frac{9t}{5} + 32$$

we would say

```
System.out.println (9 * 15 / 5 + 32);
```

which would print out

```
59
```

In Java, the normal precedence rules apply, with brackets coming before division and multiplication, which are performed before addition and subtraction.

As well as the usual four operators, use is often made in programming of finding the remainder after integer division. The operator used to represent this modulus is %. Examples of its use are:

```
23 % 2    → 1
6 % 6     → 0
81 % 11   → 4
```

While we are on the subject of writing out formulae, we note for the mathematically minded that the trigonometric functions are called with brackets like this:

```
sin x     →    Math.sin(x)
```

`Math` is a built-in class which supplies methods for trigonometry, exponentiation and other operations. Going back to the 'all on one line' restriction, we see that to raise to a power, we have to call a function, as in

```
x²        →    Math.pow(x,2)
```

Another useful method in the `Math` class is that for rounding up a real[4] number to an integer. Examples are

```
Math.round (6.6)        →    7
Math.round (6.3)        →    6
```

There is more to expressions than this short introduction reveals, but the more advanced features will be added as we need them in the next few chapters. Full details of the contents of the `Math` class are given in the Java libraries described on our web site.

Assignment

Having declared a variable, we can now use an assignment to give it the value of an expression. The assignment statement has the form:

Assignment statement
variable = expression;

The effect of an **assignment statement** is to evaluate the expression and to assign the resulting value to the variable indicated by the identifier. The equal sign which indicates the assignment is read 'becomes'. Thus we can write:

```
temperature = 24;
```

and read it 'temperature becomes 24'. The value of the expression is 24, and this is assigned to the variable `temperature`. In the next sequence:

```
oldWeight = 65;
newWeight = oldWeight - 5;
```

---

[4]The term real number has its usual meaning in this book, and includes both the `double` and `float` types that Java provides for expressing a real.

`oldWeight` is assigned the value 65, and is then used to calculate the value for the variable `newWeight` which is 60.

Assignment requires that the types of the expression and the variable are the same. Thus we cannot assign something of type `int` to a `Tree`, or even a `double` variable to an `int` variable. However, bearing in mind that even in mathematics the real numbers encompass the integers, we *can* assign integers to reals. So the following is permissible:

```
double rate;
rate = 10;
```

Printing expressions and variables

The examples so far have used calls to the `print` and `println` methods to print **strings**. It is also possible to print **numbers** and, indeed, to print the results of calculations. For example, to print 4 times 5 less 2 we would have

```
System.out.println (4 * 5 - 2);
```

which would print out

```
18
```

Similarly, we can print out the values of expressions involving variables or constants, for example,

```
static final double kmperMile = 1.609;
System.out.println (1000 * kmperMile);
```

which would print

```
1609
```

What if we want to print more than one value out, or a mixture of numbers and strings? We said in the previous section that several strings can be printed out in one print call if they are joined by a plus operator. The same applies here. However, we have to now understand what is going on behind the scenes.

The concatenate operator joins strings. When it finds something else to its left or right – for example, a number – it looks for a `toString` method defined by the class, which can convert that value to a string. All the built-in types have `toString` methods. The + operator can then perform the concatenation and the printing proceeds. For example, we can say:

```
System.out.println (1000 + " miles is "
                    + 1000 * kmperMile + " kilometres");
```

which would print

```
1000 miles is 1609 kilometres
```

Both numbers were converted to strings and joined up with the other two to make the full message. Notice that it is important to include spaces in a string that is adjacent to a number, since such spaces are not otherwise inserted.

EXAMPLE 2.2 Calculating interest

Problem The bank in the country of Savanna – called SavBank – quite often changes its interest rate for savings accounts. We would like to know what difference the change will make to the interest we may receive for the rest of the year.

Solution In this, our first real problem, we have to start by asking:

- What do we know?

- What do we want to know?

- How are we going to get there?

We know that the formula used for calculating interest, I, is the usual one of

$$I = \frac{PTR}{100}$$

where P is the principal, T is the time in years and R is the rate per annum. In this case, we know our principal – let us suppose it is G1000. (The unit of currency in Savanna is the graz, abbreviated to G.) The time is going to be $(12 - M)/12$ where M is the month we are currently in. So if we are in May, the time left will be 7/12. Finally, we must know the old rate and the new rate, for example 12.5% and 13%.

What we want to know is whether we are better off or worse off under the new rate, and by how much. We find that out by calculating the interest under both rates and finding the difference.

Algorithm The algorithm includes the names of all the values we have just been discussing.

Print out the difference between
(P * (12 – M)/12) * newRate) / 100
and
(P * (12 – M)/12) * oldRate) / 100

Program The program does just that! It initializes all the values we know, and uses expressions in the final `println` statement for the answer. Since both the expressions are the same except for the rates, we can simplify things by creating a variable which holds the value of the common part and then using this twice in the final calculation.

```
class InterestIncrease {

/*   Interest Increase Program      by J M Bishop Aug 1996

     Calculates the difference in simple interest for two
     interest rates for the remainder of the year from a
     given month.

     Illustrates declarations, assignment, constants,
     expressions and printing
*/

     static final double P       = 1000;  // in graz
     static final int M          = 4;     // for April
     static final double oldRate = 12.5;  //%
     static final double newRate = 13.00; //%

     public static void main (String [] args) {

        // Start with a title
        System.out.println("SavBank Interest Calculation");
        System.out.println("============================");

        // perform the preliminary calculation
        double PTover100 = P * (12 - M) / 12 / 100;

        // print out the results
        System.out.println("Given a change of interest rate"+
            " from " + oldRate + "% to " + newRate +
            "% in month " + M);
        System.out.println("On a principal of G" + P +
            " the interest for the rest of the year");
        System.out.print("will change by graz and cents: ");
        System.out.println(PTover100 * newRate
                      - PTover100 * oldRate);

     }
}
```

Testing   If we run the program, the output will be:

```
SavBank Interest Calculation
============================
Given a change of interest rate from 12.5% to 13% in month 4
On a principal of G1000 the interest for the rest of the year
will change by graz and cents: 3.33333
```

More on printing integers and reals

Before we leave this section, a word about the way in which numbers are converted to strings for printing. Java gives integers as many digits as they need, up to ten, with a minus sign as necessary.

Real numbers span a very wide range of values, and Java will try to convert them as sensibly as possible, but with only **six digits** maximum. If more are needed, it either rounds the decimal part up, or resorts to printing the number as a fraction and an exponent raised to the power of ten. There is one digit before the point, up to five (as required) after it and the resulting required decimal exponent comes after an E. This format is known as **scientific format**, or **E-format**. So, how would Java print the following numeric values?

```
Declaration                                     Printed as
int     taxRate = 10;                           10
int     weightLimit = 650;                      650
int     newCentury = 2001;                      2001
double  postage = 14.75;                        14.75
double  dollarsperPound = 1.6213;               1.6213
double  poundsperDollar = 1/dollarsperPound;    0.61679
double  nationalDebt = 123456789;               1.23457E+006
double  pica = 0.000000001;                     1E-009
```

Within the standard Java input–output packages, there is no way of getting a more pleasing output for a large real number.

EXAMPLE 2.3   Fleet timetables

Problem   Savanna Deliveries Inc. has acquired new vehicles which are able to travel 15% faster than the old vehicles (while still staying within the speed limit). They would like to know how this will affect journeys.

Solution   Times are represented in a 24 hour clock, such as 0930 or 1755. We need to find out how an arrival time will change, based on the reduction in the total journey time. Therefore, we need to be able to subtract times to find the journey time and multiply the result by 0.85, representing a 15% reduction. The question is how to do arithmetic on times.

Algorithm   Times consist of two parts – hours and minutes. In order to do subtraction and multiplication on times, we have to convert them to minutes first, perform the calculation, then convert back. Assuming we can do this, the overall algorithm is:

New fleet
>   Read in the departure and arrival times
>   Calculate journey time
>   Reduce journey time by 15%
>   Add to the departure time to get the new arrival time
>   Print out new journey time and arrival time.

The first conversion involves splitting an integer into two parts. To do this, we need to divide by 100, giving the hours, and get the minutes by taking the remainder. The algorithm is:

Convert to minutes

Time is	0715
Find hours from time / 100	7
Find minutes from time modulo 100	15
Set minutes to hours * 60 + minutes	435

Converting back is similar. The algorithm is:

Convert to hours and minutes

Minutes are	435
Set hours to minutes / 60	7
Set minutes from minutes modulo 60	15
Set time to hours*100+minutes	715

Program   The program to handle one journey is quite simple. The departure and arrival times of a particular vehicle are set as constants. In Chapter 4 we shall see how to read them in from the keyboard instead.

```
class NewFleet {

/*  The New Fleet Program         by J M Bishop Aug 1996
    works out the new arrival time for vehicles that are
    15% faster than before.

    Illustrates constants, expressions and assignment.
    Includes use of the modulo operator %
*/
    static final double reduction = 0.85;
    static final int depart = 900;
    static final int arrive = 1015;

    public static void main (String [] args) {

      int newArrive;          // 24 hour clock time
      long  departM,arriveM,
            oldJourneyTime,
            newJourneyTime,
            newArriveM;       // minutes in a day

    // convert the initial times to minutes
    departM = Math.round((depart / 100)*60 + depart % 100);
    arriveM = Math.round((arrive / 100)*60 + arrive % 100);

    // calculate the old and new times
    oldJourneyTime = arriveM - departM;
    newJourneyTime = Math.round(oldJourneyTime*reduction);
```

```
// create the new arrival time in minutes and
// then in a 24 hour clock time
newArriveM = departM + newJourneyTime;
newArrive = Math.round((newArriveM / 60)*100 +
                newArriveM % 60);


// Report on the findings
System.out.println("Departure time is " + depart;
System.out.println("Old arrival time is " + arrive);
System.out.println("Old journey time is " +
    oldJourneyTime + " mins ");
System.out.println("New journey time is " +
    newJourneyTime + " mins ");
System.out.println("New arrival time is " + newArrive);
  }
}
```

Notice that we use six different variables to keep all the values relevant at any one time. They are also given names which indicate their meaning well.

An interesting point in the above program is why most of the variables were declared as `long`. Java uses `long` and `double` as the default types for the result of expressions. Thus the expression

```
oldJourneyTime*reduction
```

which involves a real number will produce a `double` result. The version of `Math.round` that takes a `double` parameter produces a `long` result. In order to keep the types the same across the assignment, `newJourneyTime` must be declared as `long`. There is actually a way of changing from one type to another, but we shall delay the discussion on this to the next chapters.

Testing   Testing the program gives:

```
Departure time is 900
Old arrival time is 1015
Old journey time is 75 mins
New journey time is 64 mins
New arrival time is 1004
```

2.5   Using classes and objects

Having introduced classes and objects in Section 2.2, we can now look at how to use them. Since we are not yet far enough ahead to be able to define our own classes, we shall make use of a class already defined in Java. In so doing we shall see how:

- to import a Java package;
- to declare objects with initial values;
- to call methods from our objects.

Packages

Java is a relatively simple language in itself (with fewer features than C++, say) but it makes up for its brevity by having a set of standard packages which can be used by any program. A **package** is a collection of classes which logically fit together, and which may interact between themselves. The Java packages are:

- `applet` – for creating Java programs to run on the Web;
- `awt` – for graphics and graphical user interfacing;
- `io` – for input and output;
- `lang` – for routine language functions;
- `net` – for networking
- `util` – for additional useful utilities.

To gain access to any of these packages, except `lang` which is always available, we use the following form:

Accessing a package
import `java.package.*;`

The asterix indicates that all classes in the package must be imported into the class and made available. We can be more selective and choose just the ones we want by having several individual imports, one for each class. For example, `Date` and `Random` are classes in the `java.util` package. If we say

```
import util.Random;
import.util.Date;
```

we shall just gain access to only those two classes. If we say

```
import util.*;
```

and only use `Random` and `Date`, the effect is the same. Java is careful enough to distinguish between `import` meaning 'I may want to access' and actual use in the program. Since there is no performance degradation associated with mentioning the whole package for import, most programmers do this.

Object declarations

Once we have access to classes, we can declare objects of that class. The form of an object declaration is:

Object declaration

modifier classname objectname = **new** *classname (parameters);*

An example that we have already seen for an object declaration is:

```
Trees palm = new Trees ( );
```

An example of a modifier is `static`, indicating a class object. Other modifiers are covered later. In the form, the class name is mentioned twice. While in most cases this will be the same class name, on rare occasions we might use a different name. There was an example of this in the second starter program in Figure 2.2, line 10:

```
Frame f = new Rings ();
```

On line 2, `Rings` is declared to extend `Frame`, so there is a clear connection between the two, which is exploited when the object is declared. This is the realm of object inheritance, which is discussed fully in Chapter 8.

In any case, the object is defined to be of the class given at the start of the declaration, and it is a new object, so new storage is created for it. When an object is instantiated in this way, the class often gives the opportunity for it to be customized by providing some initial parameters. Examples of this are given in what follows.

The `Date` class

The `Date` class represents dates and times in a system-independent way. Its complete specification is given in Figure 2.9. The purpose of including the full specification is not to overwhelm you with detail, but to give an example of what a standard class in Java looks like. As you can see, it starts off with a selection of constructors. The first one, which has no parameters, will return the current date and time. Thus if we say

```
System.out.println (new Date ());
```

we create an anonymous object with today's date and time, which will then be converted to a string and printed. The conversion is carried out by the `toString` method, which should be present in all classes that want their objects to be printed. The format for the conversion means that the date will always be printed in the following form, shown with an example:

```
Day Month Date Hours:Mins:Secs Year
Sun Dec 08 17:37:01 1996
```

```
public class Date extends Object {
  //  Constructors
     public Date ();
     public Date (long Date);
     public Date (int year, int month, int date);
     public Date (int year, int month, int date,
                  int hours, int min);
     public Date (int year, int month, int date,
                  int hours, int min, int sec);
     public Date (String s);

  //  Class methods
     public static long UTC (int year, int month, int date,
                  int hours, int min, int sec);
     public static long parse (String s);

  //  Instance methods
     public boolean after (Date when);
     public boolean before (Date when);
     public boolean equals (Object obj);
     public int getDate ();
     public int getDay ();
     public int getHours ();
     public int getMinutes ();
     public int getMonth ();
     public int getSeconds ();
     public long getTime ();
     public int getTimezoneOffset ();
     public int getYear();
     public int hashCode ();
     public void setDate (int date);
     public void setDay (int day);
     public void setHours (int hours);
     public void setMinutes (int minutes);
     public void setMonth (int month);
     public void setSeconds (int seconds);
     public long setTime (long time);
     public void setYear (int year);
     public String toGMTString ();
     public string toLocaleString ();
     public string toString ();
```

Figure 2.9 *The specification of Java's* Date *class in the* util *package.*

We may not always want the time to be printed along with the date, or we may want to print the date out differently. We can get the individual parts of the full object by calling the get methods. For example:

```
Date today = new Date ();
int date, month, year;
day = today.getDate ();
month = today.getMonth ();
year = today.getYear ();
System.out.println (day + " " + month + " " + year);
```

will print out the more customary

08 Dec 1996

The other constructors provide for various ways of setting up dates, where:

• years are specified as the number of years since 1900, e.g. 96 not 1996;

• months are counted from January = 0 (not 1).

So, for example, to get the same date as the one above, we could say:

```
Date birthday = new Date (96, 11, 8);
```

The time would then be set to zero.

The set methods allow us to set individual components of a date after it has been created. The various other options look at Greenwich Mean Time, the offset which a particular computer's time is from GMT, and Universal time conversions.

EXAMPLE 2.4   Shopping days

Problem   We would like to calculate the number of shopping days to Christmas, assuming that we are already in the month of December.

Algorithm   Given the assumption that we are already in December, the algorithm is very simple, as we have only to subtract the dates of the two Dates.[5] Working from November or October would require more calculating skills than we want to use at present.

Program   This is the first program we have written which actually uses classes and objects explicitly. As such, we have put it in Figure 2.10 and numbered the lines for easy reference. The two dates are declared on lines 6 and 7. First we set up the Date object today. Then we set up Christmas, and in order to make the program last a few years, we use the year from today to set the year for Christmas. This program will not even have trouble running after the year 2000!

---

[5] Java's terminology here is potentially confusing: Date is the class, but the number of the day in the month, e.g. the 8th, is also referred to as the date, thus we have getDate and setDate. The reason for the use of date in this second context is clearly to avoid a conflict with Day, which is one of the seven Sun, Mon, Tues and so on. This is perhaps the type of confusion you should not introduce into your classes once you start defining them.

```
1.      class shopping {

2.      /* Shopping Program    by J M Bishop Dec 96
3.         calculates the number of shopping days to Christmas.
4.      */
5.        public static void main (String [] args) {

6.          Date today = new Date ();
7.          Date Christmas = New Date (today.getYear(), 11, 25);

8.          System.out.println ("Christmas is on " + Christmas);
9.          System.out.println ("Today is " + today);
10.         System.out.println ("There are " +
11.             (Christmas.getDate() - today.getDate ()) +
12.             " shopping days to Christmas.");
13.       }
14.     }
```

Figure 2.10   *An program illustrating the use of classes and objects.*

Lines 8 and 9 print out the two dates and then on line 11 we subtract their day numbers for the final message. Notice here that we have to put the subtraction expression in brackets so that the result of it, which is an integer, is the value which is converted to a string for printing. The compiler will complain if we do not do this. (Try it and see.)

Testing   The results of a test run of the program would be:

```
Christmas is on Wed Dec 25 00:00:00 1996
Today is Sun Dec 08 17:37:01 1996
There are 17 shopping days to Christmas.
```

SUMMARY

This chapter looked at programming from two levels. On the higher level, a program is composed of classes, which are composed of declarations and methods, and methods are composed of declarations and statements. Creating objects as instances of a given class led to the idea that some declarations would belong to the class, and some to each instance of it. This treatment of classes and objects was rounded off in a practical way in the last section, where we used an existing class, Date, to create and manipulate objects.

On a lower level, there are several options for declarations in the form of variables or constants . Two statements for early programming are assignment and output calls. There are eight types in Java, of which three – int, long and double – were discussed. How to write expressions within the restrictions of a single line was followed by two examples which made use of the features learnt so far. Details regarding how Java writes numbers were given. We also learnt that the output statements, strictly speaking, output only strings but that other types, such as numbers and dates, are converted into strings behind the scenes. Any data item for which the `toString` method is defined can be used in a `println`, and concatenation is a very useful facility for joining several items in a single output call.

QUIZ

2.1 Give a Java method call to draw a blue circle in the centre of a window 300 by 300 pixels, and 10 pixels from the edge of the window.

2.2 Give a Java declaration for a `Tree` object called `marula`.

2.3 If we wanted to store the names of trees, would these be declared as class variables or instance variables? Why?

2.4 Give two ways of printing your name and address in a neat label (a) using only one statement, and (b) using several statements. Explain why concatenation will almost certainly be necessary in (a).

2.5 What would be printed out on your computer from the following expressions?

```
52 % 10
9000009
Math.pow(4,3)
22 / 7
150 / 15 * 10
4 - 3 / 4 - 3
```

2.6 The `Math` package has a `sqrt` method. Give a statement to assign to x the value of

$$\sqrt{\frac{b^2 - 4ac}{2a}}$$

2.7 What actual date would the following `Date` object declaration refer to?

```
Date important = new Date (8,3,12);
```

2.8 Set up suitable declarations for the following variables: a distance in track events in the Olympics, the mass of bags of flour sold in a supermarket, the age of a child in a school, minutes in a hour, a bank balance in graz.

2.9 Referring to Example 2.4, classify each of the following as a keyword, variable, constant, method, class or package.

```
main            newArrive        Math         round
final           NewFleet         class        100
System          out              println      arrive
```

2.10 Given the following declarations in the same class, which ones would cause the compiler to report errors and why?

```
integer i, j, k;
max = 10;
double x = 1;
double K = 1,000;
static int Prize = G50;
static int 2ndPrize = G25;
int homeTime = 4.30;
static double x = 6;
```

PROBLEMS

2.1   **Singing snowman**. Using the program in Figure 2.2 as a template, construct a program to draw a singing snowman on the screen as in Figure 2.11.

2.2   **Percentage change**. Consider the program in Example 2.2. The old rate and new rate are given as constants. Instead, define a percentage change in the rate and calculate the new rate from that. For example, if the change is –20% on an old rate of 10%, then the new rate is 8%. Adapt the program and run it again.

2.3   **Banner shopping days**. Improve the program in Example 2.4 to print a banner showing the number of shopping days till Christmas, and also to omit the time from the output. (Hint: How to get dates printed without the time is explained in the last example in Section 2.5.)

2.4   **Weighted averages**. A computer science course has three parts to it: a test, an assignment and an examination, which are weighted at 20%, 30% and 50% respectively. Write a program which will set marks for the three components (out of 100) and print the final mark using the weightings.

2.5   **Fuel consumption**. A motor car uses 8 litres of fuel per 100 km on normal roads and 15% more fuel on rough roads. Write a program to print out the distance the car can travel on a full tank of 40 litres of fuel on both normal and rough roads.

2.6   **Birthdays**. The `after` and `before` methods of the `Date` class in the `util` package will return true or false depending on the relationship between the instance object and the parameter. For example,

```
new Date (96,11,25).before (new Date (96,11,1))
```

will be false. Write a program which sets up your birthday and the day of Easter this year and displays the result of each of the three relations – before, equals and after – between the two dates.

2.7 **World-wide times**. Using the time parts of the `Date` class, display the current time in a format with which you are familiar, and display the time in four other cities world-wide of your choice. To do this, you will need to know the time difference between each city and where you are.

CHAPTER 3

Structuring

3.1   On the structure of a program

The structure of a program indicates how its parts are connected together, and how sound those connections are. One can think of the structure of a bridge: each strut and rivet plays its role, and the whole performs a defined function efficiently. Bridges can even look pleasing. So it is with programs. When we create them we aim to achieve a structure that in the first instance achieves the required purpose, but then which is also readable, reusable and efficient.

Correctness

It seems obvious that a program when complete should be correct but we all know that the two properties can diverge widely. Much software these days is released to the world with errors remaining (called bugs). In defence of such software, one must say that programming is one of the most complex engineering tasks that we know, and it is also one of the newest (genetic engineering is perhaps more recent). It is only since the mid-1980s that codified books on software engineering started to appear, and standards of software reliability began to be set by international bodies. So how do we program to achieve correct software? There are two golden rules:

- Follow good programming practice while writing a program.

- Test the program thoroughly once it is done.

This book aims to instil good practice by example, and by motivating guidelines that can be followed in any programming activity. Interestingly enough, these are frequently not Java-specific.

Testing is very important, as no matter how hard we try, we cannot always imagine all possibilities that might occur when the program starts running. With simple programs, we can read through the logic and reason about what will happen. With more complex programs (extending over more than two pages, say) and, in particular, programs where the user can alter the course by supplying data, the task is very much harder. Here the careful design of test data pays off.

Readability

In order to reason about a program, we have to be able to read it, and perhaps even discuss it with others. Some of the factors which aid readability are:

- use of meaningful identifiers, e.g. noOfEnquiries instead of e;

- careful layout, especially indenting and blank lines;

- comments to explain the function of statements that follow.

One can also take readability further by starting to develop a **style** of writing which enables you to find what you are looking for quickly, and to communicate effectively within a group of programmers. For example, you may organize your methods so that their declarations always appear before the statements, at the front. Another suggestion is to arrange the methods of a large class alphabetically by name (as shown in the Date class, Figure 2.9). Software organizations will often set up such guidelines – and expect them to be followed by employees.

Reusability

While some might say that the inaccuracy of software is a major crisis in the industry, of equal concern is the inability of firms to produce software on time. One of the ways in which we aim to alleviate this position is to reuse software that has been tried and tested before. Java's packages are a classic example of reusability: instead of each of us writing a class to store and manipulate dates, one is provided.

Reusability works both ways: when writing a new program, we look around for existing classes that can be used or even adapted, and at the same time, we try to write our own classes so that they have a general appeal, without compromising their efficiency or readability in their primary program. Java has specific class constructs which aim to assist with reusability, and these are covered in Part II.

Efficiency

There is nothing more frustrating than a program which is too slow or too big. Of course, a complex task might require time, memory and disk space, but simple tasks should not. There are many small ways in which we can start out by programming thriftily, while once again not compromising our other goals. Just a few ideas for keeping a program compact are:

- declare variables as needed, do not overdo it;

- maximize the use of methods, thus avoiding copies of common statements;

- do common calculations once and store the result.

As we progress in programming maturity, more of these will be mentioned.

About what follows

This discussion introduces the rest of the chapter well. Section 3.2 looks at some more types in Java. By choosing a type to fit the items we are dealing with, readability is considerably enhanced. Efficiency is also a factor, since by selecting different numeric types, we can obtain storage correctly suited to our needs.

The next sections show different ways in which we can group statements to aid readability, reusability and efficiency. The main one is the definition of classes and their use, and considerable time is spent in Section 3.5 and the case study that follows clarifying the design principles for classes and objects.

3.2 Talking about types

Having examined integers and reals in Section 2.4, we now complete our discussion of types. The three Java types for numbers – int, long and double – are augmented by byte, short and float. Then there are the two special types, called boolean and char. We shall look at these first. When considering the numeric types again, we raise the issue of how to convert from one to the other, so that assignments can be made between different types.

Booleans

Conditions govern the decisions made in programs as to alternative paths to follow. A condition yields a value **true** or **false**. Another name for a condition is a **Boolean expression**.[1] Boolean expressions use the six comparison operators to compare the results of numeric expressions. The operators are:

[1]Booleans are named after the nineteenth century mathematician George Boole.

==	equal to
!=	not equal to
>	greater than
<	less than
>=	greater than or equal to
<=	less than or equal to

The result of such an expression can be stored in a **Boolean variable**. For example, given the declarations:

```
boolean isaMinor, isaPensioner;
int age;
```

we can store various facts about the age of someone as:

```
isaMinor = age < 18;
isaPensioner = age >=65;
```

and display these later using:

```
System.out.println
        ("Driver's licence denied:" + isaMinor);
```

If your age is 15, then `isaMinor` would be false so the statement would print:

Driver's licence denied: true

As another example,

```
System.out.println ("It is " + isaPensioner +
            " that you can ride the bus for free.");
```

will for a 15-year-old display:

It is false that you can ride the bus for free.

There are also the Boolean operators:

&	and
|	or
^	xor, the exclusive or
!	not

For the expression (x & y) to be true, both x and y must be true; for the expression (x | y) to be true, either x or y or both can be true. There is also a precedence between

and &	false	true
false	false	false
true	false	true

xor ^	false	true
false	false	true
true	true	false

or |	false	true
false	false	true
true	true	true

not !	
false	true
true	false

Figure 3.1 *Boolean operator tables.*

the operators, so that in the absence of parentheses, & will always be evaluated before |. The results of the operators are summarized in Figure 3.1.

Referring back to the earlier example with the minor and pensioner conditions, suppose we make the declarations:[2]

```
boolean isEmployed, isaYoungWorker, isaVoter, isaTaxpayer;
```

Then further facts can be deduced as follows:

```
isaYoungWorker = isaMinor & isEmployed;
isaVoter = ! isaMinor;
is a Taxpayer = isaVoter | isEmployed;
```

Boolean operators can be combined to express more complex conditions. For example, if both minors and pensioners can go free on the buses provided they are not working, then we have:

```
boolean freeBus = (isaPensioner | isaMinor) & !isEmployed;
```

The brackets are needed so that the | is evaluated first.

Boolean operators are very useful in conjunction with the comparison operators in establishing detailed conditions. An example is an expression for deciding whether school should be cancelled because it is too cold or too hot, that is:

```
goHome = temperature > 40 | temperature < 0;
```

In Java, the precedence between the comparison operators and the Boolean ones is such that the comparisons will always be executed first (that is, they have higher precedence).

[2]It is a useful habit to preface Boolean variables with 'is' or 'isa' so that statements that use them read more naturally.

In other languages, the reverse is true, and many programmers are used to putting brackets around conditions. You might often see an expression such as the go home test written as:

```
goHome = (temperature > 40) | (temperature < 0);
```

On the other hand the concatenation operator does take precedence over & and |. To print out a&b and a|b, we cannot use:

```
println(a&b + a|b);
```

because + will try to operate on the central b + a, and will report an error. Instead, we introduce parentheses:

```
println((a&b) + (a|b));
```

Java also has "short circuit" versions of *and* and *or* which are the && and || operators respectively. In the case of

```
c&&d
```

d will only be evaluated if c is true. Similarly, for ||, once c has been established as true, d is ignored.

Characters

We have already looked informally at strings in Java. They are covered more formally in Chapter 6 when we deal with arrays. A string in Java is an object, and a single character in quotes, e.g. '=' is also a string. Java provides a more simple type for single characters called CHAR. The char type encompasses all the letters, digits and symbols that appear on a keyboard, typically:

A to Z
a to z
! @ # $ % ^ & * ( ) _ + - = { } [ ] : " | ; ' ~ ` ? /

In addition, we can represent some other keyboard characters with the escape prefix:

\b   backspace
\t   tab[3]
\n   new line
\f   new page (i.e. form feed)
\r   return to the start of the line

[3]There is a sequence of fixed positions across a line on the screen, usually eight characters apart, known as **tabs**. Pressing the tab key on the keyboard or displaying the tab character via a program moves the output to the next tab position.

Notice that these particular keyboard keys cannot otherwise appear on the screen: they cause special effects when pressed.

Characters in Java are written with a single quote, e.g. '=' and the following operations are valid for them:

- assignment,

- comparison (all the six comparison operators described above),

- input and output.

The result of a comparison for less or greater depends on the order of the characters as set up in Java. What we need to know is that the letters are in order so that 'g' < 'z' , for example.

Finally, Java also provides, through the escape charater \u, space for an additional 10 000 additional characters which are not available on the usual keyboards. These are called Unicode characters and enable Java to be truly international: there are Unicode sequences for letters in Greek, Cyrillic, Hebrew, Arabic, Tibetan and so on, conforming to international standards where they exist. However, we do not need to be concerned with these while we are dealing in what is called the Latin alphabet.

Numeric types

The six numeric types are shown with their properties in Table 3.1. `byte` is typically used in programs that are dealing with data at the level of the machine. `short` can be a way of saving space, but is not often used in Java. `int` is the usual type for declaring integers, but `long` also frequently appears as it is the default for the result of an integer expression. `float` would be the natural choice for real numbers, except that `double` is the default type for the result of real expressions. That is why we introduced `int`, `long` and `double` in the previous chapter.

The numeric types have access to all the operations mentioned already, and can be output as explained in Section 2.4. In addition, there are some new and interesting operators which will be useful almost immediately. In programming, a common operation is to add one to a counter. For example, we might have the assignment:

```
int total;
total = total + 1;
```

Table 3.1 *Details of the numeric types.*

Type	Representation	Initial value	Storage	Maximum value
byte	signed integer	0	8 bits	127
short	signed integer	0	16 bits	32 767
int	signed integer	0	32 bits	2 147 483 647
long	signed integer	0	64 bits	over 10^{18}
float	floating point	0.0	32 bits	over 10^{38}
double	floating point	0.0	64 bits	over 10^{308}

Since this is such a common kind of assignment, it seems wasteful to have to type the variable's name twice in every case. Thus there are four special assignments defined to abbreviate common increments and decrements. These are shown in the next form.

Increment and decrement assignments

```
variable ++;          // add one to variable
variable --;          // subtract one from variable
variable += exp;      // add exp to variable
variable -= exp;      // subtract exp from variable
```

---

i++ or *i*+=1 mean the same thing: 'add 1 to *i*', whereas '*i*+=2' means 'add 2 to *i*', and so on. Thus the example above becomes:

```
total++;
```

If we were always adding five, then we would use

```
total += 5;
```

One way to remember that the increment operator is += and not =+ is that the latter, in an assignment, could be misinterpreted as assigning a positive value, not adding it. That is,

```
total =+ 5;
```

would treat +5 as a constant and assign it to `total`.

Conversions between types

We have hinted on several occasions that it is possible to convert between numeric types. Why would we wish to do this? A common example is that of calculations which result in real values, but which then should be displayed as integers for ease of understanding. So far, two specific conversions have been discussed:

- Rounding a `double` number up to a `long` using `Math.round`.

- Assigning an `int` to a `double` number.

Another kind of conversion applies across the board to the numeric types in order of size, which means we can assign

```
byte => short => int => long => float => double
```

or any combination of these in the same direction. For example, `byte` to `long` is allowed, and `short` to `double`. But what about the other direction? Suppose we want to 'downsize' a `double` to a `float`. In this case we have to use a **type cast**. The type cast takes the form:

Type cast
(type) *expression*

For example,

```
float kilograms;
double estimate;
kilograms = (float) (estimate * 1.2);
```

The proviso is that the value of the expression must be applicable to the values that can be stored by the type. Referring to Table 3.1, we could not cast a short value of 1000 into a byte, since it would not fit. Java will report a compilation error (if the value is deducible at compile time) or otherwise a run-time error. In the case of real to integer type casts, however, any fractional part is discarded. For example,

```
(int) 6.3  gives 6
(int) 6.8  gives 6
```

Finally, we note that type casting is allowed only between numeric types. Unlike other languages, there is no facility in Java for converting characters and Booleans into numbers and vice versa.

3.3   Repetition with for-loops

Computers, like all machines, are very good at doing the same thing over and over again. In a program, such repetition can be formulated as a **loop**. There are two kinds of loops possible in Java, as in most languages – **for-loops** and **conditional-loops**. In this section we look at for-loops; the conditional ones are introduced in Chapter 5.

The form of a for-loop

A basic Java for-loop is specified in the following form:

Simple for-statement

for (*start; check; update*) {
    body
}

The `for`, brackets and braces form the compulsory structure of the loop, and the italicized parts have to be expanded. The **start** part introduces one or more **loop variables** which are to be tested and updated. If there is more than one loop variable then their starting statements are separated by commas.

The **check** is a comparison which gives the condition for the loop to end, based on the current value of the loop variables. The **update** part consists of assignments to change the values of the loop variables each time round the loop. The **body** of the loop consists of statements. If there is only one statement, then the braces can be omitted.

Usually, there is only one loop variable. Loop variables must be numbers, and by convention they are usually integers. It is possible, but this is considered bad practice, to have a loop variable which is a real number. The reason is that a comparison on real numbers is inexact at the limits, and a loop may execute for one more or less than the number of times expected.

Consider the following example to print out five rows of stars

```
for (int i=0; i<5; i++)
    System.out.println("**********");
```

Are we sure that five and not six rows are printed? Once the initialization has been completed (and it happens only once) the sequence in which the other three parts of the loop are executed is:

    check
    body
    update

Taking it slowly, *i* starts at 0. It is checked against 5, a line of stars is printed and *i* is incremented to 1. When *i* gets to 3, the stars are printed, *i* is incremented to 4, checked against 5, more stars are printed, and *i* is incremented to 5. Now it is checked that it is *less than* 5 and fails. The loop then ends and control continues after the final brace. We can therefore verify that five rows are printed.

It is good practice to have a standard way of writing simple for-loops. If we want to run a loop *n* times, we can choose between:

```
for (int i=1; i<=n; i++)

for (int i=0; i<n; i++)
```

The first version is perhaps easier to understand. However, many related sequences in Java, such as the months of the year and arrays (as discussed in Chapter 6), use zero as a starting point. It has therefore become conventional to start loops at zero, and the second form is therefore preferred.

EXAMPLE 3.1   Multiple labels

Problem   Ms Mary Brown of 33 Charles Street, Brooklyn would like to print out several return addresses which she is going to photocopy onto sticky labels.

Solution   We checked with Ms Brown and confirmed that for the time being, she is happy to have the labels one underneath each other. (Later on we shall see how to fill a page with labels.) The solution is to take the body of the `DisplayWarning` program in Example 2.1 as a model and put it in a loop.

Program   The program follows on quite easily. Note that we follow each label by two blank lines to separate them, and use a constant, nLabels, to specify how many labels there must be.

```
class lotsaLabels {

    /* The Lots of Labels program      by J M Bishop July 1996
       prints labels one underneath each other.
       Illustrates a simple for-loop. */

static final int nLabels = 8;

  public static void main (String [] args) {

    for (int i=0; i<nLabels; i++) {
      System.out.println ("--------------------");
      System.out.println ("|                  |");
      System.out.println ("|  Ms Mary Brown   |");
      System.out.println ("|  33 Charles Street |");
      System.out.println ("|  Brooklyn         |");
      System.out.println ("|                  |");
      System.out.println ("--------------------");
      System.out.println ("\n\n");
    }
  }
}
```

Using the loop variable

The loop variable serves to record the current iteration of a loop and, its values can be used in various ways, some of which are:

- in an output statement;

- in simple arithmetic;

- as part of the bounds of another loop.

Together, these three facilities make looping much more interesting. Take the first use. We can number the star lines printed earlier as follows:

```
for (int i=0; i<5; i++) {
  System.out.print((i+1));
  System.out.println(" **********");
}
```

which would print

```
1 **********
2 **********
3 **********
4 **********
5 **********
```

Notice that the loop variable, *i*, runs from 0 to 4, but we print out (*i*+1), giving 1 to 5. If we had not put the *i*+1 in parentheses, then it would have been misinterpreted as the value of *i* plus a string concatenation with the value 1, giving 01 11 21 31 41. Check it and see.

Now consider how to print out the first 10 even numbers. There are actually two ways. We can have a loop from 0 up to and not including 10 and write out double the loop variable, as in:

```
for (int number = 0; number < 10; number++)
  System.out.println (number * 2);
System.out.println ();
```

which will produce:

```
0 2 4 6 8 10 12 14 16 18
```

The other way is to do the doubling in the update-part, which would be:

```
for (int number = 0; number < 10; number+=2)
  System.out.println (number);
System.out.println ();
```

To print the first 10 odd numbers requires a bit of thought. If number*2 is an even number, then number*2+1 or number*2-1 is an odd number. Choosing one of these expressions, we have:

```
for (int number = 0; number < 10; number++)
  System.out.println (number * 2 + 1);
System.out.println ();
```

which will produce:

```
1 3 5 7 9 11 13 15 17 19
```

EXAMPLE 3.2 Conversion table

Problem An oceanography laboratory measures temperatures of lakes in Celsius, but some of the technicians want the values in Fahrenheit. For the time being, the managers have agreed to put up conversion tables around the laboratory. You have to write the program to generate the conversion table.

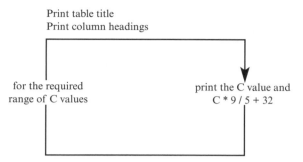

Print table title
Print column headings

for the required
range of C values

print the C value and
C * 9 / 5 + 32

Figure 3.2 *Algorithm for a conversion table.*

Solution   Use a loop to go through the range of temperatures required, writing out the one temperature and then its conversion.

Algorithm   The algorithm for a conversion table needs a heading, and then a sequence-printing loop, as described in the discussion above. Figure 3.2 shows the algorithm in diagrammatic form. What will the required range of C values be? Well, if these are water temperatures, they could range from 5 to 20.

Program   The program follows on easily. Notice that we type cast the real value produced by the expression to get the answers out as integers. To get reasonable layout, we use the escape character \t for tab.

```
class conversion {

  /* The Temperature Table Program     by J M Bishop Aug 1996
     displays a simple table converting
     Celsius to Fahrenheit for a given range.
     Illustrates using the loop variable in
     expressions in the loop */

 public static void main (String [] args) {

    System.out.println("Temperature Conversion Table");
    System.out.println("==============================");
    System.out.println();
    System.out.println("C          F");
    for (int c = 5; c <=20; c++) {
      System.out.print(c + "\t");
      System.out.println(Math.round (c*9/5 + 32));
    }
  }
}
```

Testing   The program output follows. We could redirect the output to a file, print the file and pin the table up on the wall.

```
Temperature Conversion Table
==============================
C          F
5          41
6          42
7          44
8          46
9          48
10         50
11         51
12         53
13         55
14         57
15         59
16         60
17         62
18         64
19         66
20         68
```

We note that loops can also count backwards using -- or -=. Thus, to print the sequence

```
10 9 8 7 6 5 4 3 2 1 0 -1 -2 -3 -4 -5 -6
```

we could say

```
for (int n = 10; n >=-6; n--)
   System.out.print(n);
System.out.println();
```

A nice example of counting backwards is found in the song 'One man went to mow', which is discussed in the next example.

In addition, we can have loops within loops, which is also illustrated in Example 3.3. The rule here is that the loop variables of the loops must have different identifiers to avoid confusion. Such loops are called **nested loops**.

EXAMPLE 3.3 Campfire song

Problem   A popular campfire song goes like this:

1 man went to mow, went to mow a meadow,
1 man and his dog, went to mow a meadow.

2 men went to mow, went to mow a meadow,
2 men, 1 man and his dog, went to mow a meadow.

3 men went to mow, went to mow a meadow,
3 men, 2 men, 1 man and his dog, went to mow a meadow.

We would like to print out the words up to a given number of men.

Solution   The way of tackling this problem is to take a verse from the output and under-line those parts that change each time, that is:

<u>3</u> men went to mow, went to mow a meadow,
<u>3</u> men, <u>2</u> men, <u>1</u> man and his dog, went to mow a meadow.

We have carefully used digits rather than words for the numbers, to make programming easier.

Algorithm   We set up one loop for the verses, based on how many men there are, and one loop to repeat all the men in reverse order.

Program   A first attempt at a program for five men is:

```
class mow {

    /* The Song Printing program      by J M Bishop Aug 1996
       displays the "One man went to Mow" song
       Illustrates nested and backward-counting for-loops */

    public static void main (String [] args) {

      System.out.println("****** One man went to mow ******");
      for (int man = 1; man<=5; man++) {
        System.out.println(man +
            " men went to mow, went to mow a meadow,");
        for (int companions=man; companions>=2; companions --)
            System.out.print(companions + " men, ");
        System.out.println("1 man and his dog, " +
            "went to mow a meadow. ");
        System.out.println();
      }
    }
}
```

Testing   This will produce:

```
****** One man went to mow ******
1 men went to mow, went to mow a meadow,
1 man and his dog, went to mow a meadow.

2 men went to mow, went to mow a meadow,
2 men, 1 man and his dog, went to mow a meadow.

3 men went to mow, went to mow a meadow,
3 men, 2 men, 1 man and his dog, went to mow a meadow.

4 men went to mow, went to mow a meadow,
4 men, 3 men, 2 men, 1 man and his dog, went to mow a meadow.

5 men went to mow, went to mow a meadow,
5 men, 4 men, 3 men, 2 men, 1 man and his dog, went to mow a meadow.
```

The output has one defect: the first line is written as '1 men ...' rather than '1 man ...'. To correct the program, we need to know about if-statements, covered in the next chapter.

Skipping the body of a loop

It may happen with a loop that the starting condition may already exceed the finishing one. In this case, the loop body is not executed at all. In the above example, the statement

```
for (int companions = man; companions >=2; companions --)
```

will be in this situation when man is 1. No 'men' phrases are written out for this verse, which is exactly what was intended.

3.4   Making methods

The concept of a method was introduced in Section 2.2 and used extensively in the previous chapter, where we became familiar with using methods from packages (such as `println` and `getDate`), and writing programs with a main method. We now look at how to declare our own methods.

Declaring a method

A **method** is a group of declarations and statements which is given a name and may be called upon by this name to perform a particular action. The form of a method declaration is:

```
Method declaration

modifiers kind name (parameters) {
   declarations and statements
   return expression;   // typed methods only
}
```

As before, the parts in italics are intended to be filled in. The modifiers that we have encountered so far include `public`, `static` and `final`. These can be used with their same meanings. The kind can be one of:

* `void`,

* a type,

* a class.

`void` indicates that the method can be called to perform an action in a self-standing way, for example `println`. In contrast, methods that have a type (one of the eight above, for example `int`) or a class (for example `Date`) will return a value and are called in a different way. These methods must have a **return-statement** somewhere which is executed to assign to the method a final value. The brackets after the identifier are compulsory and introduce the parameters, more about which in Section 3.5. An example of a simple void method without parameters is:

```
static void box () {
  System.out.println ("-------------");
  System.out.println ("|           |");
  System.out.println ("|           |");
  System.out.println ("|           |");
  System.out.println ("-------------");
}
```

Creating a method like this is a **declaration**. The name `box` is declared to introduce the performing of the given statements.

As an example of a typed method, consider the conversion from Celsius to Fahrenheit. If this operation is to be performed frequently, we could create a method for it as follows:

```
static int Fahrenheit (int Celsius) {
  return Celsius * 9/5 - 32;
}
```

Calling a method

If a method is declared as void, it is called by mentioning its name and parameters (if any). For example, to display a box, all we need to say is:

```
box();
```

the effect of which will be to print:

If it has a type or class (known generally as a **typed method**), then a call to it consitutes an expression and can be used wherever an expression of that type is permitted. Typically, typed methods would be called in assignments, as parts of expressions, or in output statements.

For example, referring back to the `Date` class discussed in Section 2.5, there is a method defined as

```
public int getMonth ( );
```

Within our main method we declare an object:

```
Date today = new Date (97, 6, 18);
```

and then we can find out the month by calling:

```
System.out.println (today.getMonth ( ));
```

Let us go through this example very carefully. `getMonth` is an instance method, in other words it is available for each object declared as a `Date`. It is also a typed method as opposed to a void method in that it is declared as `int`. This means that it will return an integer value when called. The method has no parameters. When we call `getMonth`, we preface it with the object we are using, and it will return the relevant information for that object, in this case the month, say of July.

Calling the conversion method defined above would be similar:

```
System.out.println (30 + "C is " + Fahrenheit (30) + "F");
```

which would print out

30C is 86F

A nuance of method calls that we have already mentioned in Section 2.2 is that the prefix depends on the method's modifiers and where it is defined relative to the call.

Method calls	
`method (parameters);`	`// declared static in this class`
`object.method (parameters);`	`// declared in another object`
`classname.method (parameters);`	`// declared static in`
	`// another class`

Specific examples of these different calls will arise in Section 3.5 as we get into the design of classes.

Defining methods, whether they are static as part of small programs, or subdivisions of a class's operation, enables us to cut down on repetition. It provides a means of creating a structure for a program, since the name of a method can be carefully chosen to reflect the action it performs. Readability is also enhanced.

Passing parameters

Methods can be made more powerful by allowing the effect to differ each time the method is called. For example, if we have a method that prints a 5 by 5 box, it would be useful if it were able to print a 10 by 10 box, or a 12 by 16 box, or whatever. In other words, the action of printing a box by means of `println` methods should appear to be independent of the number of `println`s that are actually needed. This is called **generalizing** or **parameterizing** a method and the values that are going to be different are known as **parameters**.

What we are aiming at is a means of being able to write:

```
box (5,5);
box (10,10);
box (12,16);
```

We achieve this goal by declaring the method with parameters that are given names and receive their values at the time the method is called. For the box, the declaration would become:

```
static void box (int width, int depth)
```

Although we refer to the items in the declaration and the call as parameters, strictly speaking the declaration introduces **formal** parameters, and the call provides **actual** parameters. The form for a list of formal parameters is:

Formal parameter declarations
(*type variable, type variable …*)

whereas the form for actual parameters is:

Actual parameters
(*expression, expression, …*)

The number, types and order of the formal and actual parameters must match exactly. For example, the box method can be called with:

```
int size = 60;
box (size, (int) size/2);
```

but not with any of

```
box(100);
box ("very wide");
box (12.5, 10);
```

To understand how parameters work, study Figure 3.3 carefully.

Now we note a very subtle point. Parameter passing only goes in one direction. Values can be passed into methods with parameters, but not out of them. To get a value out of a method, we use the return process of typed methods, as described above. This is not a Java restriction: it is the essence of object-oriented programming.

EXAMPLE 3.4   Large conversion tables

Problem   The oceanography laboratory was so pleased with the table we produced (Example 3.2) that they have asked us to do one for a larger range of temperatures, but to arrange it so that the whole table fits nicely on the screen or on a page.

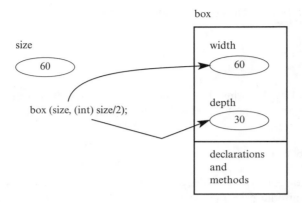

Figure 3.3 *An example of parameter passing.*

Solution We know how to do the conversion, so what we need to think about is how to arrange the layout of the table. A standard computer screen is lines 80 characters wide. Each pair of temperatures will occupy no more than 16 characters. We can therefore fit 5 columns on the screen. For temperatures from 0 to 99, this gives 20 lines, which will fit nicely on a screen or a page. We can then use nested loops to get the desired effect.

Algorithm We can tackle the solution from the top. We know how to print one line because we did it in Example 3.2. It is:

```
System.out.println (C + "\t" + Math.round(C * 9 / 5 + 32));
```

We can therefore set up a loop to print 20 such lines. The printing of the lines can go in a typed method.

Program Let us define the following constants:

```
static final int colsperline = 5;
static final int maxlineno = 20;
```

The lines will be numbered by the loop from 0 to 19 (that is, up to but not including 20) with a loop variable line. Printing one line can be put in a method, outaLine, with its own loop and loop variable, say col. Then the expression for the Celsius value on a given line and column will be:

```
thisline * colsperline + col
```

In order to clarify the program, we make some improvements at the point where the above expression would appear. Firstly, we create a typed method to perform the conversion from Celsius to Fahrenheit. Then because the Celsius value appears twice – once when it is printed out and once when it is used for the conversion – we assign it to a local variable, *C*.

Finally, tabs are set so that the columns line up, for both the headings and the values. However, notice that the numbers will be left-justified by Java, rather than lined up on the right, as would be more natural. The full program has plenty of comments to explain what is happening.

```java
class conversionTable {

  /* Conversion Table Program        by J M Bishop September 1996

     produces a conversion table from Celsius to Fahrenheit
     for values from 0 to 99.
     Illustrates static methods for structuring, as well as
     typed methods and parameters.
  */

  static final int colsperline = 5;
  static final int maxlineno = 20;
  static final String gap = "\t";

  public static void main (String [] args) {

    System.out.println("\t\tTemperature Conversion Table");

    System.out.println("\t\t============================");
    System.out.println();
    for (int col=0; col < colsperline; col++)
      System.out.print("C   F"+gap);
    System.out.println();

    // for each of the lines required, the outaLine
    // method is called with the line number r as a
    // parameter.
    for (int r = 0; r < maxlineno; r++) {
      outaLine(r);
    }
  }

  static void outaLine (int thisline) {

    /* Using the information given by the parameter as
    to which line this is, the method calculates the
    Celsius values for that line and displays them with
    their Fahrenheit equivalents */

    for (int col=0; col < colsperline; col++) {
      int C = thisline * colsperline + col;
      System.out.print (C + " ");
      System.out.print(Fahrenheit(C) + gap);
    }
    System.out.println();
  }

  // a simple conversion method
  static int Fahrenheit (int Celsius) {
    return Math.round(Celsius*9/5+32);
  }
}
```

Testing   Running the program confirms that it does produce the required effect, and the right answers.

```
                    Temperature Conversion Table
                    ==============================
    C     F     C     F     C     F     C     F     C     F
    0    32     1    33     2    35     3    37     4    39
    5    41     6    42     7    44     8    46     9    48
   10    50    11    51    12    53    13    55    14    57
   15    59    16    60    17    62    18    64    19    66
   20    68    21    69    22    71    23    73    24    75
   25    77    26    78    27    80    28    82    29    84
   30    86    31    87    32    89    33    91    34    93
   35    95    36    96    37    98    38   100    39   102
   40   104    41   105    42   107    43   109    44   111
   45   113    46   114    47   116    48   118    49   120
   50   122    51   123    52   125    53   127    54   129
   55   131    56   132    57   134    58   136    59   138
   60   140    61   141    62   143    63   145    64   147
   65   149    66   150    67   152    68   154    69   156
   70   158    71   159    72   161    73   163    74   165
   75   167    76   168    77   170    78   172    79   174
   80   176    81   177    82   179    83   181    84   183
   85   185    86   186    87   188    88   190    89   192
   90   194    91   195    92   197    93   199    94   201
   95   203    96   204    97   206    98   208    99   210
```

Example 3.4 illustrated methods and parameters well. However, the call to `outaLine` used just a single variable, `r`, each time. Methods and parameters become more interesting when the actual expression passed to the formal parameter is computed from several values, as shown in the next example.

EXAMPLE 3.5   Financial modelling

Problem   SavBank has a growth plan for savings which gives interest based on a novel formula. If the money is invested for a fixed period (say 10 years), then the interest is calculated as:

$$\frac{P \times (T + 10\%) \times R}{100}$$

where P is the principal invested, T is the number of years, and R is the rate of interest. We would like to produce a diagram of how the principal will grow, given different investment periods, say from 5 to 15 years.

Solution   We could write a program similar to the temperature conversion one, listing the years versus the final principal. However, it would be much clearer for customers if the growth was shown in a graph. How do we draw a graph?

```
SavBank Growth Plan
===================
Principal of 1000 at rate 12.5

Years
5        |**************** 1750
6        |****************** 1900
7        |****************** 2050
8        |******************** 2200
9        |********************* 2350
10       |***********************2500
11       |*************************2650
12       |**************************2800
13       |***************************2950
14       |*****************************3100
15       |******************************3250
         =========================================================
         +         +         +         +         +         +
         0        1000      2000      3000      4000      5000
                 Graz
```

Figure 3.4   *A financial modelling histogram.*

For financial modelling, a histogram is usually a good idea. We can show the number of years down the vertical axis, and draw the histogram going outwards, with graz (the currency) on the *x*-axis. Figure 3.4 shows the effect we could achieve.

In order to write a program to do this, we draw on all the techniques we have explored so far, and set up the following plan:

1.   Decide how to print a single histogram bar for a given value *h*, including scaling *h* to fit on one line. This will be the `bar` method. It has an additional parameter for the *y*-axis label (the year).

2.   Express the interest formula in proper Java.

3.   Set up a call to the `bar` method with the formula as a parameter.

4.   Put the call to `bar` in a loop over the number of possible investment periods (years).

5.   Design the `println` statements for the heading and final axis using loops.

Program   Put all together, the program is quite long, but the comments help to explain it. Notice that we have placed the main method first, and followed it by the `bar` and `axis` methods which it calls. Unlike some other languages, Java does not mind in which order methods are declared.

```
class histogram {

   /* Financial Modelling Program     by J M Bishop Aug 1996
      displays a histogram of simple interest * 1.2
      for a given principal and rate for 5 to 15 years.
```

```
        Illustrates parameter passing and for loops.*
static final double P = 1000;
static final double rate = 12.5;

public static void main (String [] args) {

  // The headings
  System.out.println("SavBank Growth Plan");
  System.out.println("===================");
  System.out.println("Principal of "+P+" at rate "+rate);
  System.out.println();
  System.out.println("Years");

  // Display a bar for each year
  // and then the final axis
  for (int year = 5; year <= 15; year++)
    bar(year, P * 1.2*year*rate/100 + P);
  axis();
}

static void bar(int label, double h) {
  /* Draws a single histogram bar
     labelled with the years and consisting of
     h/100 stars */

  System.out.print(label + "\t|");
  int stop = (int) (h/100);
  for (int star=0; star < stop; star++)
    System.out.print('*');
  System.out.println(" " + h);
}

static void axis () {
  /* Draws a horizontal axis with ticks+1 divisions
  labelled in steps of 1000. Each division is 10
  characters wide.*/

  int ticks = 5;

  // Print the bar
  System.out.print('\t');
  for (int bar=0; bar < ticks*10; bar++)
    System.out.print('=');
  System.out.println('=');

  //Print the ticks
  System.out.print('\t');
  for (int n=0; n < ticks; n++)
    System.out.print("+ ");
  System.out.println('+');

  // Label the ticks, including the last one
  System.out.print('\t');
  for (int n=0; n <= ticks; n++)
    System.out.print(n*1000 + " ");
  System.out.println();
```

```
      // Label the whole axis
    System.out.println("\t\t\t\tgraz");
  }
}
```

Testing The output is shown in Figure 3.4. This example is extended in the problems at the end of the chapter.

3.5   Guidelines for designing classes

Methods are a means of grouping statements. At the next level, classes are a means of grouping methods. Specifically, we group together methods that serve a common purpose. For example, the `Math` class in Java provides trigonometrical methods, and the `PrintStream` class provides printing methods.

In a class, we can do more than just group methods. We can also include data items. The design of the class in terms of the methods and data it provides is the cornerstone of object-oriented programming, and central to the way Java is intended to be used. We therefore consider some guiding principles for design here and follow this with an example and a case study, both of which make good use of classes and objects.

Guidelines for class design

1. **Coherence**. A class should be concerned with a single physical entity or a set of similar operations. For example, the `Date` class defines and manipulates dates; the `Math` class provides operations of a trigonometiric and exponential nature.

2. **Separation of concerns**. Even for a single entity, one can have several related classes rather than one class. For example, `Date` does not provide any output for dates, but we could imagine settting up quite a useful class which could provide various options for the popular forms of date output.

3. **Information hiding**. A class should reveal to the user only that which has to be revealed and no more. In this way data can be protected from misuse, and the class can operate on a more secure basis. There is also a case to be made for methods to be hidden if they are not relevant to users, but are needed only by the class itself. The modifier for hiding declarations is `private`. By default, all declarations are accessible.

4. **Data access via methods**. Following on from 3, a guideline that is followed in all of Java's standard classes is that most data is hidden from the user, but made accessible via appropriate methods. In this way the data is protected from inappropriate changes. For example, the `Date` class does not reveal the day, month and year fields of any `Date` instance. To access them, one uses an appropriate `get` or `set` method. A `set` method could presumably include checks that the parameter is within a valid range: for example, `setMonth(20)` would be rejected.

5.   **Object initialization**. When an object is created, it is efficient to copy in values for all its initial values, so that these can be used later. This is in preference to supplying the values repeatedly as parameters. For example, with the Date class, we set up the initial values of the date, and unless we change them, these are always available. Of course, some values must change, but the aim is to keep method calls as simple as possible. This guideline is tested to the full in the case study that follows in Section 3.6.

Other guidelines will be mentioned as the need arises.

Design notation

There are many diagrammatic notations for representing classes and objects. Some of these are quite complex and become languages in their own right. In order to keep the notation gentle, we have tried to use very simple blocks and lines here, with the meanings as laid out in Figure 3.5.

The method described is based on one of the most popular – Rumbaugh's OMT (object modelling technique) – but has been slightly adapted for use in *Java Gently*, forming what we might call JMT. The adaptations are as follows:

- Methods, variables and other detailed items have symbols, so that programs can be fully depicted with JMT.

- The class symbol is a dotted oblong, not a rectangle, as a rectangle is used for a method. This symbol is similar to that used in the Booch notation.

- The indicator for instantiating an object from a class does not necessarily have to have an arrow, since it is obvious which symbol is instantiating the other (that is, a class cannot be an instantiation of an object). Arrows tend to clutter a diagram.

- There are additional symbols for Java entites not envisaged by OMT: reference, interface, private, exception, and so on.

An alternative to the diamond in the contains relationship is a circle. The private lines apply to most of the other symbols, or they can be used down the side of a whole section of a class. The usage of the rest of the different symbols and lines will be explained as we go along.

Constructors

Every class should have at least one constructor, which is called when an object of the class is declared. We saw how to use the Date class constructors in Section 2.5. How do we create constructors for new classes? The form is:

Constructor

``
modifiers classname (parameters) {
  statements
}
``

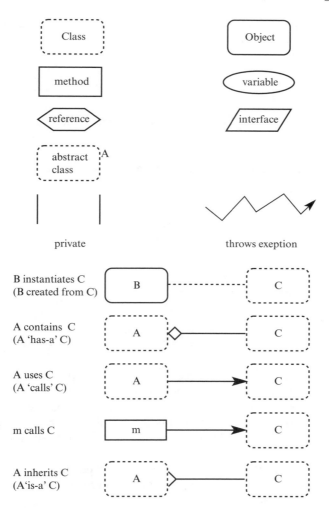

Figure 3.5 *A simple notation for class diagrams.*

In other words, a constructor is a method with the name of the class itself. A class can have several different constructors with different lists of parameters, including, often, one with no parameters at all. A constructor from the next example is:

```
Labels (int a) {
   across = a;
}
```

which has the function of storing an initial value given in a parameter into a private class variable, in accordance with guideline 5 above.

Modifiers may include only the ones used on the class itself. For simple user classes, there will be no modifiers, but for standard packages, the `public` modifier is needed, as we saw in the `Dates` class (Figure 2.10).

The next example shows how a system can be built up from two classes. It uses the JMT notation to describe their interaction.

EXAMPLE 3.6   Labels with class

Problem   We wish to print out blank labels side by side, with suitable gaps between them.

Solution   There exists a method to print a rectangle, that is:

```
static void box () {
  println ("--------------------");
  println ("|                   |");
  println ("|                   |");
  println ("|                   |");
  println ("--------------------");
}
```

but if we call

```
box(); box(); box();
```

the labels will come out one underneath each other. The Java `println` method regards the output file as consisting of lines which are written in sequence. The contents of each line have to be composed and written out before going on to the next line. This model corresponds very closely to a screen or printer. It is also possible to create a model whereby the screen or page can be drawn on freely, going up and down, back and forth, and this is discussed in Part II.

However, given the sequential nature of ordinary output, the way to get the labels side by side is to have the outer loop being concerned with rows, then for each row, consider each label across the page.

Class design   At this point we must consider the design of the classes. Clearly labels are potential objects. The question is, what operations do they need? We notice that there are two kinds of rows in a label: the one with the dashes, and the one with the uprights and spaces. The printing of these could be offered as methods by the labels class. The controlling class could then call them in loops as required.

What information should be supplied when this label class is instantiated? Since it is going to print several labels across the page, the number of labels could be set up at initialization. This number must remain the same for all the calls for a particular size of label, so it is quite correct that it be a constructor parameter, and not one for the methods themselves. The design of the program is shown in Figure 3.6.

`blankLabels` is a class which has one method, `main`. `main` has an object, `label`, instantiated from the `Labels` class. For each label there is a private variable, `across`, and two accessible methods, `printH` and `printV`. These are both called by `main`.

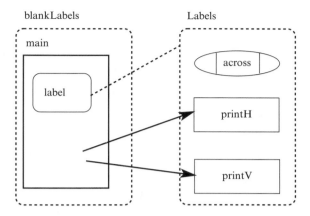

Figure 3.6   *Design for the label printing program.*

Program   First we look at the labels class.

```
class Labels {
  // A class to provide services for printing
  // a given number of labels across. The class is
  // independent of how deep the labels are going to be.

  Labels (int a) {
    across = a;
  }

  void printHorizontals () {
    for (int box = 0; box < across; box++)
      System.out.print("------------          ");
    System.out.println();
  }

  void printVerticals () {
    for (int box=0; box < across; box++)
      System.out.print("|              |      ");
    System.out.println();
  }

  private int across;

}
```

The class is neat and easy to read. Notice that the constructor parameter is copied into a private variable, which can be used by the classes methods but not seen by anyone who uses the class.

Now consider the program:

```
class blankLabels {

    /* The blank Label Printing program.      by J M Bishop
                                    revised December 1996
       Displays labels across the screen of a
       certain depth.
       Illustrates the use of a class, the use of
       instance methods and parameter passing. */

       static final int nLabels = 4;
       static final int depth = 5;

       public static void main (String [] args) {

       // Create an instance of the class that will
       // do the printing for a certain number of labels

       Labels label = new Labels (nLabels);

       // Print the two horizontal lines around the
       // required number of vertical ones.
       label.printHorizontals( );
       for (int row=0; row < depth; row++)
          label.printVerticals( );
       label.printHorizontals( );
    }
}
```

Testing Running the program will produce:

To change the number of labels across, all we need do is change the nLabels constant in the main program. Notice that the use of methods has helped in two ways:

• **Repetition**: the horizontal loop is not repeated, as it is packaged up in a method,

• **Understanding**: the nested loops are separated out, making the program easier to read.

In the exercises, we look at how to print more than one size of label in one run of the program. In the case study, we take this further by looking at different instantiations of the same object, based on variations in the constructor.

3.6 Case study 1: Price tickets

The solution to the following problem exploits classes, objects, constructors, loops, methods and parameters, showing their power fully.

Problem

Savanna High School is having a fête and has set all food and drink at prices of one, two, five or eight graz. They would like to design suitable price tickets on the computer. The G5 and G8 tickets should be bigger and more impressive than the G1 and G2 ones. Some suggestions could be:

```
-----------        ================
|2222222222|       =5555555555555=
|2222222222|       =5555555555555=
|2222222222|       =5555555555555=
-----------        =5555555555555=
                   =5555555555555=
                   ================
```

Solution

We need a method that can print a box of any size, up to a maximum of 80 wide and 20 deep. Parameters should help here, and so certainly will classes. Let us first simplify the problem by considering only the smaller tickets with a standard hyphen and bar border. Then the only variable parts are the width and depth of the ticket, and the price.

In Example 3.6, we treated the 'horizontal' and 'vertical' lines of the box separately. In fact, by using generalization, we can regard them as the same, but with different left, centre and right symbols. In other words, we have:

Line type	Left	Centre	Right
Horizontal	–	–	–
Vertical	|	price	|

Now we can define a further method to print a line with the symbols as parameters, and call it the required number of times.

Algorithm

Let us assume that the *width* and *depth* are the given measurements. Then each line consists of the following sequence:

> **aLine (left, centre, right)**
> > Draw the left symbol
> > Draw width-2 centre symbols
> > Draw the right symbol

The box itself consists of:

> **varyBox (price)**
> Draw a line with arguments (–, -, -)
> Draw depth-2 lines with arguments (|, price, |)
> Draw a line with arguments (-, -, -)

The two methods to print the smaller tickets are:

```
void aLine (char left, char centre, char right) {
    System.out.print(left);
    for (int w=2; w < width; w++)
      System.out.print (centre);
    System.out.println (right);
}

void varyBox (char price) {
  aLine('-','-','-');
  for (int d=2; d<depth; d++)
    aLine('|',price,'|');
  aLine('-','-','-');
  System.out.println();
}
```

Class design

Clearly the two methods fit together. In fact they are the basis for a `Tickets` class. What we still need to establish is the constructor. What should it contain? It must have the values for the depth and width. And at this stage we can generalize to the other kind of ticket design and let the horizontal and vertical characters be supplied as well. We do not, however, supply the price, since this could change with the same object, which encapsulates a certain design. For example, G1 and G2 tickets have everything in common except the price. The new `Tickets` class is:

```
class Tickets {

  Tickets(char h, char v, int d, int w) {
    hori = h;
    verti = v;
    depth = d;
    width = w;
  }

  void varyBox (char price) {
    aLine(hori, hori, hori);
    for (int d=2; d<depth; d++)
      aLine(verti,price,verti);
    aLine(hori, hori, hori);
    System.out.println();
  }
```

printTickets   Tickets

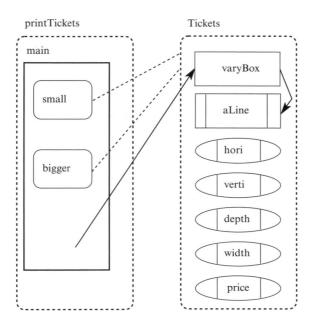

Figure 3.7   *Diagram of the ticket printing program.*

```
private void aLine (char left, char centre, char right) {
  System.out.print(left);
  for (int w=2; w < width; w++)
    System.out.print (centre);
  System.out.println (right);
}

private char hori, verti, price;
private int depth, width;

}
```

Everything that can be declared private, is. Only `varyBox` and the constructor are available. Notice the clustering of the private method and variables at the end of the class: this helps to remove them from the eye of the reader. At this point we can envisage the class diagram, as in Figure 3.7.

And now for the program. It is very simple, declaring two objects and then using each of these twice to print different valued tickets. In so doing, it very clearly shows the difference between objects and method calls on those objects.

```
class printTickets {

  /* The Ticket printing program      by J M Bishop Sept 1996
                                       revised Dec 1996
     Prints out four tickets from two different designs.

  public static void main (String [] args) {
```

```
System.out.println
   ("Suggested Price Tags for the fete");
priceTickets small = new priceTickets ('-','|',5,11);
small.varyBox ('2');
small.varyBox ('1');

priceTickets bigger = new priceTickets ('=','=',7,15);
bigger.varyBox ('5');
bigger.varyBox ('8');
   }
}
```

Testing

The output from the program above is:

```
Suggested Price Tags for the fete

-----------
|222222222|
|222222222|
|222222222|
-----------


-----------
|111111111|
|111111111|
|111111111|
-----------


===============
=5555555555555=
=5555555555555=
=5555555555555=
=5555555555555=
=5555555555555=
===============


===============
=8888888888888=
=8888888888888=
=8888888888888=
=8888888888888=
=8888888888888=
===============
```

SUMMARY

Programs need to be properly structured to achieve correctness, readability, reusability and efficiency. Contributing to proper structure are types (for data items), methods and parameters (for grouping statements) and classes (for modelling objects and grouping methods).

Apart from the numeric types, Java has types for `Boolean` and `char`. The numeric types can be converted into each other. Methods fall into two kinds: typed and void. Typed methods return values and are used in expressions. Methods can be prefaced with modifiers such as `static` and `private` which govern how they may be called. Parameters generalize methods, with values being able to be passed in but not out again.

For-loops provide for repeated execution of statements. The loop variables can be used in the loop, and loops can be nested inside each other as well as run 'backwards': that is, from a higher number to a lower one.

The design of classes is a crucial part of programming, and a simple notation for describing the design is useful. Guidelines for design included coherence, separation of concerns, information hiding, and careful access to and initialization of data.

QUIZ

3.1 How many stars would the following loop print out?

```
for (int star = 9; star<0; star++){
   System.out.print('*');
}
```

3.2 The following statements are meant to print a sequence consisting of a number and then that many equal signs followed by a plus, each on a new line. For example:

```
4 = = = = +
```

Can you work out what they actually print, and how to fix them?

```
int number;
for (number = 1; number < 5; number++) {
    System.out.println(number);
}
for (int sign = 1; sign < number; sign++) {
    System.out.println(sign);
}
System.out.println('+');
```

3.3 How would you display your name in the middle of a line 80 characters wide?

3.4 Write a loop to print out the decades of the 20th century (e.g. 1900, 1910 ...).

3.5 Write declarations of Boolean variables and suitable assignment statements to record whether a prospective student has the following school-leaving qualifications: a score of 20 and a C or more in maths or a D or more in maths and a C or more in computer science.

3.6 The `Tickets` class can be used to print blank tickets. Give an object declaration and a call to `varyBox` which will accomplish this.

3.7 Why was the price parameter of `varyBox` declared as `char` and not `int`?

3.8 Give the equivalent decrement assignment statement for

```
taxrate = taxrate - 0.5;
```

3.9 Given the declaration of a `mountain` method, namely:

```
static void mountain (int size; char symbol);
```

decide which of the following calls are valid or not, giving reasons:

```
mountain (0,0);
mountain (8, '8');
mountain (6);
```

3.10 Suppose we wished to print just a single line of `Ticket`, for testing purposes. Could we call the `aLine` method to do this?

PROBLEMS

3.1 **Interest changes**. In Example 2.2, we looked at how the interest received would change depending on a change of rate in a given month. In order to plan ahead, we would like to know how the interest would change based on the month in which the rate change is announced. Write a program to print out a table showing how the interest would change from January to November. Use the same data as in Example 2.2.

3.2 **Another song**. Another song that can go on a bit is:

There were 10 green bottles hanging on the wall,
10 green bottles hanging on the wall
And if one green bottle should accidentally fall
There'll be 9 green bottles hanging on the wall.

9 green bottles hanging on the wall
And if one green bottle should accidentally fall
There'll be 8 green bottles hanging on the wall.
etc.

1 green bottle hanging on the wall
And if one green bottle should accidentally fall
There'll be 0 green bottles hanging on the wall.

Using the technique discussed in Example 2.7, design an algorithm to print out such a song, and program it to start with 5 green bottles.

3.3 **A number triangle**. Write a program which uses for-statements and `print/println` statements to produce the following triangle:

```
1
2 2
3 3 3
4 4 4 4
5 5 5 5 5
```

Adapt the program to print the triangle so that the numbers are centred, as below. Adapt it again to print the triangle upside down.

```
    1
   2 2
  3 3 3
 4 4 4 4
5 5 5 5 5
```

3.4 **Shaded boxes**. Write a program to print out boxes consisting of 'darker' and 'lighter' sides, like this:

```
+--
++-
+++-
++++
```

3.5 **Conversions**. A conversion table can be viewed as a general algorithm. Establish this fact by adapting the program in Example 3.4 to print out the conversion from miles to kilometres (1 mile = 1.6 km) and again to print dollars to graz (1$ = 0.45G).

3.6 **Printing names**. Write methods to print out the letters of the alphabet that form your name, in a large format using asterisks. Each letter is formed on a 7 by 9 grid and drawn downwards, so that when the letters are printed out underneath each other, the name can be turned sideways and read. For example, for William, we need five methods, one to do each of the letters W, i, l, a and m, and the letters might look like this:

Create a class containing the methods, then write a program to call the methods in the right order to print your name. Should the methods be class methods or instance methods?

3.7 **Labels**. Adapt the program in Example 3.6 to print three labels with your name and address across the page, and do this eight times to fill the page. If you line the output up carefully, you can photocopy this on to standard-sized sticky labels.

3.8 **Clearer tables**. The conversion table of Example 3.4 is not quite right because the values increase across the page, rather than down, which is more normal. Can you work out how to change the program so as to print the values increasing in columns?

3.9 **Times tables**. In the olden days, exercise books used to have multiplication tables printed neatly on the back. These would be arranged three across and four down, with each row being of the form:

```
4 times table       5 times table       6 times table
1 × 4 = 4           1 × 5 = 5           1 × 6 = 6
2 × 4 = 8           2 × 5 = 10          2 × 6 = 12
3 × 4 = 12          3 × 5 = 15          3 × 6 = 18
4 × 4 = 16          4 × 5 = 20          4 × 6 = 24
5 × 4 = 20          5 × 5 = 25          5 × 6 = 30
6 × 4 = 24          6 × 5 = 30          6 × 6 = 36
```

```
 7 × 4 = 28          7 × 5 = 35          7 × 6 = 42
 8 × 4 = 32          8 × 5 = 40          8 × 6 = 48
 9 × 4 = 36          9 × 5 = 45          9 × 6 = 54
10 × 4 = 40         10 × 5 = 50         10 × 6 = 60
11 × 4 = 44         11 × 5 = 55         11 × 6 = 66
12 × 4 = 48         12 × 5 = 60         12 × 6 = 72
```

Write a program which makes good use of methods and parameters to print out a complete set of all the first 12 multiplication tables.

3.10 **Timetable**. It is always useful to have a blank timetable to fill in for one's lectures. Write a program that will print out such a timetable, with Monday to Friday across the top, and the hours 8 to 15 down the left. The timetable should have suitable borders.

3.11 **Histogram**. A histogram is generally a useful graph to draw. See if you can create a class based on that in Example 3.5 which includes bar and axis methods and can be called to print histograms for a variety of data. Test it by mapping the value of sin *x* against values of degrees from 0 to 90. Think of other examples that could be tried. (Note: they will have to be based on calculations since we have not learnt to read in values yet, or you could come back to this problem after Chapter 4.)

CHAPTER 4

Changing the state

4.1   Inputting interactively

A program will most often need to acquire values for its variables from the outside world. Such values form the **data** for the program and could consist of tables stored on disk, replies to questions or just lists of values to be typed in. The term **stream** is applied to the sequence of data items that will come from one source. Thus the keyboard is modelled by a stream, as is a file on disk. In this section we look at keyboard input, and follow it by looking at file input and output in Section 4.3.

Input files

The Java equivalent of `System.out` is `System.in`. Although `System.in` is also a predeclared item, its class is `InputStream`, which is an **abstract** class in Java terms. Abstract classes are covered fully in Chapter 8, but what we need to know here is that we cannot create objects of abstract classes. The `System.in` item must be supplied as a constructor parameter to another class called `DataInputStream`, thereby creating a usable object. We acknowledge that this is a complex way of handling matters, but the following form shows that the actual programming involved is not excessive.

```
┌─────────────────────────────────────────────────────────────┐
│ Declaring the keyboard for input                              │
├─────────────────────────────────────────────────────────────┤
│ import java.io.*;                                             │
│ DataInputStream stream = new DataInputStream(System.in);      │
└─────────────────────────────────────────────────────────────┘
```

Before the class statement, we must import the `java.io` package in which the `InputStream` and `DataInputStream` classes are defined. Then the declaration declares a new stream, connected to `System.in`, with all the facilities of the `DataInputStream` class. A typical such declaration is:

```
DataInputStream in = new DataInputStream (System.in);
```

which will declare `in` as the stream that is connected to the keyboard. In Section 4.3 we shall see how to connect streams to files as well.

One side effect of reading is that something could go wrong, for example the data might end unexpectedly. Such events are called **exceptions** and we shall see later in the chapter how to deal with them. Java requires that we indicate in every method which exceptions can occur. Therefore if we are going to read, we need to add the phrase

```
throws IOException
```

after the appropriate method.

Reading strings

Similar to the `println` method, the `DataInputStream` class provides a `readLine` method which will read in a full line of text to the given string. The form is:

```
┌─────────────────────────────────────────┐
│ Reading a string                         │
├─────────────────────────────────────────┤
│ string = readLine(stream);               │
└─────────────────────────────────────────┘
```

Notice two differences between this form and that for printing:

- The suffix is `-Line` not `-ln`;

- The method is typed, not void, so is called in an assignment, not on its own.

So for example, a simple program to greet someone in French would be:

```
import java.io.*;

class Greetings {
  public static void main (String [] args) throws IOException {
    DataInputStream in = new DataInputStream (System.in);
```

```
        System.out.println("What is your name?");
        String name = readLine(in);
        System.out.println("Bonjour " + name);
        }
    }
```

What is your name?
Pierre Marchand
Bonjour Pierre Marchand

ReadLine reads a whole line from the keyboard, up until return is pressed.

Java's approach to reading numbers

Java can read values of the other types of data if they are already in binary form and stored in a file. However, the language does not have a class for reading and converting numeric values written in textual form. Thus if we want to interact with a program from the keyboard, the idea is that we should read a string and do the conversion ourselves. This could be tedious, and is, after all, an operation that we may need to perform frequently. Therefore, most books create a little class which will provide the functionality required. *Java Gently* is no exception.

4.2 *Java Gently's* Text class

The class defined for *Java Gently* is called Text and it provides among others the methods shown in the following form:

The Text Class
| ```
void    prompt (String s);
int     readInt (DataInputStream in);
double  readDouble (DataInputStream in);
String  readString (DataInputStream in);
char    readChar (DataInputStream in);
``` |

prompt is a method that will print out a string, but then keep the cursor on the same line so that a reply can follow immediately. readInt and readDouble return numbers as required. readString is not exactly the same as the built-in method readLine because all of the Text class's methods have the property that multiple values can be typed on a single line. This feature is illustrated in the next example and exploited in the Olympic medals example (4.6). readChar reads a single character. The class is stored in a package called javagently and so in order to access it, a suitable import statement must be added to the program.

    The class is not at all long, and is discussed in full in Chapter 6. Now we look at an example that uses Text to good advantage.
```

Summing a list of numbers
Read in the count
Set the total to zero

Count times | Read a number
Add it to the total

Figure 4.1 *Algorithm for summing a sequence of numbers.*

EXAMPLE 4.1 Summing a sequence of numbers

Problem There is a sequence of numbers that needs to be summed, and the precise length of the sequence is not known.

Solution It is quite straightforward to read the numbers into the computer, adding each one in turn to a total. The problem is how to know when the end of the numbers has been reached. There are actually four ways:

1. **State in advance** how many items there must be and keep a running count.

2. **Precede the data by a count** of how many items there actually are, and keep a running count.

3. Make use of an **end-of-file exception** to mark the end of the items.

4. Put a **special terminating value** at the end of the items, such as zero or 999.

The first two methods are applicable to counting-loops, since they rely on the number of items being known before reading starts. In method 3 the number of items is not relevant; rather, the reading stops when a certain condition is achieved, and we show how to detect it in the next section. The last one is applicable to conditional loops, and is discussed in the next chapter.

Of the two methods for counting-loops, the second is more general, since the same program will be able to read in 10 numbers, or 55, or 1000, with just the data being changed. Let us consider it as a model for our solution.

Algorithm The algorithm is depicted in Figure 4.1.

Program

```
import java.io.*;
import javagently.*;
```

```
class summation1 {
  /* The first Summation program       by J M Bishop Aug 1996
     Reads in numbers interactively and
     displays their sum.
     Illustrates the declaration of an input stream
     and simple use of the Text class. */

public static void main (String [] args) throws IOException {

  DataInputStream in = new DataInputStream(System.in);

  int count;
  double total=0;
  double number;

  System.out.println("****** Summing numbers ******");
  Text.prompt("How many numbers?");
  count=Text.readInt(System.in);

  for (int i=1; i <= count; i++) {
    Text.prompt (i+"> ");
    number = Text.readDouble(System.in);
    total += number;
  }

  System.out.println("That's enough, thanks.");
  System.out.println("The total is " + total);
  }
}
```

Testing   Running the program will produce the following dialogue on the screen.

```
****** Summing numbers ******
How many numbers?   5
1>   23
2>   -18
3>   45
4>   11
5>   2
That's enough, thanks.
The total is 63
```

The plain type indicates the values that are typed in; bold type indicates output from the program. Notice that we try to make the running of the program as helpful to the user as possible. In Java, there are very fancy ways of doing this, as we shall investigate in Part II.

The flexible features of *Java Gently's* Text class

The Text class has a forgiving nature: it will detect bad numbers and permit you to type them in again. It allows – and ignores – blank lines and spaces between data items. It does not allow them inside strings, so, if we write a Text version of the greeting program, only one of Pierre's names would appear:

```
import java.io.*;
import javagently.*;

class Greetings2 {
  public static void main (String [] args) throws IOException {

    DataInputStream in = new DataInputStream (System.in);

    Text.prompt("What is your name?");
    String name = Text.readString(in);
    System.out.println("Bonjour " + name);
  }
}
```

What is your name? Pierre Marchand
Bonjour Pierre

`Greeting2` detects only a single word: that is, Pierre, not Pierre Marchand.

Text does actually allow multiple items on a line, we just have to be aware that we want them. So a third version of the greetings program for a two word name would be:

```
import java.io.*;
import javagently.*;

class Greetings3 {
  public static void main (String [] args) throws IOException {

    DataInputStream in = new DataInputStream (System.in);

    Text.prompt("What is your name?");
    String firstname = Text.readString(in);
    String secondname = Text.readString(in);
    System.out.println("Bonjour " + firstname+" "+secondname);
  }
}
```

What is your name? Pierre Marchand
Bonjour Pierre Marchand

Although forgiving, Text is very firm, and if it wants two names it will get them or die in the attempt. Thus the second call to `readString` will wait until another string is entered.

4.3   File input and output

Although it is a relief to be able to enter input to programs at last, interactive testing can rapidly become tedious. It is often better to keep the data in a file and read it from there. Certainly for large amounts of data this is essential. The extension to the stream declaration for declaring a file is:

Declaring a file for input

```
DataInputStream stream = new DataInputStream
                      (new FileInputStream("filename"));
```

Instead of supplying `System.in` as the parameter to the `DataInputStream` constructor, we create a new object of the `FileInputStream` class initialized with the actual file name. For example, to read data from a file called 'numbers' we would define a stream as

```
DataInputStream fin = new DataInputStream
                (new FileInputStream("numbers"));
```

`fin` is a `DataInputStream` and therefore it can be passed to any of the `Text` methods. In a program, one can have several streams open for input. For example, suppose we adapt the `summation1` program so that the count is read from the keyboard, but the numbers themselves are read from a file. We could dispense with the prompts in this case. The program becomes:

```
import java.io.*;
import javagently.*;

import java.io.*;

class summation2 {
   /* The second Summation program      by J M Bishop Dec 1996

      Reads in numbers from a file and
      displays their sum.
      Illustrates the declaration of two input streams. */

  public static void main (String [] args) throws IOException {

   DataInputStream in = new DataInputStream(System.in);
   DataInputStream fin = new DataInputStream
                (new FileInputStream("numbers"));
   int count;
   double total=0;
   double number;

// Gets the count from the keyboard
   System.out.println("**** Summing from numbers file ****");
   Text.prompt("How many numbers? ");
   count=Text.readInt(System.in);

// Reads the numbers from a file called "numbers"
   for (int i=1; i <= count; i++) {
     number = Text.readDouble(fin);
     total += number;
   }

   System.out.println("That's enough, thanks.");
   System.out.println("The total is " + total);
  }
}
```

If the same five numbers given in Example 4.1 were on the file, then the screen output would be:

```
**** Summing from numbers file ****
How many numbers? 5
That's enough, thanks.
The total is 63
```

Outputting to a file

It is very useful to be able to send output to a file. Not only does it make it easy to retain the results and print them out, but very often programs produce too much output to appear sensibly on the screen. In the same way as we set up a file input stream, we can set up a file output stream. The form is:

Output to a file

```
PrintStream stream = new PrintStream
                (new FileOutputStream ("filename"));
```

We recall that `println` and so on are part of the `PrintStream` class. In order to use them on the file, we create another `PrintStream` object. The object supplied to initialize it is a new `FileOutputStream` object, created with the file name that we want. So an example would be:

```
PrintStream fout = new PrintStream
            (new FileOutputStream("results"));
```

As a simple example, consider printing a label directly to a file. The program would be:

```
import java.io.*;

class printaLabel {

/* File printing program      by J M Bishop revised Dec 1996
   Prints a single label to a file.
   Illustrates file declarations and writing
   to a file and the screen in the same program */

public static void main (String [] args) throws IOException {

  PrintStream fout = new PrintStream
            (new FileOutputStream ("label.out"));

  System.out.println ("Printing the label to label.out");
  fout.println ("------------------------");
  fout.println ("|                       |");
  fout.println ("|  Ms Mary Brown        |");
  fout.println ("|  33 Charles Street    |");
  fout.println ("|  Brooklyn             |");
  fout.println ("|                       |");
  fout.println ("------------------------");
  System.out.println ("Program finished");
  }
}
```

The output produced by this program would be:

```
On the screen:
Printing the label to label.out
Program finished

In the file label.out
------------------------
|                      |
|   Ms Mary Brown      |
|   33 Charles Street  |
|   Brooklyn           |
|                      |
------------------------
```

4.4   Selection with if-else

Two methods of changing the values of variables have been covered so far: assignment and reading in. We now consider how to check the values in variables, and choose alternative actions based on the result of the check. Java has two **selection** statements known as the **if-statement** and the **switch-statement**. We look at the if-statement here, and the switch-statement in the next chapter.

Form of the if-statement

The general form of the if-statement is:

If-statement
```if``` (*condition*) *statement* ```else``` *statement*;

The condition is a Boolean expression as covered in Section 3.2. Examples are:

```
speed > speedlimit
(age >= 16) & (age < 75)
isaMinor
year == 1066
day != 29
initial != 'J'
```

In the if-statement we refer to the statement following the parentheses as the **then-part** and to the statement following the ```else``` as the **else-part**. The whole if-statement is executed as follows. First, the condition is evaluated. If this result is true, the then-part is executed, and the else-part is skipped. If the result is false, the then-part is skipped and the else-part is executed. A simple example would be:

```
if (number >= 0) System.out.println("Positive")
else System.out.println("Negative");
```

The following diagram explains the example further:

true   → write out Positive
number >=0
false   → write out Negative

In the form of the if-statement, the `else` is given in italics. This means that it is optional and the statement can be used in an 'if-then' version. For example,

```
if (day == 25) System.out.println("Christmas, Hooray");
```

In either case, the then- and else-statements can be blocks, which would be surrounded by braces.

EXAMPLE 4.2   Summing three ways

Problem   A sequence of numbers needs to be summed, and separate sums kept of the positive and negative numbers as well.

Solution   Start with the `Summation1` program in Example 4.1. Add in two new totalling variables, and use an if-statement to cause values to be added to one or the other.

Algorithm   The loop in algorithm form is shown in Figure 4.2.

Program   The program implements the algorithm by reusing the `Summation` program and adding the if-statements required. Notice that we start out with the most common case – greater than zero. The remaining, and less common case, comes next by default: that is, we do not even ask whether a number is negative since if it is not positive it *must* be negative.

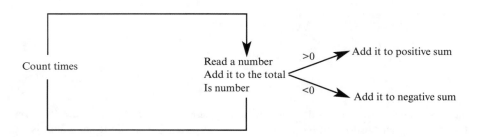

Figure 4.2   *Algorithm to add numbers three ways.*

But, what if it is zero? In this program it does not matter, since adding zero to either total has no effect! Notice, however, that adding zero takes place in the less common case, with the negative numbers.

```java
import java.io.*;

class threeSums {

  /* The Three sums program      by J M Bishop Sept 1996
     adds a sequence of numbers and also keeps
     totals of the positive and negative ones separately.
     Illustrates the if-statement. */

  public static void main (String [] args) throws IOException {

    DataInputStream in = new DataInputStream(System.in);

    int count;
    double total=0, postotal =0, negtotal =0;
    double number;

    System.out.println("****** Three sums ******");
    Text.prompt("How many numbers? ");
    count=Text.readInt(in);

    for (int i=1; i <= count; i++) {
      Text.prompt(i+"> ");
      number = Text.readDouble(in);
      total = total + number;
      if (number > 0) postotal += number;
      else negtotal += number;
    }

    System.out.println("That's enough, thanks.");
    System.out.println("The total is " + total);
    System.out.println("The positive total is " + postotal);
    System.out.println("The negative total is " + negtotal);
  }
}
```

Testing   A complete run would look like this:

```
****** Three sums ******
How many numbers?  5
1>   20
2>   11
3>   -3
4>   0
5>   -2
That's enough, thanks.
The total is 26
The positive total is 31
The negative total is -5
```

Blocks in then- and else-parts

Suppose that in the `threeSums` program, it is also required to know how many positive and negative numbers were read. Then two more counters are needed and, to each part of the if-statement, an extra statement is added to do the counting. Thus, the if-statement would become:

```
int posCount, negCount;

if (number >= 0) {
   posTotal += number;
   posCount++;
   }
else {
   negTotal += number;
   negCount++;
   }
```

Successive else-ifs

Sometimes, there are more than two possibilities that need to be considered. One way in which this is done is by **successive else-ifs**. The condition of the first if-statement eliminates one case, leaving the rest to the else-part. The else-part in its turn introduces another if-statement which selects out another condition and leaves the rest to its else-part, and so on. Else-ifs are illustrated nicely in an example that assigns a grade for various ranges of marks, thus:

```
int marks;
char grade;
if (marks >= 80) grade='A';
else if (marks >= 70) grade='B';
else if (marks >= 60) grade='C';
else if (marks >= 50) grade='D';
else                  grade='E';
```

Notice a few points about this statement:

- The conditions are carefully ordered, so that each eliminates a certain range of marks. Thus, the line that writes out a D for anything over 50 will be reached only when it has already been established that the mark is under 60.

- The last class, E, is given for all the rest of the marks, and does not need a condition.

- The layout of successive if-statements is important for readability, and should try to reflect the pattern of conditions as much as possible.

A secondary consideration is that the most frequently occurring conditions should be checked first. If it is more likely that people will fail, then it will be marginally more efficient to arrange the order of the conditions thus:

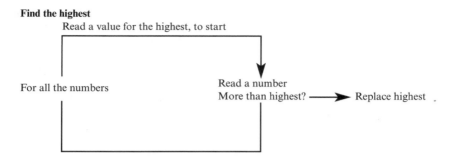

Find the highest

Figure 4.3   *Algorithm for finding the highest number.*

```
int marks;
char grade;
if       (marks < 50)  grade='E';
else if (marks < 60)  grade='D';
else if (marks < 70)  grade='C';
else if (marks < 80)  grade='B';
else                   grade='A';
```

EXAMPLE 4.3   The highest number

Problem   Find the largest in a sequence of numbers.

Solution   A program can read in the numbers one at a time, remembering the highest so far, and updating this if necessary. We note that negative numbers should be catered for as well.

Algorithm   This is a very interesting algorithm. We start by assuming that we have found the highest of *n* numbers. Then the *n*+1th number is read. To find the highest of the *n*+1 numbers, all that needs to be done is to compare the new number with the highest so far, and if it is higher, to replace the highest. This process can then be repeated for as long as required.

The question is, how does the process start? Well, the highest number of a sequence that is one long must be just that number. So we start by reading in one number, make it the highest and proceed from there. The algorithm is shown in Figure 4.3.

Program

```
import java.io.*;

class highestValue {

  /* The Highest Value Program       by   J M Bishop   Aug 1996
        Finds the highest in a list of numbers.
        Illustrates the if-statement */
```

```
public static void main (String [] args) throws IOException {

    DataInputStream in = new DataInputStream(System.in);

    System.out.println("*****  Finding the highest number *****");

    // Find out how many numbers will be coming
    Text.prompt("How many numbers (1 or more)? ");
    int n = Text.readInt(in);

    // Start off the sequence
    System.out.println("Type them in");
    Text.prompt("1> ");
    int highest = Text.readInt(in);

    // Read and check the rest of the numbers
    int number;
    for (int i= 2; i<=n; i++) {
      Text.prompt(i+"> ");
      number = Text.readInt(in);
      if (number > highest) highest = number;
    }
    System.out.println("That's enough, thanks");
    System.out.println("The highest number was "+ highest);
  }
}
```

Testing   It is a good idea to test such an algorithm with the first number being the highest, then with the last, and then with one in the middle. Another test would be to have all the numbers except one equal. This is left up to the reader, but here is one run:

```
*****  Finding the highest number *****
How many numbers (1 or more)?   5
Type them in
1>   56
2>   -99
3>   23
4>   70
5>   -4
That's enough, thanks
The highest number was 70
```

The next example has a more complex structure, and requires if-statements, coupled with methods. It also uses characters rather than integers for the data that is to be compared.

EXAMPLE 4.4   Counterfeit cheques

Problem   Counterfeit cheques are in circulation and the banks have discovered that they all have the same distinctive properties. In the 10-digit cheque number, if there are:

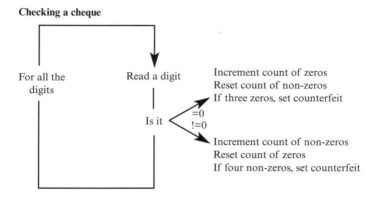

Checking a cheque

For all the digits → Read a digit

Is it =0 → Increment count of zeros / Reset count of non-zeros / If three zeros, set counterfeit

Is it !=0 → Increment count of non-zeros / Reset count of zeros / If four non-zeros, set counterfeit

Figure 4.4 *Algorithm for checking a cheque.*

- three or more zeros in succession,
- and/or four or more non-zeros in succession,

then the cheque could be counterfeit. We would like the computer to assist in warning of a possible counterfeit.

Solution When the cheques are handled by the banks' computers, the first thing that is read is the number. For the purposes of this example, we could write a program to read in cheque numbers and to analyse them for the above properties. The analysis could detect the occurrence of either of the runs described above and if either is found then the cheque can be marked as suspect.

Algorithm The algorithm for analysing a number involves reading it in, digit by digit, and counting the number of zeros and non-zeros. However, these have to occur in runs, so once a run is 'broken', the relevant count will be reset. It will therefore be necessary to remember that a critical count was reached at some stage: this is best done with a Boolean variable. Figure 4.4 shows what the algorithm looks like.

Program The program follows the algorithm closely, making use of two methods for clarity. The digits will be read as characters, but one of the features of the Text class is that any items must be delimited by what is known as 'white space' – spaces, ends-of-lines, tabs. Thus the digits of the cheque have to be entered with spaces following each one, so that they can be read using readChar.

```
import java.io.*;

class Cheque {
   // Checking the occurrence of >= 3 zeros
   // or >= 4 non-zeros in a row
```

```
    DataInputStream in = new DataInputStream (System.in);
    static final int NoofDigits = 10;
    static boolean counterfeit = false;
    static int CountofZeros = 0;
    static int CountofNonzeros = 0;

    static void RecordZero () {
      CountofZeros ++;
      CountofNonzeros = 0;
      if (CountofZeros == 3) counterfeit = true;
    }

    static void RecordNonzero () {
      CountofNonzeros ++;
      CountofZeros = 0;
      if (CountofNonzeros == 4) counterfeit = true;
    }

    public static void main (String [] args)throws IOException {

      DataInputStream in = new DataInputStream (System.in);

      System.out.println("***** Checking for counterfeits *****");
      System.out.println("Enter a cheque number with " +
            "digits separated by a space");
      char digit;
      for (int i =0 ; i < NoofDigits; i++) {
        digit = Text.readChar(in);
        if (digit == '0') RecordZero ();
        else RecordNonzero();
      }
      if (counterfeit) System.out.println("        COUNTERFEIT");
      else System.out.println("        OK");
    }
}
```

Testing   Cheque numbers should be chosen so as to test the special cases. For example, a sample run of the program with input and output might be:

```
****** Checking for counterfeits ******
Enter a cheque number with digits separated by a space
0 0 0 3 3 0 0 4 4 0
        COUNTERFEIT

****** Checking for counterfeits ******
Enter a cheque number with digits separated by a space
0 0 3 3 3 0 0 3 3 3
        OK

****** Checking for counterfeits ******
Enter a cheque number with digits separated by a space
4 4 4 4 0 0 5 5 0 0
        COUNTERFEIT
```

4.5   Introduction to exceptions

If-statements provide a means of control over the state of the current method. We can check the values of data to which we have access and react accordingly. But what happens if a condition is set in another method and we, the caller of the method, should react to it? The if-statement is not powerful enough to handle this. We need another construct.

Java's role in Web programming puts it in the position of the old adage that 'if things can go wrong they will': a user could disconnect, a file could have been deleted, incorrect input could be entered, a host server might be unavailable. In order to operate within such a volatile environment, Java has a special concept known as an **exception**.

An exception is an object which signals that some unusual condition has occurred. Java has many predefined exception objects, and we can also create our own. The point about exceptions is that they are intended to be **detected** and **handled**, so that the program can continue in a sensible way if at all possible. Should an exception occur outside our immediate environment, we shall be informed as to what has happened. We then have the opportunity to handle the situation that has arisen. If we do not react, the method we are in is terminated and the exception is sent up to the method that called us. This process may repeat until eventually an unhandled exception will pass to the Java virtual machine which will terminate the program.

Figure 4.5 illustrates the process of one method calling another and having a handler ready for a possible exception. Depending on how the rest of A is structured, it may be able to continue operating after it handles the exception, or it may exit.

Now let us consider a concrete example related to the summation program. It is unlikely that a user of a program will wish to count precisely the number of values to be entered beforehand. It would therefore be useful to be able to detect in some other way that the data is at an end. The third method mentioned in the list in Example 4.1 is to use Java's exceptions. In the reading methods supplied with Java, a check is made each time as to whether the input has been exhausted (either by the file ending or by the user indicating end-of-input in the usual way on the keyboard). If the check turns up true, then the read method causes an EOFException (for end-of-file exception). The summation program must then react to this.[1]

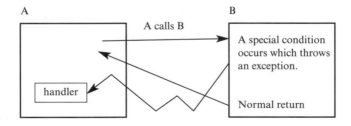

Figure 4.5   *The process of exception handling.*

---

[1]In other languages, the end of input condition can be checked separately in advance using an if-statement and the method can decide how to proceed based on the outcome. This is not the case in Java: in order to handle variable length input, we **must** use exceptions.

The four essentials of exceptions

To use exceptions, we have to do four things:

1.   Try: create a block around statements where the result of any method calls or other operations might cause an exception and preface them with the keyword **try**.

2.   Catch: follow the try-statement with one or more handlers prefaced by the keyword **catch**.

3.   Throw: if the exception is not dealt with at all, it will automatically be passed up to the calling method; if we catch it and deal with it partially, we can still send it up with a **throw** statement.

4.   Declare: mention in the method declaration which exceptions it may throw back to its caller.

In general, but not always, the event which causes the exception is triggered in a method lower down the calling path, and we do not know the precise reason why it is thrown at us. That is why exceptions have very explanatory names, which are usually enough to guide us in their handling.

Indeterminate loops

If there are indeterminate amounts of data, then the loop must similarly be an indeterminate one. The for-statement is powerful enough to handle this variation. All we do is omit any ending condition. The loop will then continue, until presumably an exception gets in the way and causes control to transfer out of the loop. In fact, all three parts of the for-statement are optional. The really basic indeterminate loop is:

```
for (; ;)
```

However, while the loop is in progress, it is often necessary to keep count of iterations, so that more probably we would have

```
for (int count; ; count++)
```

Although exceptions are one way of getting out of a loop, Java does provide another way using a break-statement. However, the break can only be activated by an if-statement based on conditions that are calculable in the loop itself. Thus we can say

```
if (number == 999) break;
```

but we cannot, in Java, use the if-statement and break-statement to detect the end of data.

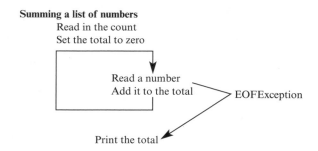

Figure 4.6 *Algorithm for summation with an exception.*

The end-of-file exception

One of the most useful exceptions is that which signals the end of data. On the keyboard, the user types in data and when finished, presses the character which the system uses for ending the stream. This may be cntrl-D, cntrl-Z or esc, for example. The presence of this special character is detected by the `Text` class and is relayed to the caller by throwing the `EOFException`. It is therefore up to us to catch it. How this is done is shown in the next example.

EXAMPLE 4.5   Summation with exceptions

Problem   There is a sequence of numbers that needs to be summed, but we do not know how many initially.

Solution   For the sake of explanation, let us assume that the numbers will be read in from the keyboard. We shall make use of `Text`, `prompt` and `readDouble` to obtain the same sequence of interaction as in Example 4.2. But now we have to be able to detect and react to the `EOFException`.

Algorithm   Figure 4.6 shows the algorithm.

Program   The loop has to be an indeterminate one: we achieve this by leaving the check-part blank in the for-loop. Since we shall now want to know how many numbers were read, the for-loop serves the purpose of keeping track of the tally.

```
import java.io.*;
import javagently.*;

class summation2 {
```

```
/* The Second Summation program      by J M Bishop Aug 1996
   Reads and sums numbers until the end of data is indicated.
   Illustrates the correct use of the EOFException. */

public static void main (String [] args) throws IOException {

  DataInputStream in = new DataInputStream(System.in);

  int count;
  double total=0;
  double number;

  System.out.println("****** Summing n numbers ******");
  System.out.println("Type numbers, ending with cntrl-D");

  try {
    for (int count=1; ; count++) {
      Text.prompt (count+"> ");
      number = Text.readDouble(in);
      total += number;
    }
  }
  catch (EOFException e) {
    System.out.println("That's enough, thanks.");
    System.out.println("The total of the "+ count +
      " numbers is " + total);
  }
}
}
```

Testing   If this program was run then the screen might have the following on it:

```
****** Summing numbers ******
Type numbers, ending with cntrl-D
1>   23
2>   -18
3>   45
4>   11
5>   2
That's enough, thanks.
The total is 63
```

Notice that the control-D typed is not visible on the output, but it was there!

Recovering from an exception

The previous example showed how we could handle an exception in order to conclude a program gracefully. There may also be cases where we do not wish to end the method, but to go back and retry the operation that caused the exception. An example of such a situation is the opening of a file. If we have the file name incorrect, we may wish to give the user the chance to enter another name. The algorithm is shown in pseudo-code in Figure 4.7. This algorithm is used in the next example.

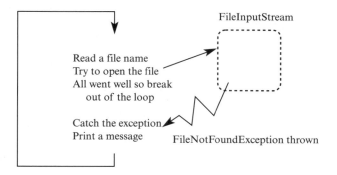

Figure 4.7 *An algorithm for opening a file securely.*

EXAMPLE 4.6 Olympic medals

Problem   The number of gold, silver and bronze medals for each country has been stored on file. We would like to display these results, as well as a total number of medals for each country.

Solution   Set up a loop very similar to the summation one, using the EOFException, but do not prompt for input (since it is coming from a file), and get four values at a time – country, gold, silver and bronze. However, we should also check whether the file name is valid. Here we can use the FileNotFoundException as described earlier. We shall write out the program first this time, and then explain it.

Program

```
import java.io.*;

class Olympics {

   /* Olympic medals program      revised J M Bishop Dec 1996
      Reads in and totals medals gained by
      countries in an Olympic Games.
      Illustrates recovering from an exception
      and using an exception to detect end of file */

  public static void main (String [] args) throws IOException {

    System.out.println("**** Olympic medals ****");
    System.out.println();

    // Declare the keyboard stream, and initialize
    // the file stream to go there too.
    // Java requires that objects used later on definitely
    // have a value, and within a try one cannot be sure.
    // The same applies to giving filename an initial value.
```

```
DataInputStream in = new DataInputStream (System.in);
DataInputStream fin = new DataInputStream(System.in);
String filename = "";

for (;;) {
  try {
    Text.prompt("What file for the medals statistics?");
    filename = Text.readString(in);
    fin = new DataInputStream (new FileInputStream (filename));

    // Success, so break out of the loop
    break;
  }
  catch (FileNotFoundException e) {
    System.out.println(filename + " does not exist.");
    System.out.println("Try again");
    // loop back
  }
}
String country;
int gold, silver, bronze, total, all = 0;
System.out.println
      ("\nCountry\t\tGold\tSilver\tBronze\tTotal");
try {
  for (; ;) {
    country=Text.readString(fin);
    gold   = Text.readInt (fin);
    silver = Text.readInt (fin);
    bronze = Text.readInt (fin);
    total  = gold + silver + bronze;
    System.out.print(country);
    if (country.length()<8) System.out.print("\t");
    System.out.println
        ("\t"+gold+"\t"+silver+"\t"+bronze+"\t"+total);
    all += total;
    }
  }
  catch (EOFException e) {
    System.out.println(all+" medals won.");
  }
 }
}
```

Algorithm   The first point to discuss is why the `FileNotFoundException` requires a for-try sequence, and the `EOFException` uses a try-for sequence. What exactly is the difference? The for-try sequence is shown diagrammatically in Figure 4.7. It is used when we want to try something repeatedly. After the catch statement, control passes back up to the front of the loop. In the case of the try-for sequence, once the exception is detected, the loop should end. Hence the catch statement appears outside of the loop, and the loop is terminated by replacing it with this handler.

The second point concerns the comment on initial values for objects. It is the case that any assignments made within try-statements cannot be guaranteed to have happened.

The Java compiler will therefore complain if variables and objects are not given default values before we embark on a try statement.

Notice that the first for-loop could have had the option of including a count on the number of times the user can retry. After say, five, unsuccessful tries, the loop could end naturally. At this point, `fin` will still have its default value, being the keyboard, and the program will limp along reading data from there instead of from a file.

Testing The output from the program is:

```
**** Olympic medals ****

What file for the medals statistics? medals
medlas does not exist.
Try again
What file for the medals statistics? medals

Country           Gold      Silver    Bronze    Total
Australia         9         9         22        40
China             16        22        12        50
Cuba              9         8         8         25
France            15        7         15        37
Germany           20        18        27        65
Hungary           7         4         10        21
Italy             13        9         12        34
Poland            7         5         5         17
Russia            26        21        16        63
South.Korea       7         15        5         27
Spain             5         6         6         17
Ukraine           9         2         12        23
United.States     43        32        25        100
519 medals won.
```

User-defined exceptions

Apart from the exceptions already defined in the Java library packages, users can also set up their own exceptions, peculiar to the situation in hand. To define such an exception, the form is:

Defining a new exception

```
class name extends Exception {
  public name () {super (); }
  public name (String s) {super(s); }
}
```

We now have an exception class called `name` and we can throw exception objects of this class as in:

Throwing a new exception

```
throw new name ("message");
```

The message can be used by the exception handler (the catch statement) to give information to the user, or it can be empty (accounting for the two options in the declaration above). Opportunities for using user-defined exceptions will arise later in the book.

SUMMARY

There are two ways of changing the state of a variable: by assignment and by reading in values. In order to read in Java, we have first to connect a stream. Thereafter we can read strings. Through the `javagently` class we can also read numbers and characters. In addition, files can be declared for both input and output and programs, and can receive and send data to multiple streams.

There are also two ways of changing the course of the program based on conditions that occur. The if-statement is suitable for checking the local state within a method. It can have an else-part, as well as successive else-ifs. When the condition occurs in another method, it is signalled back by means of an exception. Exceptions can be caught and handled. There are standard ways of recovering from an exception and trying again.

QUIZ

4.1   The following program extract is meant to swap the integer values in *x* and *y* if necessary, so that *x* lands up with the lower one. What will actually happen? Correct the extract.

```
if (x > y)
    int temp = x;
    x = y;
    y = x;
```

4.2   Give declarations to set up an input file called 'marks' which will have the name `marksIn` in the program.

4.3   What will the `Text` class do if a string is typed in where a number is required?

4.4   Given the suggestion in Example 4.3, devise another set of test data for exercising the `highestValue` program.

4.5   In the following try-statement, where could exceptions occur? What are their names?

```
try {
  for (int count = 0; ; count++) {
    x = Text.readDouble (in);
    y = 1/x;
    System.out.println (x, y);
  }
}
```

4.6   In Example 4.6 (Olympic medals), why was it necessary to use a dot in the country with more than one word, rather than a space, for example United.States instead of United States?

4.7   How is end-of-file signalled on your system when inputting from the keyboard?

4.8   Given the following statements and data, what will be printed out?

```
int i, j, k;                        Data
Text.readInt (i);                   67   56
Text.readInt (i);                   98   kilos
Text.readInt (j);                   11.5 33
Text.readInt (k);
System.out.println (i, j, k);
```

4.9   The following set of statements is inefficient. Why is this so? Rewrite it more efficiently.

```
if (pre == 'm') System.out.print("milli");
if (pre == 'c') System.out.print("centi");
if (pre == 'K') System.out.print("kilo");
System.out.println("metre");
```

4.10   If one wanted to read in amounts such as 65kg or 7s, how could the data be set up so that this could be done simply?

PROBLEMS

4.1   **Conversions**. Adapt the program in Example 3.4 so as to read in the limits required for the table.

4.2   **Fibonacci**. The Fibonacci series consists of a series of numbers in which the first two are 1 and each successive number is the sum of the two that precede it, that is:

1 1 2 3 5 8 13 21 34 55 ...

Write a program to print the first 50 terms of the series.

4.3   **Average ages**. A Youth Club has 24 children grouped in four 'rings'. The children are aged 7 to 11. Write an interactive program to read in the ages for each ring and to work out the average age per ring for a group of 24 children, as well as the average overall age.

4.4   **Fuel consumption**. Adapt the program written for Problem 2.5 so as to read in all the values that may vary.

4.5   **Weighted averages**. Adapt the program in Problem 2.4 to read in the marks from a file and print each student's average as well as the overall average. Use exceptions to detect the end of the file.

4.6   **One man went to mow**. Fix Example 3.3 so that the last line is correctly printed out for one *man*.

4.7   **Olympics tries**. Change the Olympic medals program (Example 4.6) so that it tries to get a correct file name five times, and then gives up.

CHAPTER 5

Controlling the flow

5.1   Conditional loops with `while` and `do`

This book introduced loops early in order to emphasize the power of programming in handling repetitive tasks in a simple way. The two kinds of loops examined so far have been:

- counting loops based on the for-statement;

- indeterminate loops based on the for-statement, but with breaks and exceptions providing for exits from the loop when certain conditions or signals are encountered.

As was explained in the discussion on exceptions, the place where the exception is thrown is often one level lower than the place where it is caught. The implication is then that the condition for the loop to end is hidden, except in so far as it is conveyed in a meaningful exception name, such as `EOFException`.

We now consider a third and important group of loops, those that are based on conditions which are visible and detectable where the loop itself is defined.

The form of conditional loops

Conditional loops are phrased in terms of while- or do-statements. A general form of a loop using the while-statement is:

> **While-statement**
> ```
> Initialize the conditions
> while (conditions) {
>   Statements to perform the loop
>     and change the conditions
> }
> ```

After statements to initialize variables involved in the conditions, the loop itself starts by checking the conditions. If they evaluate to true, the body of the while-statement is entered and executed. When the end of the loop is reached, control goes around again to the beginning and the conditions are checked again. This process is repeated until the test of the conditions evaluates to false, at which point the looping stops, and control is passed to the statement following the body of the loop.

EXAMPLE 5.1   Highest common factor

Problem   We wish to find the highest common factor (HCF) of two numbers.[1]

Solution   One possible solution would be to find all the factors of each number and then compare both lists for the highest one. Fortunately, there is a quicker way!
   Suppose a and b are the numbers, a is larger than b and their HCF is f. Then $a - b$ and b will also have an HCF of f. If we use this fact, repeatedly replacing the larger of the two numbers by their difference, until the two numbers are the same, then this figure will be the HCF, even if it is 1.

Algorithm   The above discussion can be expressed in the algorithm in Figure 5.1.

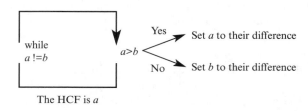

Figure 5.1   *Algorithm for finding the HCF.*

[1]Some might know the HCF as the GCD – greatest common divisor.

Examples

a	b	|a – b|
65	39	26
26	39	13
26	13	13
13	13 HCF	

a	b	|a – b|
99	66	33
33	66	33
33	33 HCF	

Program   Notice that the loop only has one statement, and therefore the braces were omitted.

```java
import java.io.*;

class findHCF {

  /* The HCF Program      by J M Bishop Aug 1996
     Calculates the highest common factor of two integers.
     Illustrates a while loop. */

  public static void main (String [] args) throws IOException {

    DataInputStream in = new DataInputStream (System.in);

    System.out.println("***** Finding the HCF *****");
    Text.prompt("What are the two integers? ");
    int a = Text.readInt (in);
    int b = Text.readInt (in);
    System.out.print("The HCF of "+a+" and "+b+" is ");

    while (a != b)
      if (a > b) a -=b;
      else       b -=a;
    System.out.println(a);
  }
}
```

The general form of the do-statement is similar, as shown below. The do-loop starts off by going through its body at least once before checking the conditions. This can sometimes be a desirable property, but in general the while-statement is favoured by programmers.

Do-statement

Initialize the conditions
do
  Statements to perform the loop
  and change the conditions
while *condition;*

The two very important points about conditional loops are that:

- the condition must be initialized;
- the condition must change during the loop.

If the condition is not initialized, then the loop will be working on incorrect or even undefined information. If it is not altered during the loop, then there will be no chance of it changing and causing the loop to end.

Before going on to a problem, consider a small illustrative example of conditional loops, bearing in mind the importance of formulating them correctly. In order to convey the sense of the looping process, the example makes use of Booleans and methods, which have the effect suggested by their names.

Developing a conditional loop

The first example simulates trying to find a pair from a drawerful of mixed coloured socks.

```
PickaSock();
PickAnotherSock();
while (!aPair()) {
  DiscardaSock ();
  PickAnotherSock ();
}
```

The loop is initialized by having two socks in hand: this is essential so that the check for a pair can be correctly performed. The loop is correctly formulated in that the condition will change each time round, as a new sock is selected. There are, however, two crucial flaws in the loop.

Suppose a pair is never found. The condition is not met so the loop continues, but the method to `PickAnotherSock` will eventually fail, and the whole operation will crash. The other problem is similar – suppose there were no socks in the drawer to start with. In this case, neither of the initializing statements can be performed, and the program as it stands will not be able to execute. These two situations can be summed up as:

- guard against not being able to begin;
- guard against never ending.

The remedy is to provide additional conditions as the guards. In this case, we need to know if sufficient socks (that is, at least two) exist to be able to test for a pair, and then we need to know when the drawer becomes empty. Both conditions are based on the number of socks in the drawer, and we assume that this figure can be provided in some way. The corrected version of the loop then becomes:

```
if (NumberofSocksinDrawer >= 2) {
  PickaSock ();
  PickAnotherSock ();
}
```

```
while (NumberofSocksinDrawer > 0 and !aPair()) {
  DiscardaSock () ;
  PickAnotherSock () ;
}
```

```
{At this point, a pair may or may not have been found}
```

There is one final consideration with any conditional loop. If there is more than one part to the condition governing the loop, it may be necessary to know at the end which part caused the loop to stop. In the example, it seems sensible to be able to decide whether the search was successful or not. This is called **a follow-up action**, and is performed by re-checking some of the conditions, as in:

```
if (aPair()) System.out.println("Got a pair of socks.");
else System.out.println("Bad luck, no pair found.");
```

Notice that when conditions are connected (as they often are), one must be careful as to which is tested. In this case, it would not have been correct to test for the drawer being empty as in:

```
if (NumberofSocksinDrawer == 0)
   System.out.println("Bad luck, no pair found.");
else System.out.println("Got a pair of socks.");
```

since the pair could have been found on the very last time round the loop. The drawer would also be empty, but that is irrelevant for this purpose.

Exercise   Write the necessary if-statements to report on whether a pair was found or not, whether the drawer was empty initially, or whether it became empty during the search.

5.2   The switch-statement

The if-statement is a two-way selection statement based on conditions. However, if there are several simple tests for given values, successive else-if statements can become unwieldy. Java provides for so-called **keyed selection** with the switch-statement. The form of the switch-statement is:

Switch-statement

```
switch (switch-expression) {
  case value : statement; break;
  case value : statement; break;
  . . .
  default : statement; break;
}
```

The switch-statement considers the value of the switch-expression and, starting at the first case value, endeavours to find a match. If a match is found, then the corresponding statement is executed and the **break** causes control to pass to the end of the whole switch. The **default** keyword is a catch-all for values that have not been mentioned. The break statements and the default part are not strictly compulsory but it is considered good programming practice to have them. Without a break, control falls through to the next case. This could be useful if the statement part is empty, as shown in the examples that follow.

The switch-expression must produce a value which is an integer or character. It may not be real. The case values are expressions of the same type as the key-expression, and there may be one or more case value for a given statement. The key-values do not have to be in any order but may occur only once.

As an example, consider the little jingle which gives the number of days in a month:

Thirty days hath September, April, June and November.
All the rest have thirty-one, excepting February alone,
Which has but twenty-eight days clear,
And twenty-nine in each leap year.

If we assume that month has an integer value, then a switch-statement can be used to look at the month and set days to the appropriate value as follows (ignoring leap years):

```
switch (month) {
   case 9:
   case 4:
   case 6:
   case 11: days = 30; break;
   case 2: days = 28; break;
   default: days = 31; break;
}
```

As always, the statement mentioned after each case can be a compound statement and include several statements. Such is the situation when establishing the correct number of days for February, taking account of leap years. Instead of doing a calculation of the year (divisible by 4 and so on), we simply ask whether the year is leap or not:

```
switch (month) {
   case 9:
   case 4:
   case 6:
   case 11:
     days = 30; break;
   case 2: {
     System.out.println("Is this a leap year?");
     char ans = Text.readChar(in);
     if (ans == 'Y') days = 29 else days = 28;
   };   break;
   default: days = 31; break;
}
```

Switch-statements are the subject of the next example. The switch expressions are characters, which is quite often the case.

EXAMPLE 5.2   Exchange rates

Problem   SavBank issues foreign exchange in four major currencies for customers, but the rates change daily.

Solution   Set up a method which uses a switch to convert graz into one of the major currencies. These are Y (yen), $ (dollars), D (marks) and F (francs). The rates should be read in with suitable prompts each morning. (You could also include sterling if your keyboard has a pound sign.)

Algorithm   The solution can be divided into two parts: the entry of the exchange rates, and the method which does the conversion and prints the foreign currency value. Clearly a switch-statement is ideal for the second part, and it will look something like this:

```
switch (currencySymbol) {
  case 'Y': factor = yenExchange; break;
  case '$': factor = dollarExchange; break;
  case 'D': factor = markExchange; break;
  case 'F': factor = francExchange; break;
  default : .....;
}
```

What should be done in the default case, which would be reached if an invalid symbol is entered? Obviously, a message must be displayed, informing the user that the symbol was invalid. But how to try again? One possibility would be to declare and raise an exception. This would be overkill, however, since we have all the information to hand, and we stipulated repeatedly in Chapter 4 that exceptions are for cross-method communication.

   Instead we declare a simple Boolean variable which will be set to false, and should the currency symbol be valid, it will be set to true. The switch-statement is then encased in a while-statement based on the Boolean. Figure 5.2 sums this up.

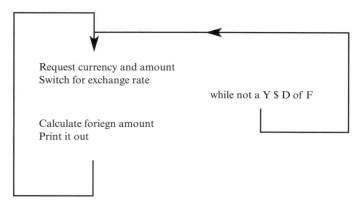

Figure 5.2   *Algorithm for handling currency symbols.*

A further question is how to interact with the user. A question and answer session can become tedious and unclear. Instead, we use a tabular format, where the user fills in the first two columns and presses return, then the program tabs to the third column and gives the result. The output would then look like this:

```
SavBank Foreign Exchange Section
================================
Graz    into    gives
1000    $
                217.391 dollars
1000    Y
                25000 yen
1000    M
                Valid currencies are Y$DF. Try again
        D
                333.333 marks
1000    F
                1098.9 francs
```

Program   This version of the program sets up the exchange rates as constants, to emphasize the use of the switch-statements.

```
import java.io.*;

class ForeignExchange {

  /* The Foreign exchange program      by J M Bishop Oct 1996
     changes graz into yen, dollars, marks for francs.
     Illustrates the use of switches. */

  static final double yenExchange = 0.04;
  static final double dollarExchange = 4.6;
  static final double markExchange = 3.0;
  static final double francExchange = 0.91;

  public static void main (String [] args) throws IOException {

    DataInputStream in = new DataInputStream (System.in);
    double amount;
    double factor = 0;
    char c = '$'; // by default

    System.out.println("SavBank Foreign Exchange Section");
    System.out.println("================================");
    System.out.println("Graz");
    for (; ;) {
    try {
      amount = Text.readDouble (in);

      boolean found = false;
      while (! found) {
        c = Text.readChar (in);
        Text.prompt ("\t\t");
```

```
        switch (c) {
          case 'Y' : factor = yenExchange; break;
          case '$' : factor = dollarExchange; break;
          case 'D' : factor = markExchange; break;
          case 'F' : factor = francExchange; break;
          default  : System.out.println
                       ("Valid currencies are Y$DF. Try again");
                     Text.prompt ("\t");
        }
        found = (c=='Y' | c=='$' | c=='D' | c=='F');
      }

      System.out.print (amount / factor);
      switch (c) {
        case 'Y' : System.out.println (" yen"); break;
        case '$' : System.out.println (" dollars"); break;
        case 'D' : System.out.println (" marks"); break;
        case 'F' : System.out.println (" francs"); break;
      }
    }
    catch (EOFException e) {}
    }
  }
}
```

Case ranges

In the previous example, the switch expression was a single variable, and it mapped directly on to the case values. Sometimes, there are many values for each statement, but there is a simple way of adjusting them so that there is only one per statement. For example, suppose that given an examination mark, it is required to set a symbol depending on the multiple of ten, with anything over 80 being A, over 70 being B, and so on down to anything under 40 being F. The switch to achieve such a mapping is:

```
switch ((int) (mark / 10)) {
  case 10:
  case 9:
  case 8:  symbol = 'A'; break;
  case 7:  symbol = 'B'; break;
  case 6:  symbol = 'C'; break;
  case 5:  symbol = 'D'; break;
  case 4:  symbol = 'E'; break;
  default: symbol = 'F'; break;
}
```

This is the clearest and most efficient way of solving this problem, but it is not the only way. The same effect could be achieved using successive if-else-statements as described in Section 4.4. However, it is usually easier to see what is going on in a table as opposed to a calculation, so switch-statements should be used in preference to if-statements where possible.

When not to use switches

The clarity of the switch makes it a natural choice for many types of selections. However, it cannot be used in situations where the selection is based on conditions. For example, the following is not valid Java:

```
/* NOT VALID JAVA */
switch (number) {
  case < 0    : Addtonegatives;
  case = 0    : Donothing;
  case > 0    : Addtopositives;
}
```

The cases must be actual values. A suitable approach here would employ successive if-else-statements.

Another place where switch-statements are inappropriate for checking strings. A string is a more complex entity than a switch can handle. Later on we shall see how to match strings as keys to values (Chapter 6).

5.3   Conditional loops and input data

Dealing with the outside world in the form of a user's input is a very important part of a program. In Chapter 4, we assumed that the input would end when the end of data was detected by an exception. There are other more subtle ways of telling the program to stop, and the next two examples explore these.

EXAMPLE 5.3   Controlling an engine

Problem   An engine is controlled by numbers that may change, but must always be in descending order. As soon as the sequence is no longer descending, the engine stops. How would this aspect of its operation be programmed?

Solution   We assume that the numbers will be read into a program, and that for the purposes of the investigation they can then be ignored. What is important is to get the algorithm for checking on the sequence correct.

Algorithm   To check that a number is in sequence, we have to have both it and the previous number in hand. Each time round the loop, we replace the previous number with the one read in. As far as starting off goes, we cannot make an assumption as to the value of the first number, so the remembered number cannot be preset to a special value. Instead, the first number is read in separately, and then the loop starts.

Program   The relevant loop would be:

```
int n = Text.readInt(in);
do {
  previous = n;
  n = Text.readInt(in);
}
while (n <= previous);
```

Extension   Since we have established that a program to control the engine is feasible, the maker of the engine has asked that it be written, but with the following additional conditions:

- the first number must be positive;

- the numbers must not go below 0.

For each number, he asks that we print out that many dots.

Algorithm   The condition on the while-statement will need two parts now: to check the new number against 0 and to check it against `previous`. In addition, an if-statement is needed at the beginning to check that the very first number is positive. Printing the dots is best done in a separate method. Since it will depend upon n, we give the method a parameter to make this easy to do.

Program

```
import java.io.*;

class controller {

  /* The Engine controller program      by J M Bishop Aug 1996
     reflects the operation of an engine until it
     is shut down by a change in the sequence of
     numbers expected.
     Illustrates multiple conditions for starting
     and ending a loop. */

  static void react (int dotcount) {
    for (int dot = 0; dot < dotcount; dot ++)
      System.out.print(".");
    System.out.println();
  }

  static void instructions () {
    System.out.println("Type in the readings as they come");
    System.out.println("The engine will keep working while"+
      " readings are the same");
    System.out.println("or decreasing. It stops normally on" +
      " an increased reading and");
    System.out.println(" abnormally on a negative one.");
  }
```

```
public static void main (String [] args) throws IOException {

    DataInputStream in = new DataInputStream(System.in);
    System.out.println("***** Controlling an engine *****");

    Text.prompt("Type in the start-up value");
    int n = Text.readInt(in);
    if (n <= 0)
      System.out.println("The engine cannot work on that.");
    else {
      instructions ();
      int previous;
    do {
      react (n);
      previous = n;
      n = Text.readInt(in);
    }
    while (n>=0 & n <= previous);
    if (n<0) System.out.println("Abnormal shutdown");
    else System.out.println("Engine shut down okay");
   }
  }
}
```

Testing   Sample input and output for the program would be:

```
***** Controlling an apparatus *****
Type in the start-up value
Type in the readings as they come
The engine will keep working while readings are the same
or decreasing. It stops normally on an increased reading and
abnormally on a negative one.
............
11
..........
9
.........
5
.....
2
..
4
Engine shut down okay
```

The testing should include the cases for abnormal shutdown and where the data starts off negative.

The next example looks at how to design a loop that can take care of all possible happenings in the input data.

EXAMPLE 5.4   Missing the target

Problem   We would like to show how loops can handle the three cases of guarding against

- not being able to begin;
- never ending;
- reaching the end.

Solution   We shall work with the following simple loop:

```
int target = Text.readInt(in);
do
   int number = Text.readInt(in);
while (number != target);
```

Reading is a special operation in a loop, in that it involves processing data, and it *also* changes the outcome of the value of variables. Thus, a read performs the dual function of the body of a loop and changing the conditions.

Algorithm   Now consider the first two guards mentioned previously: the loop may not be able to start if no data exists, and it may never end if the target does not appear. If the target does not appear, then the data has ended, so both cases reduce to an end of data condition, both of which which will be signalled by the EOFException. So the simple try- and catch-statements with the loop are:

```
try {
  int target = Text.readInt(in);
  do
    int number = Text.readInt(in);
  while (number != target);
}
catch (EOFException e) {
  System.out.println("The data has run out.");
}
```

This loop is unsatisfactory because the catch is a catch-all: we would like to be able to distinguish between the two reasons for an EOFException to be raised. One way is to add more try-statements, and then record the status in a Boolean which protects the next stage:

```
boolean endofdata = false;
try {
  int target = Text.readInt(in);
}
catch (EOFException e) {
  System.out.println("No starting value.");
  endofdata = true;
}
if (!endofdata) {
try {
```

```
    do
       int number = Text.readInt(in);
    while (number != target);
    System.out.println("Finished correctly");
  }
  catch (EOFException e) {
    System.out.println("Target not found.");
    endofdata = true;
  }
}
```

Algorithm 2 This version is not easily understandable. With exceptions, it is better to keep try-statements to a minimum and handle catches together. One way of doing this is to use nested trys, and to throw an inner exception out to the outermost level. In so doing, we can change its name to a user-defined exception. Since an exception is a class declaration, it appears before the one for the class containing the main program. Thus we have:

```java
import java.io.*;

class TargetNotFoundException extends Exception {} ;

class exceptions {
  public static void main (String [] args) throws IOException {

    DataInputStream in = new DataInputStream (System.in);

    try {
      int target = Text.readInt(in);
      try {
        do
           int number = Text.readInt(in);
        while (number != target);
      }
      catch (EOFException e) {
        throw new TargetNotFoundException();
      }
    }
    catch (EOFException e) {
      System.out.println("No starting value.");
    }
    catch (TargetNotFoundException e) {
      System.out.println("Target not found.");
    }
  }
}
```

5.4 Case study 2: Rock–scissors–paper game

There is a popular two-person game in which each player makes a choice of rock, scissors or paper, and who is the winner depends on the following rules:

- rock beats scissors (it can smash them);

- scissors beat paper (they can cut it);

- paper beats rock (it can wrap it).

If both players make the same choice, then it is a draw.

We would like to program the computer to play this game against a human. Each will make a choice and the computer will work out who won.

Solution

Programming any two-person game involves seven steps:

1. Give instructions (or omit them if requested to do so).

2. Initialize the game, if necessary.

3. Set up a loop to play the game repeatedly until told to stop.

4. Generate the computer's choice.

5. Get the user's choice.

6. Decide who has won.

7. Play again, or if no more, sign off.

We shall look at each step in turn.

Step 1: instructions

Computer games should always give instructions for new users. These should include not only a description of the rules, but also how to enter replies. Two issues which should always be addressed here are whether replies need to be followed by return, and whether capital letters are acceptable as well as lower-case letters. We shall require the user to type in R, S, P or a Q to end. We shall not permit lower-case letters.

Step 2: initialize

We need to ask the question here as to how the computer is to make its choice. Ideally, we want a random choice, and therefore need to use random numbers. Java provides a class in the `util` package called `Random`. The specification of `Random` is given in Figure 5.3.

Once a `Random` object is created (with or without a starting value, called a *seed*), the next random number of any of the four types mentioned can be obtained. We want an integer, and we would like to seed it from data supplied by the user, so we could use:

```
private static Random dice(Text.readInt(in));
int next = dice.nextInt ();
```

```
public class Random extends Object {
  // constructors
    public Random ();
    public Random (long seed);
  // instance methods
    public double nextDouble ();
    public float nextFloat ();
  public syncronized double nextGaussian ();
  public int nextInt ();
  public long nextLong ();
  public syncronized void setSeed (long seed);
```

Figure 5.3 *The specification of the Random class.*

The problem is that next will have any integer value, and we want one between 0 and 2. We can obtain this simply by taking the remainder after dividing by 3, thus:

```
if (next < 0) next = -next;
mychoice = next % 3;
```

Step 3: set up a loop

We are going to use an indeterminate while-loop because the place where we stop the loop (based on a Q being input) is in between getting our choice and getting the computer's choice. We exit the loop with a break. The loop is the main feature of the main class that plays the game, as follows:

```
import java.io.*;

class playGame {

  /* The Playing Game program      by J M Bishop   Aug 1996
     Calls methods in the RSP class to get
     my choice and the computer's choice and
     display who has won until Q is typed.
     Illustrates conditional loops and objects */

  public static void main (String [] args) throws IOException {

  DataInputStream in = new DataInputStream(System.in);

  RSPGame mygame = new RSPGame ();
  mygame.startGame (in);
  while (true) {
    mygame.makemyChoice();
    if (mygame.getyourChoice (in)=='Q') break;
    mygame.winner ();
  }
```

```
        System.out.println("Thanks for playing");
    }
    }
```

Step 4: generate the computer's choice

We have already seen that this will be done by random numbers. The computer will be submitting 0, 1 or 2 and the user will be submitting R, S or P. In fact, this will not cause problems.

Step 5: getting the user's choice

Here we have to program defensively. We must check that the character entered is indeed one of the permissible ones. If it is not, we should give a message and try again. A do-loop is in order because the test comes after the input has been done. The basic sequence is:

```
do {
    Text.prompt("Your choice of R S P or Q to stop ?");
    yourchoice = Text.readChar(in);
} while (yourchoice!='R' & yourchoice != 'S'
        & yourchoice != 'P' & yourchoice != 'Q');
```

This sequence will force the player to use capital letters. Notice that the initial message serves as an error message as well.

Step 6: decide who has won

This is algorithmically the most intricate part. We have three choices for the computer, and each of these has three outcomes, depending on the player's choice. This could mean a selection statement with nine arms! Fortunately, there is a better way, using a method with parameters.

Let us consider the first case of the computer having a rock. Then, depending on the player's choice, the computer judges the result as:

- scissors – win,
- paper – lose,
- rock – draw.

The same process is repeated for the computer having a scissors, except that the list of player's choices is in a different order. Clearly, a method will be appropriate here, and the result is shown in the program below.

Step 7: sign off

We can have a very simple sign off, such as thanking the user, or we can print out statistics on how many games were won either way.

Program

The program follows the strategy outlined above, and makes good use of all the control instructions introduced in this chapter. The program is arranged in two classes: the structure of the `playGame` class is more or less independent of the game being played, except that it refers to the `makemyChoice` and `getyourChoice` methods as belonging to `RSPGame`. In the `RSPGame` class, there are three private variables/objects and one private method. Figure 5.4 gives the class and method diagram for the program.

```
import java.io.*;
import java.util.Random;

class RSPGame {

    /* The RSP Game class       by J M Bishop Aug 1996
       offers four methods:
       startGame, getmyChoice, getyourChoice and Winner.
       getyourChoice returns a character so
       that we can stop if it was a Q.
       Illustrates typed methods switches, loops and Random. */

    void RSP ( ) { } ;
    private static int mychoice;
    private static char yourchoice; // R S P
    private static Random dice;
```

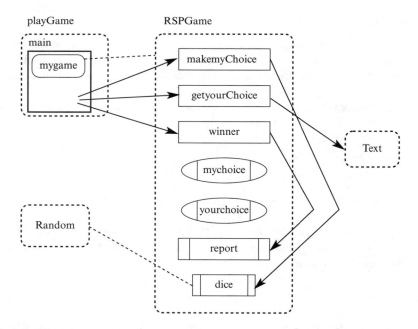

Figure 5.4   *Class and object diagram for the rock–stone–paper game.*

```
void startGame (DataInputStream in) throws IOException {
  System.out.println("Let's play RSP");
  System.out.println("To show I'm not cheating, start me off by"+
    " giving me a number.");
  dice = new Random(Text.readInt(in));
}

void winner () {
  // In the calls to report, the first parameter is my choice.
  // The second one is the choice that I could beat.
  // The third one is the choice that would beat me.

  switch (mychoice) {
    case 0 : report ('R','S','P'); break;
    case 1 : report ('S','P','R'); break;
    case 2 : report ('P','R','S'); break;
  }
}

void makemyChoice () {
  // nextInt returns an integer in its full range.
  // We have to reduce it to 0, 1, 2

  int next = dice.nextInt();
  if (next < 0) next = -next;
  mychoice = next % 3;
}

char getyourChoice (DataInputStream in) throws IOException {
  do {
    Text.prompt("Your choice of R S P or Q to stop ?");
    yourchoice = Text.readChar(in);
  } while (yourchoice!='R' & yourchoice != 'S'
          & yourchoice != 'P' & yourchoice != 'Q');
  if (yourchoice != 'Q')
    System.out.print("You drew "+yourchoice+" and ");
  return yourchoice;
}

private static void report (char me, char Iwin, char youWin) {
  System.out.println("I drew a "+me);
  if (yourchoice == Iwin)
    System.out.println("I win");
  else if (yourchoice == youWin)
    System.out.println("You win");
  else
    System.out.println("It's a draw");
  }
}
```

Testing

A typical run could go something like this:

```
Let's play RSP
To show I'm not cheating, start me off by giving me a number.
67
Your choice of R S P or Q to stop ? R
You drew R and I drew a S
You win
Your choice of R S P or Q to stop ? S
You drew S and I drew a R
I win
Your choice of R S P or Q to stop ? P
You drew P and I drew a R
You win
Your choice of R S P or Q to stop ? P
You drew P and I drew a P
It's a draw
Your choice of R S P or Q to stop ? S
You drew S and I drew a P
You win
Your choice of R S P or Q to stop ? R
You drew R and I drew a S
You win
Your choice of R S P or Q to stop ? Q
Thanks for playing
```

As you can see, the computer's choices are random, and it does lose sometimes!

SUMMARY

The while-loop is the basic controlling loop. It checks the condition at the start of the loop. The do-loop checks the condition at the end. In either case, we can check one or more conditions in the middle and exit the loop using a break-statement. Boolean variables are useful when programming while-loops, in order to keep the value of conditions established before the time comes to check whether to continue. The use of while-loops is intimately entwined with reading input data, and, as was explained in the previous chapters, it is necessary to handle some of the ending conditions via exceptions.

The switch-statement provides for multi-way decision making based on values. Several values can lead to the same statement. The values may only be integers or characters.

QUIZ

5.1   Each of the following three loops is meant to read characters until a $ is found. One of them will not work correctly. Explain why and show how it could be fixed.

```
char ch;
for (;;) {
  ch = Text.readChar(in);
  if (ch == '$') break;
}

char ch;
do
  ch = Text.readChar(in);
while (ch != '$');
```

```
char ch;
while (ch != '$')
  ch = Text.readChar(in);
```

5.2   Write a switch-statement that will print out the name for each of the days of the week, given a number from 0 to 6.

5.3   What would be suitable target ending values for the following sets of data:

- ages of people

- air temperatures

- years

5.4   Write out suitable instructions for the RSP game in the case study.

5.5   What happens when a switch statement is entered with a case value that is not one of those listed and there is no default case?

5.6   What would be the while-statement equivalent of the indeterminate for-statement

`for (;;)`

5.7   If we want to have the chance of trying an operation again once an exception has been thrown into a while-statement, should we use a do-try or a try-do sequence? (Hint: See Examples 4.6 and 5.4 for explanations of the difference.)

5.8   Write a while-loop which will print out all the even numbers between 0 and 20.

5.9   Draw an algorithm diagram for the last program in Example 5.4.

5.10 Suppose we decided to change the `getyourChoice` method in the case study into a boolean method and return

`return yourchoice == 'Q';`

How would the calling method change?

PROBLEMS

5.1   **Postage stamps**. Savanna Mail has decided to have machines that print out postage stamps up to a maximum value of G99.99. The stamps have a basic design as follows:

```
--------------------

|  SAVANNA  |

|   G14.30   |

|   BY AIR   |

--------------------
```

The three zones of postage rates per 10 grams are as follows:

A   50c
B   90c
C   G1.10

and the postage is doubled for airmail. Write a program that prompts the user for the mass of an article, the zone to which it is going and whether it should go by air or not, and then prints out the correct stamp. Use a class for the stamps, and create three objects for the different zones. Refer to the case study in Section 3.6 for a model.

5.2   **Rainfall figures**. The rainfall figures in mm are available for each day of the past four weeks. We want to know the total rainfall for each week, the most recent wettest day and the driest week.

Write a program that will read in several sets of 28 rainfall figures and print out the three bits of information required. Sample data and results would be:

```
Sample data           Sample results
3  0  0  7  8  21  0   39 mm
0  1  1  0  0  0   4   6 mm
9  6  7  0  0  0   0   22 mm
0  0  0  0  0  0   1   1 mm
The wettest day was day 6.
The driest week was week 4.
```

5.3   **Golf scores**. The Savanna Golf Course has nine holes. At each hole, a player is expected to be able to sink the ball in the hole in one to five shots. This gives a course average or par of 30. A player's score for the course is the sum of the numbers of shots for each hole. Depending on past performance, a player is granted a handicap which is subtracted from his or her score to give his or her actual result for a game. Players are also interested in knowing whether they have scored under par or not. When players play together, the winner is the one with the lowest score. If the scoring of a golf game were computerized, sample input and output might be:

```
Player   Handicap   Shots per hole        Total   Result   Under Par?
1        6          1 3 6 2 1 4 3 2 4      26      20       yes
2        3          2 2 2 2 4 4 4 2 2      24      21       yes
3        2          4 5 4 3 4 1 3 5 4      33      31       no
The winner is player 1 with a handicapped result of 20
```

Write a program which

- reads in the shots per hole for several players;

- calculates each total score, handicapped score and par decision;

- determines the winning player and the winning score.

5.4   **Sensitive drugs**. A sensitive drug cannot sustain a change in temperature of more that 30 °C in a 24 hour period. The temperatures are monitored and recorded every two hours. Write a program the laboratory technician can run once a day to determine whether or not to throw the drug away.

5.5   **Parking meters**. The Savanna Traffic Department wants to decide whether or not to mount a campaign against illegal parking. A number of traffic inspectors are sent to different zones in the city where parking time is restricted. The different zones have different time restrictions. Each of the traffic officers has to monitor any 10 cars in their zone and record the actual time the vehicle was parked in the time restricted zone. If 50% or more of the cars were parked for a longer period than allowed, the traffic department will decide to launch a massive campaign. Write a program that

- reads in the number of zones;

- reads the time limit and actual parking-time for ten vehicles for each of the zones;

- determines the number of cars exceeding the time limit in each of the zones;

- decides whether a campaign should be mounted or not;

- identifies the zone where the situation is the worst.

Sample input and output might be:

```
Please enter the number of zones: 3
Area        Limit                 Parking times              Over limit
1            60        20 40 70 35 45 78   34 56 73   5      3
2            45        62 47 68 40 53 62 120    8 15 72      7
3            30        66 32 41 89   7 25   29 33 54 17      6
A campaign must be mounted.
Concentrate on area 2
```

5.6   **Engineering apparatus.** A certain engineering apparatus is controlled by the input of successive numbers. If there is a run of the same number, the apparatus can optimize its performance. Hence we would like to arrange the data so as to indicate that a run is coming. Write a program that reads a sequence of numbers and prints out each run of numbers in the form (n^*m) where m is the number to be repeated n times. These instructions are printed in brackets on a new line, to indicate that they are going to the apparatus. Note that a run could just consist of a single number. The numbers are terminated by a zero, which halts the apparatus. Sample input and output would be:

```
Sample input and output
20 20 20 20 20 20 20 20 20 20 50
(10*20)
50 50 50 50 60
(5*50)
60 60 60 60 20
(5*60)
30
(1*20)
30 30 30 90
(4*30)
0
(1*90)
(0)
```

5.7   **Rabbits!** A scientist needs to determine when she will run out of space to house her rabbits. She starts with two rabbits and it is known that a pair of adult rabbits (those more than three months old) produce on average two rabbits every three months. The scientist has space to house 500 rabbits. Write a program which will determine how many months it will be before she runs out of space. Adapt the program to print out a table of the rabbit populations (adult, non-adult and total) every three months for five years. Assume no rabbits die.

5.8   **Fibonacci again.** Problem 4.2 involved printing out the Fibonacci sequence. Alter the program so that only every third value is printed out. What do you notice about these values?

5.9   **Setting exchange rates.** Improve the Exchange rates program (Example 5.2) so that the rates can be read in before trade begins each day.

CHAPTER 6

Arrays and tables

6.1 Simple arrays

We are beginning to realize that there is a need to be able to store and manipulate multiple values in a program. If there are relatively few values, simple variables can possibly be used, but consider the following example.

Suppose we have several hundred scores between 0 and 19 which have to be analysed for frequency of occurrence of each score. We could set up 20 counters, one for each score. As the scores are read in, the counter corresponding to the score could be incremented. It would be very unwieldy if we had to invent 20 different names for the counters, and then use a big switch-statement every time one of them needed updating. What we need is the concept of the ***i*th variable** so that we can read a value, say i, and then update $counter_i$. Programming languages provide for this facility with the **array**.

Form of an array

An array is a bounded collection of elements of the same type, each of which can be selected by indexing with an integer from 0 upwards to a limit specified when the array is created. The relevant form is:

Array declaration

```
type arrayname [ ] = new type [limit];
type arrayname [ ] = {values};
```

Arrays can be declared to contain any type or class, but the index and hence the limit must always be an integer. The limit gives the number of elements in the array, with each element being indexed by a number in the range from 0 to *limit* – 1. Examples of array declarations of the first form shown above are:

```
int frequencies [] = new int [20];
Date holidays [] = new Date [16];
String countries [] = new String [175];
```

The `frequencies` array will have 20 integers, numbered 0 to 19. There will be 16 dates in the `holidays` array, numbered 0 to 15, and 175 strings stored in the `countries` array numbered 0 to 174. Notice that array names are frequently given as plurals.

The second form creates an array with initial values. The size of the array is then deduced from the number of values given, for example:

```
char vowels [ ] = {'a','e','i','o','u'}
```

The `vowels` array has five characters, numbered from 0 to 4.

To access an array element, we give the name of the array variable and an index expression enclosed in square brackets. The index is sometimes known as the **subscript**. For example, we could have:

```
for (int i=0; i<20; i++) frequencies[i] = 0;
holidays [0] = new Date (97,1,1);
countries[44] = "Great Britain";
System.out.println(vowels[3]);
```

Remember that arrays are always indexed starting at 0, so that the last example here will print the fourth element, which is 'o', not 'i'.

EXAMPLE 6.1   Frequency count

Problem   The frequencies of several hundred scores between 0 and 19 have to be calculated.

Solution   The solution has already been outlined at the beginning of the section. We set up an array and as each score is calculated or read, the appropriate element of the array is incremented. The algorithm is so simple that we go straight on to the program.

Program   The program uses the random number generator to create 100 numbers between 0 and 19 for testing purposes. The important line is

```
    scoreFreqs [score]++;
```

which is where the relevant element of the array is incremented.

```
    import java.util.Random;

    class Frequencies {
      /* The Frequencies Program      by J M Bishop Dec 1996
         counts the frequencies of scores from 0 to 19.
         Tested by generating random numbers.
         Illustrates simple array handling */

      static final int maxscore = 20;
      static final int n = 100;

      public static void main (String [] args) {

        int scoreFreqs [] = new int [maxscore];
        int score;
        Random TestScore = new Random ();

        for (int i=0; i<n; i++) {
            score = Math.abs(TestScore.nextInt() % 20);
            scoreFreqs [score]++;
        }

        System.out.println("Table of score Frequencies\n"+
                        "===========================\n");
        for (int i = 0; i<maxscore; i++)
          System.out.println(i + "\t\t" + scoreFreqs[i]);
      }
    }
```

Testing   Sample output would be

```
Table of score Frequencies
===========================
0           4
1           3
2           5
3           4
4           8
5           3
6           4
7           4
8           3
9           9
10          4
11          4
12          4
13          6
14          4
```

```
15        4
16        9
17        6
18        6
19        6
```

This program has been written without methods or classes. Clearly, it could have been formally broken up and parameter interfaces created. However, in this case, we deemed it simpler to present the program as one unit, so that the idea of arrays can be understood on its own. In later examples, we shall see how arrays interface with classes in different ways. We now consider the properties of arrays in a formal way.

Properties of arrays

1. **Element type.** Arrays can be formed of any type or class, from integers to dates to arrays themselves. The last leads to multi-dimensional arrays, discussed in detail in Section 6.2.

2. **Size.** The size of an array is limited only by the computer's memory, which is usually adequate for most applications. The size is **fixed** at the time that the array is created, and cannot be changed thereafter.

3. **References.** When an array is declared, a **reference** is set up for it. This reference will point to the place where the array's elements are stored. The declaration

    ```
    int A [] = new int [4];
    ```

    therefore has the effect shown in Figure 6.1. The declaration can be done in two stages: one to declare the array name and create the reference, and then later another to set up the storage. The equivalent Java statements would be:

    ```
    int A [];
    A = new int [4];
    ```

4. **Operator.** The only operator that applies to a whole array is assignment. Assigning one array to another, though, does not create a copy of the whole array. Instead, it copies the references, so that both arrays will refer to the same storage, and changes made to one will affect the other. Copies of the actual values of arrays can be made in the same way as copies of objects can, by a method called **cloning**, and this topic is taken up in Section 7.2. Should we wish to copy an array at this point, we could do it simply by creating a new array and copying each element over using a loop.

Figure 6.1   *Diagram of an array declaration.*

5. **Element access.** Java is quite firm about allowing access only to array elements that actually exist. Every time an array is accessed, the index supplied is checked against the bounds given in the array declaration. If the index is out of bounds, an `ArrayIndexOutOfBoundsException` is raised. The exception can be caught and handled, and if it is not, the program halts. For example, with the above declarations, both `frequencies[100]` and `vowels[5]` would cause errors.

6. **Length.** The length of an array can be established by means of a special property associated with every array, called `length`. Thus

    ```
    frequency.length
    ```

    will yield 20. In other words, `length` returns the limit used in the declaration. Notice that `length` is not a method, but a property, and therefore does not have parentheses after it.

7. **Parameters.** Arrays can be passed as parameters to methods. A very convenient feature of Java is that the formal parameter in the method does not have to specify the length of the array it expects. The method can accept arrays of the correct type of any length, and processes them by using the `length` property described in point 5. A prime example is the main method which declares

    ```
    main (String [] args)
    ```

    If there are any arguments, `main` could print them out using a for-loop as follows:

    ```
    for (int i=0; i<args.length; i++)
      System.out.println(args[i]);
    ```

Array and class interaction

There are at least three different ways in which arrays and classes can interact.

1. An array of a class of objects (Figure 6.2).

    ```
    Dates holidays [] = new Dates [4];
    ```

2. A class containing an array and methods that operate on it (Figure 6.3).

Figure 6.2 *Diagram of an array of a class of objects.*

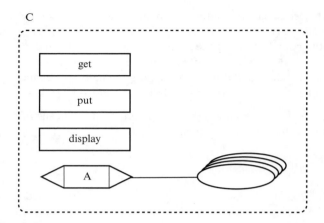

C

Figure 6.3 *Diagram of a class containing an array.*

```
class C {

   int get (int i) {
     return A[i];
   }
   void put (int i, int x) {
     A[i] = x;
   }
   void display () {
     for (int i=0; i<A.length, i++)
         System.out.println(A[i]);
   }

   private int A [] = new int [4];
}
```

A is marked as private because in this class, the only access to the array is via the methods. Notice that A is not static: objects of class C can be declared, and each one will get its own instance of the A array.

3.   A class containing methods that operate on array parameters (Figure 6.4).

```
int marks [] = new int [n];
Sort (marks);
System.out.println(max(marks));
```

Figure 6.4 shows that there exists only one array, marks. The methods in C have formal parameters which are array references. When the call is made, the reference is directed to marks, and the method operates on that array.

The first technique was used in Example 6.1. The others are illustrated in examples that follow.

C

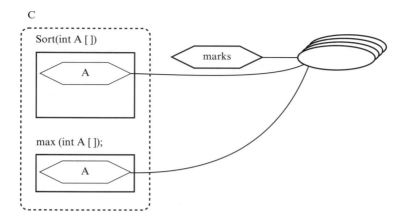

Figure 6.4   *Diagram of methods that have array parameters.*

Arrays as an abstraction

In this book, we delayed introducing arrays in order to emphasize the control operations in processing data. Very often, one will find a solution to a problem that makes use of an array, where in fact it is not strictly necessary. Is this wrong? No, it is not wrong; it merely represents a different abstraction of a solution.

Consider the following problem: we need to read in 20 values and find the smallest and the largest. There are two approaches to the solution:

- Read in the 20 values, keeping track of the smallest and largest 'on the fly'.

- Read the 20 values into an array, then scan the array through twice to find the smallest and then the largest values.

Instinctively, the first approach seems more efficient, and on the face of it, it is no more complicated than the second. But the balance changes if we take into account methods that we already have in stock.

Suppose we already have methods to calculate the minimum and maximum values from a given array. Then, the comparative algorithms would be as shown in Figure 6.5.

The concept we are highlighting here is called *separation of concerns*. In the first algorithm, all the operations are mixed up in one process. In the second, we identify three concerns which can be handled separately in both time and space. These are the reading, finding the minimum and finding the maximum. The development of each process can proceed independently in time, and they are also identified separately in space as three different methods. In the long run, the second approach can enable us to reap the benefits of readability and be more easier to manage.

These ideas are illustrated in Example 6.2 which, strictly speaking, does not *need* an array, but which uses one to good effect to make an easily understandable program. On the other hand, later examples do need an arrays, as did Example 6.1.

Min and max on the fly

Initialize min and max

For each value

Read in a value
Reset min and max
if appropriate

Print out min and max

Min and max arrays with functions

Read the values into array A
Print out min(A) and max(A)

Figure 6.5 *Two algorithms for finding the min and max in an array.*

EXAMPLE 6.2 Diving competitions

Problem   The judging of diving competitions relies on judges from several countries. In order to avoid bias, such as judges rewarding competitors from their home country with higher scores, the result for a single dive is calculated as the average of all the scores, less the highest and lowest score. We would like to computerize these calculations.

Algorithm   As outlined just above, there are two possible approaches to this problem. The three values required – that is, the sum, the lowest and the highest scores – can all be calculated on the fly while the scores are read in. Alternatively, we can read the values in and then assess them. Assuming we choose the second approach, then there are once again two options. These are to compute the three values simultaneously in a single loop, or to have three different loops, perhaps in three different methods, to calculate them. Since the calculations are really so simple, we shall adopt the first approach this time, and do them all together.

Class design   The program breaks naturally into two parts. There is a class for reading in the scores, eliminating the outer ones, and so on. Then the main program is concerned with computing the final result for each dive.

The relationship between a class for judges and the array of scores falls into the second category of array and class interaction described above. The scores are kept in a class and we have two methods, getScores and assessScores, to read them in and total them. The broad outline of the class relationship is shown in Figure 6.6.

The array declaration is:

```
private int score [];
```

The number of judges is set up by the constructor, so that we also have the case here where the array is introduced, and then its size created later:

```
Judge (int n) {
  noofJudges = n;
  score = new int [noofJudges];
}
```

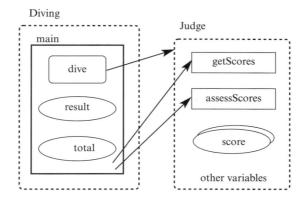

Figure 6.6 *Class diagram for the diving program.*

In addition, associated with the array are four other variables, notably:

```
int minJudge, maxJudge, minScore, maxScore;
```

While `score` is private and accessible only through the methods, these other variables can be accessed directly. It would be too tedious to create additional methods just to send them across as values: moderation in everything!

Program   Here follows the class:

```java
import java.io.*;

class Judge {
  /* The Judge Class by       J M Bishop Dec 1996
     Stores and assesses diving scores.
     All the variables are visible, except the
     array of scores itself.
     Illustrates arrays */

  static final int noofJudges = 8;
  int minJudge, maxJudge, minScore, maxScore;

  Judge (int n) {
    noofJudges = n;
    score = new int [noofJudges]
  };

  void getScores (DataInputStream in) throws IOException {
    System.out.println("Type in the "+noofJudges
                     +" scores in order");
    for (int i=0; i < noofJudges; i++)
      score [i] = Text.readInt(in);
  }

  int assessScores () {
    minScore = 10;
    maxScore = 0;
```

```
      int sum = 0;
      for (int i=0; i < noofJudges; i++) {
        sum += score[i];
        if (score[i] <= minScore) {
          minScore = score[i]; minJudge = i;
        }
        if (score[i] > maxScore) {
          maxScore = score[i]; maxJudge = i;
        }
      }
      minJudge++; maxJudge++;
      return sum;
    }

  private int score [];

}
```

And here is the program:

```
class Diving {
  /* The Diving program        by J M Bishop Dec 1996
     Uses the Judge class to record the
     correct scores for dives.
     Illustrates class methods, arrays
     and typed functions. */

  static final int noofDives = 3;

  public static void main (String [] args) throws IOException {
    System.out.println ("Diving Score Calculator\n" +
                        "=======================\n");
    DataInputStream in = new DataInputStream(System.in);
    double result, total = 0;
    Judge dive = new Judge (8);

    for (int i=0; i < noofDives; i++) {
      System.out.println("Dive no: "+(i+1));
      dive.getScores (in);
      result = (double) (dive.assessScores ()
            - dive.minScore - dive.maxScore)
            / (double) (dive.noofJudges - 2);
      total += result;
      System.out.println("Scores " + dive.minScore
          + " from judge "
          + dive.minJudge + " and " + dive.maxScore
          + " from judge "
        + dive.maxJudge + " excluded.");
      System.out.println("Result is: " + result);
    }
      System.out.println("Diving average is : "+
          total/noofDives);
  }
}
```

Testing   A test run of the program would produce:

```
Diving Score Calculator
=========================
Dive no: 1
Type in the 8 scores in order
7 8 7 4 8 6 9 7
Scores 4 from judge 4 and 10 from judge 8 excluded.
Result is: 7.16667
Dive no: 2
Type in the 8 scores in order
8 8 8 8 4 8 10 8
Scores 6 from judge 5 and 10 from judge 6 excluded.
Result is: 8.33333
Dive no: 3
Type in the 8 scores in order
7 7 7 7 7 7 7 7
Scores 7 from judge 8 and 7 from judge 1 excluded.
Result is: 7
Diving average is : 7.5
```

6.2   Multi-dimensional arrays

Multi-dimensional arrays are very useful for storing data in rows and columns, often known as matrices. Since Java permits array elements to be of any type, including arrays themselves, arrays of multiple dimensions can be built up. For a typical matrix such as that shown in Figure 6.7, the declaration would be:

```
int matrix [][] = new double [4][5];
```

Rows are always mentioned first in the declaration. This enables a single row of the matrix to be represented. For example,

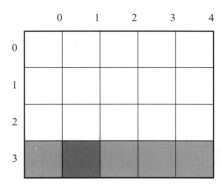

Figure 6.7   *A typical matrix.*

```
matrix[3]
```

would give the shaded row in Figure 6.7. Each element of the row can be selected by indexing twice, as in:

```
matrix [3] [1]
```

which would give the darker element. To swap two rows, *i* and *j*, of the matrix, we could say:

```
int row [] = new int [5];
row = matrix[i];
matrix[i] = matrix[j];
matrix[j] = row;
```

EXAMPLE 6.3   Gold exploration

Problem   Savanna Exploration Inc. has obtained data of infrared readings of a portion of desert where gold is believed to be present. The data should show up the boundaries of a gold reef, based on readings which are greater than the average of those around them. Can you help find the gold?

Solution   The map of the readings can be considered, a point at a time, and a corresponding map printed out showing those with higher than average infrared levels. For example, given the following data on a sample 8×8 grid:

```
21 21 22 30 40 21 34 45
21 22 23 30 45 21 37 40
22 23 24 45 46 47 38 39
22 23 24 35 46 47 38 38
23 24 25 36 46 49 37 36
23 24 25 37 39 48 36 35
23 24 25 25 26 25 26 25
23 25 26 27 28 29 30 31
```

we could deduce the corresponding map:

```
******* Savanna Exploration Inc. *****
We shall find gold!

Map of possible boundaries of the gold reef
==========================================
  0 1 2 3 4 5 6 7
0
1           *     *
2     *   * * *
3           * *
4     *   * * *
5         *     *
6
7
Good luck prospecting!
```

Algorithm   The high-level algorithm is:

Gold exploration
Read in the data
Assess each point, creating the corresponding map of blanks and asterisks
Print the map

Each of these steps can be refined into double loops scanning the whole matrix. For example, assessing a point consists of adding up the values to its north, south, east and west and dividing by 4. If the point itself has a higher reading than its neighbours, we mark it as part of the reef on the map. Thus there are two matrices: data and map.

```
point = data[i][j];
average = (data[i-1][j]+data[i+1][j]
             +data[i][j-1]+data[i][j+1])/4;
if (point > average) map[i][j] = cover;
```

We must also consider how to deal with data points on the edge of the grid. We shall assume that there is sufficient redundancy in the data to allow us to ignore the points on the boundary. Thus we run the assessing loops from 1 to rowmax-1 and 1 to colmax-1 respectively.

Class design   The design consists of two classes: one concerned with the gold maps, and one concerned with activating them. The design of the Gold class is once again category two: there is a class containing arrays with methods that can be called to act upon them. The arrays and all their supporting variables and constants are private as there is no need for them to be known outside the class. The class diagram is very similar to that of Example 6.2. This time you are encouraged to draw it yourself.

Program   The Gold class is:

```
import java.io.*;

class Gold {

  /* The Gold class      by J M Bishop   Jan 1997
     Transforms raw geological
     readings into a character map of a possible
     gold reef.
     Illustrates two different multi-dimensional
     arrays in a class. */

  Gold (int r, int c) {
    rowmax = r;
    colmax = c;
    data = new double [rowmax] [colmax];
    map = new char [rowmax] [colmax];
  }
```

```
void readIn (DataInputStream in) throws IOException {
  for (int i=0; i<rowmax; i++)
    for (int j=0; j<colmax; j++)
      data[i][j] = Text.readDouble(in);
}

void assess () {
  double point, average;
  for (int i=0; i<rowmax; i++)
    for (int j=0; j<colmax; j++)
      map[i][j] = blank;
  for (int i=1; i<rowmax-1; i++)
    for (int j=1; j<colmax-1; j++) {
      point = data[i][j];
      average = (data[i-1][j]+data[i+1][j]
                 +data[i][j+-1]+data[i][j+1])/4;
      if (point > average) map[i][j]=cover;
    }
}

void print () {
  System.out.println("Map of possible boundaries " +
                     "of the gold reef");
  System.out.println("==============================" +
            "=============\n");
  for (int j=0; j<colmax; j++) System.out.print(j+" ");
  System.out.println();
  for (int i=0; i<rowmax; i++) {
    System.out.print(i+" ");
    for (int j=0; j<colmax; j++)
      System.out.print(map[i][j]+" ");
    System.out.println();
  }
  System.out.println("Good luck prospecting!");
}

private int rowmax, colmax;
private double data [][];
private char map [][];
private static final char blank = ' ';
private static final char cover = '*';
}
```

Then calling it we have the short `Explore` class:

```
import java.io.*;

class Explore {

  public static void main (String [] args) throws IOException {

    DataInputStream fin = new DataInputStream(new FileInputStream
                    ("gold.dat"));
```

```
    System.out.println("******* Savanna Exploration Inc. *****");
    System.out.println("We shall find gold!");
    Gold mine = new Gold (8,8);
    mine.readIn(fin);
    mine.assess();
    mine.print();
  }
}
```

Only one instance of the `Gold` class is created, but of course we could have several, and thus process several sets of data and make several maps.

Testing   The expected output to the file has already been given.

The next example illustrates the use of the third technique for the array-class interaction that we mentioned. It is typical of statistical type programs, where a bank of functions is programmed separately for arrays and matrices which are passed as parameters. Fortunately, the reference facility that Java uses for arrays enables the methods to be written independently of the size of the arrays, thus achieving considerable generality. In Chapter 8 we shall see how this generality can be extended to the types of the elements as well.

EXAMPLE 6.4   Rainfall statistics

Problem   The Savanna Weather Department has kept statistics on monthly rainfall figures for the past 20 years. Now they would like to calculate:

● the average rainfall for each month, and

● the standard deviation for each month.

Solution   The table of rainfall figures that is provided by a clerk will look something like this:

Year	Jan	Feb	Mar	Apr	May	Jun	Jul	Aug	Sep	Oct	Nov	Dec
1987	20	22	17	14	5	0	0	0	7	12	30	20
1988	22	24	19	12	0	0	3	0	8	15	20	25
1989	17	17	17	15	0	0	0	0	6	17	8	20
1990	10	10	10	5	0	0	0	0	0	12	10	15
1991	10	10	10	5	0	0	0	0	0	12	10	15
1992	20	22	17	14	5	0	0	0	7	12	30	20
1993	22	24	19	12	0	0	3	0	8	15	20	25
1994	17	17	17	15	0	0	0	0	6	17	8	20
1995	25	30	25	15	7	0	0	0	20	15	20	30
1996	25	30	25	15	7	0	0	0	20	15	20	30

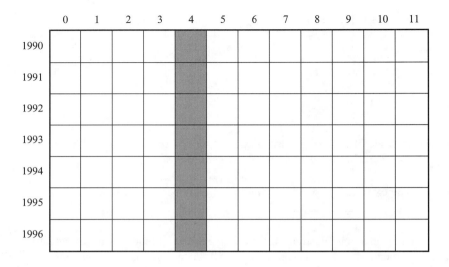

Figure 6.8   *Diagram of part of a matrix for rainfall data.*

The data can be read in by drawing such a table on the screen and letting the user type in each value in turn, or by reading the values from a file. As the values are read in, they are stored in a matrix which is indexed by both the months and the years. Since the rainfall for a month seems to be the crucial figure, the matrix should be structured so that a whole column can be moved around at once. In other words, we would like to represent the matrix as in Figure 6.8.

To do this, we make months the first subscript, and the range of years the second, that is:

```
static final int maxyear = 7;
double rainTable [] [] = new double [12][maxyear];
```

`rainTable[5]` then gives all rainfall for all the available years for June (remember arrays start at 0, so June is 5). This is the shaded area in Figure 6.8.

Once the rainfall figures are safely in the matrix, methods can be designed to perform the required calculations. Each will make use of the matrix and be passed a column of one month's rainfall figures.

Solution   Some elementary statistics is in order at this point. If we have a set of measurements x_i we can analyse them to find the mean $\bar{x}$ which gives the average measurement, and the standard deviation s, which shows the amount by which measurements are likely to differ from the mean. In other words, the standard deviation indicates the spread of the measurements.

The mean of a set of measurements x_i ($i = 1, n$) is defined to be:

$$\bar{x} = \frac{\sum\limits_{i=1}^{n} x_i}{n}$$

and the formula for the standard deviation is:

$$S = \sqrt{\frac{\sum\limits_{i=1}^{n} (x_i - \bar{x})^2}{n - 1}}$$

We can allow for expected errors and intrinsic randomness by saying that the result of a set of measurements will be within a certain standard deviation. In many cases we can say that the true result is in the range $\bar{x} \pm 2s$: that is, the mean plus or minus twice the standard deviation.

Class design   Calculating the mean – or average – could be done fairly simply as we read in each new value. However, because the formula for the standard deviation uses the mean, we have to calculate it after the mean has been arrived at. Thus, we store the values in an array, and process them from there in a second stage. If we adopt technique three for class–array interaction and have the matrix in the main class, with columns of it being repeatedly passed as parameters to methods in another class, then the method to calculate the monthly average could be declared as:

```
static double monthlyAverage (double monthlyRain [], int n)
```

Alternatively, the declaration could be:

```
double monthlyAverage (int m, int n) ;
```

where the first parameter indicates an index into the rain table, and the rain table is stored in the class itself (technique two). If the whole column is sent, accessing the elements is by single indexing. If the index alone is sent as a parameter, then the method has to perform double indexing to get to each element. On balance, technique three is a better choice.

If the value calculated by `monthlyAverage` is assigned to a variable a, it can be passed to the next method which uses it to calculate the standard deviation. The declaration for this function is therefore:

```
double monthlyStdDev
   (double monthlyRain [], int n, double mean);
```

Program   This version of the program assumes input from a file called `rain.dat` with output to `rain.out`. First of all, here is the `Rain` class with the two statistical methods.

```
class Rain {

   /* The Rain class      by J M Bishop    Jan 1997
      Has methods for calculating the mean and standard
      deviation.
```

```
            Illusrates passing arrays as parameters. */

    static double monthlyAverage (double monthlyRain [], int n) {
      double total = 0;
      for (int y=0; y<n; y++)
        total += monthlyRain[y];
      return total / n;
    }

    static double monthlyStdDev (double monthlyRain [],
                               int n, double mean) {
      double total = 0;
      for (int y=0; y<n; y++)
        total += (mean-monthlyRain[y])*(mean-monthlyRain[y]);
      return Math.sqrt(total/(n-1));
    }
  }
```

And here is the main class that declares the matrix, reads in the data, and then makes use of the `Rain` class.

```
  import java.io.*;

  class Weather {

    /* The Weather program      by J M Bishop Jan 1997
       Calculates mean and standard deviation of rainfall
       for each month over the number of years provided.
       Illustrates handling of a matrix and passing columns
       as parameters.
       The data must be in the form:
       year followed by the 12 rainfall figures for
       the months of that year. */

    static int startYear, endYear = 0;
    static double rainTable [] [] = new double [12] [70];

    static void readIn () throws IOException {

      DataInputStream fin = new DataInputStream
          (new FileInputStream("rain.dat"));

      int actualYear = 0; // e.g. 1985
      int yearIndex = 0;

      // The actual years are read in and might not be sorted
      // or contiguous. The yearIndex starts at 0 and is used
      // to store the data in an orderly manner.

      try {
        while (true) {
          actualYear = Text.readInt(fin);
          System.out.print(actualYear +" ");
```

```
      if (yearIndex == 0) startYear = actualYear;
      for (int m = 0; m<12; m++) {
        rainTable[m][yearIndex] = Text.readDouble(fin);
        System.out.print(rainTable[m][yearIndex]+" ");
      }
      System.out.println();
      yearIndex++;
    }
  }
  catch (EOFException e) {

    // Pick up the last year of data read in.
    endYear = actualYear;
    System.out.println("Data read for "+startyear+" to "+
        endyear+"\n\n");
  }
}


static void showResults () {
  System.out.println("Rainfall statistics for " +
    startYear + " to " + endYear);
  System.out.println("=========================" +
      "============\n");
  System.out.println("Month\tMean\tStd.Deviation");
  int nyears = endYear-startYear+1;
  double a, s;
  for (int m=0; m<12; m++) {
    a = Rain.monthlyAverage (rainTable[m], nyears);
    s = Rain.monthlyStdDev (rainTable[m], nyears, a);
    System.out.println((m+1)+"\t"+a+"\t"+s);
  }
}


  public static void main (String [] args) throws IOException {
    readIn ();
    showResults ();
  }
}
```

Testing   For the data shown above, the output to the file would be:

1985	20	22	17	14	5	0	0	0	7	12	30	20
1986	22	24	19	12	0	0	3	0	8	15	20	25
1987	17	17	17	15	0	0	0	0	6	17	8	20
1988	10	10	10	5	0	0	0	0	0	12	10	15
1989	20	22	17	14	5	0	0	0	7	12	30	20
1990	22	24	19	12	0	0	3	0	8	15	20	25
1991	17	17	17	15	0	0	0	0	6	17	8	20
1992	25	30	25	15	7	0	0	0	20	15	20	30
1993	25	30	25	15	7	0	0	0	20	15	20	30
1994	10	10	10	5	0	0	0	0	0	12	10	45

Data read for 1985 to 1994

```
Rainfall statistics for 1985 to 1994
=====================================
Month    Mean     Std Deviation
1        18.8     8.26667
2        20.6     9.8813
3        17.6     7.74711
4        12.2     5.68077
5        2.4      3.26871
6        0        0
7        0.6      1.28062
8        0        0
9        8.2      7.4
10       14.2     5.1558
11       17.6     10.2207
12       25       11.9024
```

Unfortunately, as we have noted before, Java does not have neat output formatting facilities for numbers of variable sizes.

6.3 Strings

Strings were the first data items that we introduced in *Java Gently* and they have been used extensively since. It is now time to take a formal look at what they really are and what facilities are available for them. Strings are special in Java for several reasons:

- `String` is a class so that strings are objects and not variables along with items defined from one of the primitive types such as `int` or `char`.

- There is a special notation for string constants which also creates a shorthand when new string objects are instantiated.

- Once created, the contents of a string cannot be changed.

So, for example, if we make the declaration:

```
String bigOne = "hippopotamus";
```

an object will automatically be created and initialized (without us using `new`) and will contain a reference called `bigOne`, as in Figure 6.9.

Compare this declaration with a similar one for dates:

```
Date graduation = new Date (1998,5,4);
```

Here the constant is given in parentheses and the new operator is used.

The strings created in quotes or read into objects of the `String` class cannot be altered. There is another Java class, `StringBuffer`, which allows for this sort of thing. The `String` class has 24 different methods, some of which are shown in the next form:

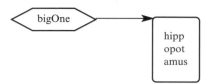

Figure 6.9   *Diagram of a* `string` *declaration.*

String class methods	
int	length ()
char	charAt (int *index*)
boolean	equals (Object *obj*)
int	compareTo (String *S*)
int	indexOf (String *S*)
String	substring (int *begin*, int *end*)
char []	toCharArray ()

`length` will give the length of string. Notice that unlike for an array, this is a method call, so the parentheses are required. Although a string cannot be indexed directly, it is made up of characters and the character at any index position can be obtained via `indexAt`. The whole string can also be transformed into a character array if required. For example,

```
String bigOne = "hippopotamus";
char study [];
study = toCharArray (bigOne);
```

produces an array of length 12 with each character from the original string. `indexOf` operates as a searching mechanism, enabling one to find a substring in a string. So, for example,

```
String bigOne = "hippopotamus";
int bang = bigOne.indexOf("pop");
int fizz = bigOne indexOf("up");
```

will produce 3 in `pop` but –1 in `fizz`. Similarly, a substring can be extracted, as in

```
String bigOne = "hippopotamus";
String small = bigOne.substring(3,5);
```

which would give `"pop"`.

`compareTo` and `equals` enable whole strings to be compared. The comparison operators and `==` should not be used for this purpose. The reason is connected with the fact that strings are objects; the full implications are carefully discussed in Section 7.2. The difference between assigning string values and their references is also covered in Section 7.2. Meanwhile, we note how the comparison methods would be used. `equals` returns a Boolean as expected, for example:

```
String bigOne = "hippopotamus";
String small = bigOne.substring(3,5);
System.out.println (bigOne.equals(small));
```

will give false. The comparison works as follows:

```
a.compareTo(b) a less than b      -1
               a same as b         0
               a greater than b    1
```

The comparison is a straight alphabetical one. So, for example,

```
String bigOne = "hippopotamus";
String small = bigOne.substring(3,5);
System.out.println (bigOne.compareTo(small));
```

will produce −1. In other words, 'hippopotamus' does come alphabetically before 'pop'.

One of the common operations in programming is to convert strings to numbers and back again. In fact, this is what has to be done when we read and write numbers. In this book, reading numbers is done through the Text class, and in this section we can look at the inside of that class, to see how it actually performs its task. But first we have to examine two more Java features: envelopes and tokenizers.

Envelopes

One of the strict rules in Java is that variables and objects cannot be mixed in any way. For most of the time, this causes little inconvenience, but there are times when a standard package requires an object, and we wish to send it, say, an integer. In order to do so, we first place it in what is known as an **envelope** class. The envelope class provides access to the value and also has various conversion methods available.

The Java lang package has four envelope classes associated with numbers, namely Double, Float, Integer and Long. As their names suggest, they provide class-level versions of their respective primitive data types. There are also similar classes called Character and Boolean for char and boolean types, respectively.

As an example, the important methods of the Integer class are given in the following form:

Integer and int conversions
Integer (int *value*);
int   intValue ();
int   parseInt (String *s*);
Integer valueOf (String *s*);

The first two provide for moving back and forth between types and classes. Thus if *i* is an int,

```
Integer Iobj = new Integer (i)
```

makes an object out of it. To get the `int` back in order, say, to print it, we use:

```
System.out.println(Iobj.intValue());
```

The other two selected methods convert from strings and back: more of this below. The other three numeric envelope classes – `Double`, `Long` and `Float` – have identical methods.

Tokenizers

We have already mentioned that Java is slightly deficient in the input arena, and that the `Text` class was created to make up for the problem. In fact, Java can read strings, and also provides a very efficient means of breaking a string up into tokens. Tokens are substrings separated by characters such as a comma, a space or a tab. In this way we can pick off substrings from the input and pass them to the string versions of the envelope class routines for conversion in order to get the values we want.

Some of the methods provided by the `StringTokenizer` class, which is in `java.util`, are:

`StringTokenizer` declaration and access

`StringTokenizer (String s);`
`String   nextToken ();`
`String   nextToken (String delimiter);`
`boolean hasMoreTokens ();`

There are additional methods for changing the delimiters, counting tokens and so on. We now consider how envelopes and tokenizers are used in the Text class.

EXAMPLE 6.5   The `Text` class

Problem   What really goes on behind the scenes in the `Text` class?

Solution   We now have covered enough of the language to explain the `Text` class. The class is not long, but it does make use of tokenizers and envelopes. The methods provided by the class are:

The `Text` class methods

`public static void prompt (String s);`
`public static int readInt (DataInputStream in);`
`public static int readDouble (DataInputStream in);`
`public static int readString (DataInputStream in);`
`public static int readChar (DataInputStream in);`

Obviously, the list could be extended to include methods applicable to the other primitive types.

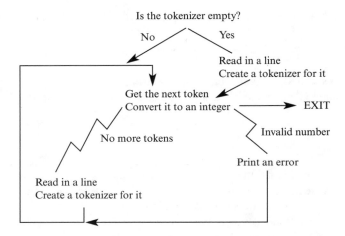

Figure 6.10 *Algorithm showing the Text. readInt method in action.*

Algorithm The `Text` class is composed of a set of methods which can be called in any order. There is no initializing to be done, so the methods must be sure to initialize themselves. The methods are static, and the class is not intended to be instantiated. It operates as a service provider in the same way as the `Math` class.

The general algorithm for each of the reading methods is illustrated by that for reading an integer (Figure 6.10). The routine can initialize itself by detecting a null token. If this is the case, it reads a line and creates a token. It then calls `nextToken` and tries to convert the token to a number. Both statements can go wrong:

●   The call to `nextToken` can fail if there are no more tokens. The appropriate action is therefore to read another line.

●   The conversion can fail if the substring forming the token does not represent a number of the proper kind. Again an exception is raised. Here we just print a message and try again.

If both statements complete successfully, the method exits.

The class also has a prompt method for writing out a short message and staying on the same line.

Program The program contains a particularly interesting statement in each of the numeric conversion methods. The integer one is:

```
return Integer.valueOf (item.trim()).intValue();
```

Let us consider what this does. `item` is a string returned from the tokenizer. Working from the inside outwards, we first trim it of spaces, using a method from the `String` class. Then we call the `Integer.valueOf` method to convert the string to an object of type `Integer`. Finally, we take the object out of its envelope and turn it into an `int` type. This statement is worth putting into a typed method!

```
import java.io.*;
import java.util.*;

class Text {

  /* The famous Text class      by J M Bishop   Aug 1996
     provides simple input from the keyboard and files.
     Routines provided are:
  public static void prompt (String s);
  public static int readInt (DataInputStream in);
  public static int readDouble (DataInputStream in);
  public static int readString (DataInputStream in);
  public static int readChar (DataInputStream in); */

  public Text () {}  ;

  private static StringTokenizer T;
  private static String S;

  public static void prompt (String s) {
    System.out.print(s + " ");
    System.out.flush();
  }

  public static int readInt (DataInputStream in) throws IOException {
    if (T==null) refresh(in);
    while (true) {
      try {
        String item = T.nextToken();
        return Integer.valueOf (item.trim()).intValue();
      }
      catch (NoSuchElementException e1) {
        refresh (in);
      }
      catch (NumberFormatException e2) {
        System.out.println("Error in number, try again.");
      }
    }
  }

  public static char readChar (DataInputStream in) throws IOException {
    if (T==null) refresh(in);
    while (true) {
      try {
        return T.nextToken().charAt(0);
      }
      catch (NoSuchElementException e1) {
        refresh (in);
      }
    }
  }

  public static double readDouble (DataInputStream in) throws
                                                    IOException {
    if (T==null) refresh(in);
    while (true) {
```

```
        try {
          String item = T.nextToken();
          return Double.valueOf (item.trim()).doubleValue();
        }
        catch (NoSuchElementException e1) {
          refresh (in);
        }
        catch (NumberFormatException e2) {
          System.out.println("Error in number, try again.");
        }
      }
    }

    public static String readString (DataInputStream in) throws
                                                  IOException {
      if (T==null) refresh (in);
      while (true) {
        try {
          return T.nextToken();
        }
        catch (NoSuchElementException e1) {
          refresh (in);
        }
      }
    }

    private static void refresh (DataInputStream in) throws
                                                  IOException {
      S = in.readLine ();
      if (S==null) throw new EOFException();
      T = new StringTokenizer (S);
    }
  }
```

Testing   The class has been extensively tested in the book already. See also Section 4.2.

6.4   Sorting

Sorting is a very common operation in computing, and many systems provide high-level commands which enable data to be sorted in any specified way. These commands rely on one of a number of sorting algorithms, and every programmer should know at least one such sorting algorithm by heart. We start by introducing a simple one – selection sort – which performs in time proportional to the square of the number of items being sorted. Other algorithms (for example, Quicksort) perform faster, but are perhaps more difficult to understand and remember. Quicksort is covered in Chapter 12.

Selection sort

Sorting items means moving them around in a methodical way until they are all in order. A method used by some card players is to sort cards by holding them in the right hand, finding the lowest one and taking it out into the left hand, then finding the next lowest and taking it out, until all the cards have been selected, and the left hand holds the cards in order. The following sequence illustrates how this method works.

Left hand	Right hand
	7 3 9 0 2 5
0	7 3 9 – 2 5
0 2	7 3 9 – – 5
0 2 3	7 – 9 – – 5
0 2 3 5	7 – 9 – – –
0 2 3 5 7	– – 9 – – –
0 2 3 5 7 9	– – – – – –

We could implement this by having two arrays and picking the numbers out of one, adding them to the other. However, there is a way of keeping both lists in the same array, the one growing as the other shrinks. Each time an element is picked out, the gap it leaves is moved to one end, thus creating a contiguous area, which is used to hold the new list. The move is done by a simple swap with the leftmost element of the right hand. So, the example would proceed as follows:

Left hand	Right hand
	7 3 9 0 2 5
0	3 9 7 2 5
0 2	9 7 3 5
0 2 3	7 9 5
0 2 3 5	9 7
0 2 3 5 7	9
0 2 3 5 7 9	

The underlined digits are those that moved at each phase. Each time, a reduced list is considered, until only one element is left. The algorithm can be phrased more precisely as shown in Figure 6.11.

Because sorting is clearly going to be useful in many contexts, it makes sense to put it in a method from the beginning. The parameters would be the array to be sorted, and the number of items that are active in it. Of course, we shall have to say in the formal parameter what type of items are being sorted. In Section 8.2 we explain how we can relax this requirement. The example sort given here sorts an array of doubles.

```
static void selectionSort (double [ ] a, int n) {
  double temp;
  int chosen;

  for (int leftmost = 0; leftmost < n-1; leftmost++) {
    chosen = leftmost;
    for (int j = leftmost+1; j < n; j++)
      if (a[j].lessThan(a[chosen])) chosen = j;
    temp = a[chosen];
```

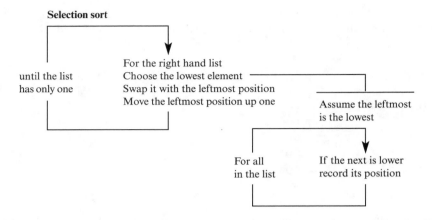

Figure 6.11 *Algorithm for selection sorting.*

```
        a[chosen] = a[leftmost];
        a[leftmost] = temp;
    }
}
```

Sorting is a frequent requirement in computing, and it is useful to have a sorting algorithm handy. The algorithm can be applied to arrays of any size, and containing any elements, and can be used to sort in ascending order just by changing the comparison from < to >. Notice, however, that if we wish to sort from highest to lowest, then the value that moves to the left each time will be the largest, not the smallest. Simple examples illustrating sorting are easy to construct. Let us instead investigate how to sort classes.

EXAMPLE 6.6 Sorting names and marks

Problem Suppose that the names and marks of a class of students have to be printed in alphabetical order.

Solution Use a computer. Read all the name–mark pairs into an array, sort them according to the name using selection sort, and then print out the contents of the array.

Algorithm The first step is to define the data and the data structure. The data will look like this:

```
    Jones 67
    MacDeedle 51
    Abbott 90
```

We define a class with two variables – one for the name and one for the mark. The array will be declared of this class, for example:

```
class Students { ... }
Students group [] = new Students [50];
```

In the sorting process, the name is used in the comparison part, but when the swapping is done, the whole object is copied. Thus, the mark will move around with the name while sorting is proceeding. The class design is an example of technique one, as discussed in Section 6.1.

Program   The program is really just a rework of the sort given in the previous example. The reader is encouraged to produce it. Remember that because the types of the array being sorted are different, the sort method has had to be changed accordingly.

6.5   Hash tables

There are two problems with arrays:

- an array is of fixed size, set at declaration time;
- the index to an array is always an integer.

Consider the following, fairly common, requirement: we would like to store values for each of the letters of the alphabet. An array would be the ideal choice, but we cannot index one with `char`, nor can we convert `chars` to `integers` and back.

Fortunately, Java provides help in the form of standard classes in the `java.util` package.

The `Vector` class

The `Vector` class defines sequences of objects where the sequence can grow in size as required. In fact, it grows automatically, without even being explicitly asked to! Objects are put in and out of the vector using methods. A method is also used to access elements. We shall not look further at vectors in this chapter for two reasons: firstly, the next class is more general and interesting, and, secondly, the terminology used for defining vectors is quite different from Java's other classes, and is generally considered to be most confusing.

Hash tables

What we really want is a dynamically sized structure, which also has the property that the indices can be, well, anything. Java's hash tables fit this bill completely. A hash table is an collection of pairs of items (key,value). The key is the index (in array terms) and the value is what is associated with the key. We can therefore see that an array is a special case of a hash table, with the key being of type `int`. With hash tables, though, the key can be of any type or class, including `double`, `String`, `Students` or whatever.

A word about the term 'hash' table. Hash refers to the fact that the items are not stored sequentially in the table, but in a manner which makes them efficient to retrieve. In fact, in a fairly empty table, the efficiency can approach that of an array. As a result, hash tables are not ordered by key, and if we print out what is in one, it will appear in some seemingly random order.

The declaration of, and operations available on, a hash table are summarized in the form:

Hash table declaration and access

```
Hashtable name = new Hashtable ( );

void     put (Object key, Object value);
Object   get (Object key);
boolean  containsKey (Object key);
boolean  contains (Object value);
void     remove (Object key);
```

The class `Object` is defined by Java as the superclass of all classes. There will be more about it in the next two chapters. In the meantime all we need to know is that `Hashtable` is defined based on `Object` so that it can be used with any class.

For example, suppose we wish to associate names with dates. We could do the following:

```
Hashtable holidays = new Hashtable ();
Date d;

// remember months are indexed from 0!
holidays.put ("Christmas", new Date (97,11,25));
holidays.put ("New Year", new Date (97,0,1));
d = (Date) holidays.get ("Christmas");
```

The last statement will successfully get the date 25 Dec 1997 out of the table. But why does the prefix (Date) appear in the assignment? The reason is that hash tables are potentially available for any kinds of objects. The result type of a `get` is `Object`. In order to ensure that we have obtained a `Date`, Java requires that we **cast** the `Object`. The format for doing this is the same as for casting primitive types, which we discussed in Section 3.2. There is more on casting in Section 7.2.

Enumerations

Another class that is closely associated with hash tables is `Enumeration`. In fact, `Enumeration` is not a class: it is a special kind of class called an interface.[1] Interfaces are discussed in Section 8.2, but for now we can just make use of the facilities offered for the purposes of enhancing the power of hash tables.

---

[1] A term commonly used in other languages for an enumeration is an **iterator**.

Enumerations provide a means for iterating over a collection of objects. There are only two methods:

Enumerations
```Object   nextElement ();```   ```boolean hasMoreElements ();```

Once we declare an enumeration, `nextElement` will repeatedly provide the next element, and we can do this until `hasMoreElements` becomes false. For example, if `table` is a `Hashtable` and has been filled with keys that are `Strings` (the type of the values does not matter at this point), then the loop for printing out the keys will be:

```
System.out.println("In the table");
for (Enumeration e = table.keys(); e.hasMoreElements();) {
  String s = (String) e.nextElement();
  System.out.println(s);
}
```

Notice that because of the casting required (as explained just above), the update part of the loop is done as a separate assignment in the body, rather than along with the initialize and check parts, as is usual. Putting this all together, we can tackle Example 6.7.

EXAMPLE 6.7   Student marker

Problem   We would like to store student marks and query them, based on names.

Solution   Here we have a classic case for a hash table. The names and marks can be read in and each pair can be put in the hash table. Then querying is a simple `get` operation, perhaps preceded by a `containsKey`, just to check that the name was spelt correctly. We shall assume that there are six marks per student and that the program must in addition calculate a final mark based on a weighted average. This gives us more scope to practise arrays as well.

Class design   There should obviously be a student class, with the three items, name, marks and final mark. The technique for array–class interaction is the first one: the table is declared as being a collection of objects of the class `Student`. The class diagram would be as shown in Figure 6.12.

Program   Here is the `Student` class:

```
import java.io.*;

class Students {
  /* The Students class by J M Bishop Dec 1996
     Stores names and marks.
     Everything is directly accessible
     by users of the class. */
```

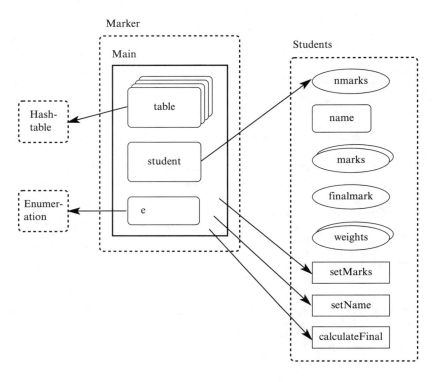

Figure 6.12 *Class diagram for the Student Marks program.*

```
static final int nmarks = 6;
String name;
int marks [] = new int [nmarks];
int finalMark;
int weights [] = {5,10,5,15,25,50};

Students () { }  ;

void setMarks (DataInputStream in) throws IOException {
  for (int i=0; i<nmarks; i++)
    marks[i] = Text.readInt(in);
}

void setName (DataInputStream in) throws IOException {
  name = Text.readString(in) + " " + Text.readString(in);
}

void calculateFinal () {
  finalMark = 0;
  for (int i=0; i< nmarks; i++)
    finalMark += marks[i]*weights[i];
  finalMark = finalMark/100;
}
}
```

The Marker program follows the lines set out above. Of interest are the lines where objects from the hash table are retrieved, and a type cast must be done.

```java
import java.io.*;
import java.util.*;

class Marker {
  /* The Marker Program      by J M Bishop   Dec 1996
     registers the marks of students
     and enables them to be queried.
     Illustrates the use of a hash table */

  public static void main (String [] args) throws IOException {
    DataInputStream fin = new DataInputStream (
      new FileInputStream("marks.dat"));
    DataInputStream in = new DataInputStream (System.in);

    Hashtable table = new Hashtable (20);

    for (int i=0; i<10; i++) {
      Students student = new Students ();
      student.setName (fin);
      student.setMarks (fin);
      student.calculateFinal();
      table.put(student.name,new Integer(student.finalMark));
    }

    System.out.println("In the table");
    for (Enumeration e = table.keys(); e.hasMoreElements();) {
      String name = (String) e.nextElement();
      System.out.println(name);
    }

    while (true) {
      try {
        Text.prompt("Whose mark would you like to know?");
        String s = Text.readString(in) + " " + Text.readString(in);
        if (table.containsKey(s)) {
          Integer Iobj = (Integer) table.get(s);
          System.out.println(Iobj.intValue());
        }
        else System.out.println("Sorry, try again.");
      }
      catch (EOFException e) { break;}
    }
  }
}
```

Testing The following test was run on a set of test data:

```
In the table
Derrick Kourie
Mary Brown
```

```
John Botha
Carol Steele
Peter Beukes
Francois Jacot
Elizabeth Rogers
Louis Botha
Jean Barkhuizen
William Bishop
Whose mark would you like to know? Mary Brown
86
Whose mark would you like to know? William Bishop
90
Whose mark would you like to know? Carol Steele
97
Whose mark would you like to know? Francios Jacot
Sorry, try again.
Whose mark would you like to know? Francois Jacot
81
Whose mark would you like to know?
```

The program could detect that Francios Jacot – a misspelling – was not in the table, through the `containsKey` call, and reacted appropriately.

SUMMARY

Arrays provide for multiple values referred to by the same name. Arrays in Java are of fixed size, but they can have multiple dimensions. There are several ways in which arrays and classes interact, and the correct technique must be chosen for each problem's solution. A useful feature in Java is the ability to declare a method with an array parameter whose length is not specified.

Strings are not arrays in the Java context, but are objects instantiated from a special `String` class. They have their own properties and characteristics. Conversion methods between strings and character arrays and between strings and numbers do exist. In order to round off the family of arrays and strings, there are two other Java concepts – envelopes and tokenizers. Together these combine to provide the power needed by the `Text` class, which is used for all the simple input in this book. Sorting also makes use of arrays, and the selection sort is explained and presented in as general a way as possible.

Finally, we consider how the restrictions of fixed size arrays as well as indexing only with integers can be relaxed. The best answer is to use Java's hash tables which can store values of any class, indexed by any other class, and enable the table to be interrogated and values or keys retrieved. To iterate through the hash tables, we use the enumeration interface supplied along with hash.

QUIZ

6.1   Draw diagrams to show the references and storage created by the following declarations:

```
int counters [] = new int [5];
String names [] = {"Adam", "Eve", "Joseph", "Sarah");
```

6.2   Write a loop to go through the array of names in 6.1 and print out the first position of the letter 'e' in each name, if it exists.

6.3   In Example 6.2 (Diving competitions), the array of scores is declared as:

```
private int score [];
```

Where is it given a length and by which class?

6.4   What is wrong with the following statements?

```
int A [] = new int A[10];
System.out.println (A[A.length()]);
```

6.5   We have declared an array:

```
double B [] = new double [100];
```

Would it be possible to send it to the monthlyAverage method defined in Example 6.4 to calculate the mean and, if so, what would the call look like?

6.6   If "yen" and 167.9 form a pair of a double number, with a string key, what would be the statement required to put the pair into a hash table called exchangeRates? What would be the statement required to get the 167.9 out again and print it, given the key "yen"?

6.7   What would be printed from the following statements?

```
String a = "abcdefg";
System.out.println(a.compareTo("aabcde"));
```

6.8   In which package can the Hashtable class be found?

6.9   The following statements will not compile. What is wrong? Can you fix them?

```
Hashtable holidays = new Hashtable ();
holidays.put ("Foundation Day", new Date (97,6,6));
Dates d = holidays.get ("Foundation Day");
```

6.10   What would be the substring produced by the following:

```
String bigOne = "hippopotamus";
String s = bigOne.substring(1,1);
```

PROBLEMS

6.1   **Mains voltage.** The mains voltage supplied by a substation is measured at hourly intervals over a 72 hour period, and a report made. Write a program to read in the 72 readings and determine:

● the mean voltage measured;

● the hours at which the recorded voltage varies from the mean by more than 10%;

● any adjacent hours when the change from one reading to the next is greater than 15% of the mean value.

Include in your program an option to display a histogram of the voltage over the 72 hours, using the method developed in Example 3.5.

6.2   **Useful methods**. Write a class with methods which take an array of integers as one of their parameters and do the following:

● find the maximum of all the elements;

● determine whether all the quantities in the array are equal;

● determine the number of times a value greater than a given level occurs.

We would also like to add the following facilities:

● find the maximum of all the elements, plus all the positions where it occurs;

● determine the range of values spanned by the array.

Discuss why this may be more difficult and propose a class–array design that might be able to provide for the methods.

6.3   **Sum of squares**. Write a typed method which is given two integers as parameters, and returns as its value the sum of the squares of the numbers between and inclusive of the two parameters. Show how to call the method to print the value of Σi^2 where i runs from 1 to 10. How would the program change if the data was to be read in and stored initially in an array?

6.4   **Validating codes**. Course codes at Savanna University have a precise form: four capital letters followed immediately by three digits. Write a class for such codes, and include methods to read, write and check a code for validity.

6.5   **Standard passes**. The Senate at Savanna University has decreed that at least 75% of students in each course must pass. This means that the pass mark for each course will differ. Write a program that will read in a file of marks and determine the highest pass such that the Senate's rule applies.

6.6   **Palindromes**. A palindrome is a word or sentence that reads the same forwards as backwards, disregarding punctuation. Famous palindromes are:

Madam, I'm Adam

Able was I ere I saw Elba.

Write a boolean method which will check whether a given string is a palindrome or not. Call the method from a test program.

6.7   **Concordance**. A concordance is a list of words similar to an index, where the position of each word – its page number and line number – in a piece of text is indicated. The difference between a concordance and an index is that a concordance considers all words except common ones such as 'and', 'the' and 'is'. Write a Java system to create a concordance from a piece of text at your disposal. Use hash tables. (Hint: the hash table will have the words as keys and the page/line numbers as values. Since the words could occur more than once, the value will have to be an array of numbers, and will have to have an upper limit, say 10 occurrences recorded.)

6.8   **Judges' countries**. In Example 6.2, instead of printing out the judges' numbers, we would like to print out the country from which they come. Use an array to set up a list of country names for the judges on duty, and adapt the program to make the output more explanatory. Consider carefully whether to have an array of countries in Judge alongside the scores, or whether to create another class consisting of a name and a score.

6.9 **Population increase**. Since 1980, the Savanna population statistics have been stored on a computer file, with each line containing the year followed by the total people counted for that year. Write a program that will read this file and find the two consecutive years in which there was the greatest percentage increase in population. The data is not guaranteed to be in strict year order and may need to be sorted first.

6.10 **Bilingual calendars**. Design a program to print out a calendar, one month underneath each other. Then using hash tables, set up versions for the months and days of the week in another language (say, French, Spanish or German), and let the user select which language the calendar should be printed in.

PART II

Power

CHAPTER 7

Objects at work

7.1 Designing an object-oriented program

Java is an object-oriented language and, in Part I, we introduced and used both objects and classes in many examples. Now that we have covered the basic constructs of Java, it is time to look at the real power of objects, and how they are used in larger programs. In this chapter we discuss objects using a case study of a typical inventory program. In the next chapter we go on to look at further capabilities of objects, such as inheritance and abstract classes, and explore some more examples. Before we look at the example, let us consider once again the concept of object modifiers.

Object modifiers

The general form of an object declaration is:

```
Object declaration
modifier classname objectname;
modifier classname objectname = new classname ( );
modifier classname objectname = new classname (parameters);
```

Table 7.1 *Some of the modifiers applicable to objects.*

Modifier	Visibility and use
No modifier	The object is visible within its package.
public	The object is visible anywhere its class is visible.
private	The object is visible only within its own class.
final	The object may not be changed.
static	The object is a class object. There is only one of it in its class. It is accessed through its class name.

where the modifier may be any one of those shown in Table 7.1.

Object declarations

To reinforce the different concepts of classes and objects instantiated from them, let us go back through a few examples of object declarations from previous chapters.

```
// Example 1
PrintStream fout = new PrintStream
                   (new FileOutputStream ("marks.out"));
DataInputStream in = new DataInputStream (System.in);
```

The first example follows the form given in Section 2.5 closely. The objects created are `fout` and `in`, plus the anonymous `FileOutputStream` object passed to the `PrintStream` constructor. `System.in` is also an object, predeclared in the `System` class and passed here to `DataInputStream`'s constructor.

```
// Example 2
String country;
country = Text.readString(fin);
```

Example 2 shows how an object name can be introduced, and the creation of the object handled later. `country` is declared as a `String` object, but it is left to the `readString` method to create the object using `new` and to give it its values. The reference to this new object is then assigned to `country`. (More about references in the next section.)

```
//Example 3
private static Random dice;
dice = new Random (Text.readInt(in));
```

The `dice` example is similar. The name of an object is `dice`. Later on an object is created for the dice via `new Random` and values are given to the `Random` object from `Text.ReadInt(in)`.

```
//Example 4
throw new TargetNotFoundException ();
catch (TargetNotFoundException e);
```

Finally, exceptions are objects too, and when we throw one it is a new one, different from others thrown. The catcher gives it a name, in this case e. The name is seldom used within the catch clause, though.

We now consider the design and development of an example which will make considerable use of classes and have many objects instantiated from them.

EXAMPLE 7.1   Nelson's Coffee Shop

Problem   Nelson's Coffee Shop is looking to computerize its inventory. It would like to investigate what information it needs about coffee stocks and what operations it should incorporate to handle them.

Solution   At this stage we are not going to write the whole inventory program! We are just looking at the definition of the objects. In so doing, though, we shall bear in mind that while coffee may be the main selling item at the shop, it may in the future also sell pastries, ice-creams and so on, and these developments should be borne in mind.

Definition   The shop does not sell just one kind of coffee, but many kinds, such as Java, Columbian and Kenyan. Coffee is going to be a class, and we shall create different coffee objects. In looking at stocks of coffee, we can list the data items that need to be taken into account when recording information about a particular blend. Such a list is the starting point for an object definition. At the same time, we take a guess at the general type of each data item. The first such list is shown in Table 7.2. String, real, integer and date all have existing equivalents in Java.

Looking at this list, we notice that it is too simple. Whereas the first five properties refer to coffee in general, the sell-by-date is going to differ for each *batch* of coffee as it comes into the shop. What this means is that a batch is another object. Not only must it record the date, but it also keeps a count of the number of kilograms of coffee for that date. The main coffee object will keep a cummulative total. This relationship is illustrated in Figure 7.1.

The next part of the definition concerns the operations. We treat these in two groups: those for a blend of coffee (Table 7.3) and those for particular batches (Table 7.4). Starting with the coffee, there is a list of operations that seem likely. Some of these have implications for batches.

We can see that there is a hierarchy between the two types of objects: coffee objects call batch operations, but not vice versa. The method to remove old stock will consider

Table 7.2   *Data items for the cofffee class.*

Item	Type
Name	String
Price	Double (graz)
Amount in stock	Integer (kilograms)
Reorder level	Integer (kilograms)
Barcode	String
Sell-by-date	Date

The kinds of coffee in stock

Batches with different sell-by dates for each coffee

Figure 7.1 *Multiple classes and objects for the Coffee Shop.*

each batch in turn and nullify a batch if it finds it is too old. Similarly, selling coffee could bring a batch down to zero.

How can an object be removed? It will all depend on how the batch objects are arranged. The only grouping structure we know of so far is an array, and we can immediately see that it is a singularly inappropriate structure if we want to delete items: all those following will have to move up, or we have to handle gaps.

Of course there is a better way, but in order not to extend this part of the example for too long, we shall tackle that in Section 7.3, and return to the coffee shop in Section 7.4. Consequently, we will not implement the methods to sell coffee or remove old stock at this point, and will be content to keep batches in an array.

Table 7.3

Operations on coffee	Implications for batches
Prepare to enter stock	
Display coffee blend's data	
Check reorder level	
Change price	
Add stock	Add a new batch
Sell coffee	Subtract stock from relevant batches
Remove old stock	Check sell by date

Table 7.4

Operations on batches	Implications for coffee
Add a new batch	
Display data about a batch	
Check how much is available	
Check sell-by date	
Sell	

Classes   Now we can try to express the design in Java. Starting with the specification of the `Batch` class:

```
import java.util.*

class Batch {

  /* The Batch class       by J M Bishop Oct 1996
     for products with sell-by-dates.
     Can be tested with the Coffee class main program. */

  Batch (double k, Date d);
  double available ( );
  void sell (double k);
  void display ();
  boolean pastSellByDate();

  private double inStock;
  private Date sellByDate;
}
```

The details of the methods have not yet been filled in. Let us first look at how they are used. To create a new batch, the `Coffee` class will include a statement of the form:

```
freshBatch = new Batch (kilos, roastDay);
```

The new batch will have to be linked to the other batches in some way, but we shall leave that issue for the time being. When coffee is sold, the method responsible must first check the availability in the oldest batch and sell as much as it can there. If the order is not complete, the next batch is offered. Let us assume that in an array of batches, batch `b[i]` contains the oldest coffee. The statement to call it to sell d kilograms will be:

```
b[i].sell(d);
```

If we needed to reduce stock from another batch, identified by `b[j]`, then

```
b[j].sell(d);
```

would refer to a different stock and date. The two would not be confused, because they are in different objects. The definition of the Coffee object proceeds in a similar way. Its outline is:

```
import java.util.*;

class Coffee {

  /* The Coffee class       by J M Bishop Oct 1996
     keeps an inventory of batches of coffee of a
     particular kind or blend */

  Coffee ( ) ;
```

```
       void prepareToStock (DataInputStream in);
       void display ();
       void sell (double k);
       boolean stocksLow ();
       void changePrice (double p);
       void checkSellByDates ();

       private boolean newBatchIn (DataInputStream in);
       private String name;
       private double price;    // per kg
       private double stock;    // kgs
       private double reorder;  // kgs;

       private Batch B [ ] = new Batch [10];
       private int batches;
   }
```

As with a batch, the variables are all declared as private, which means that they cannot be altered from outside, only from methods within the class itself. The constructor has no parameters, and in fact does nothing either: all the setting of values is done inside prepareToStock. Why did we do it this way? The reason is that the details of the coffee will be read from a file; they are not available in the program itself. In the next version of the program, we will add a second constructor.

Both the prepareToStock method and newBatchIn will be reading data, and they both get passed the data stream concerned from the main program, which creates coffee objects. The class diagram so far is shown in Figure 7.2. Notice that Coffee uses some of the methods of Batch, and there is therefore a solid arrowed line to it. Also, the array of batches kept in Coffee is declared as of the class Batch, and this instantiation is shown by a plain line. The private variables and methods are shown grouped with private lines down the side of the class. (See Figure 3.5 for the class notation.)

Data An important consideration for the operation of the reading in of coffee is how the data should be arranged. We choose to keep it on file at this stage, but as soon as we get to Chapter 9 (not very far away now) we shall be able to input data with a graphical user interface. The alternative, that of prompting the user on the screen, line by line, is really very tedious and not part of modern programming any more.

The data can be arranged on file as follows:

```
name
price reorder-level
stock sell-by-date      (repeated for each batch)
0
```

with an example being

```
Columbian
60 10
10 1997/Apr/15
25 1997/May/31
0
```

Coffee

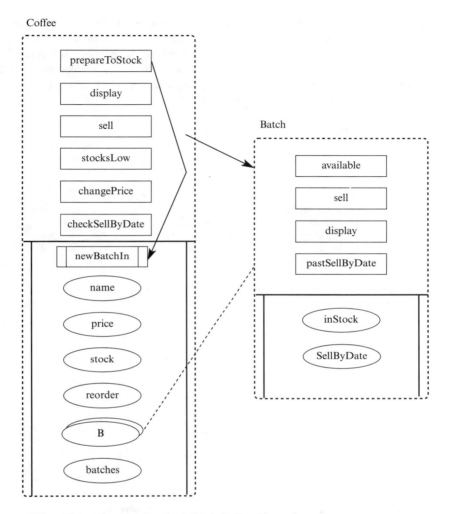

Figure 7.2   *Class diagram for the initial Coffee Shop classes.*

```
Java
64 30
20 1997/May/23
100 1997/Jul/12
12 1997/Aug/1
0
Kenyan
59 10
15 1997/May/20
0
```

The zero after each set of batches is necessary to enable the loop to end. (See Section 5.3 for a discussion on this issue.) The date is going to be read in as a string and converted to a Date object. How this is done was discussed in Chapter 6.

Program And finally we have the program. It consists of three classes, `Batch`, `Coffee` and main program, `CoffeeShop`. The latter contains a little test main program which causes the data to be read in and printed out. Nothing else happens at this stage, but of course we have achieved a lot: we have written a large-ish object-oriented program, and it contains two kinds of user-defined objects. Just as a matter of interest, can you count how many other kinds of objects it contains as well?

```java
import java.io.*;
import java.util.*;

class Batch {

/* The Batch class      by J M Bishop Oct 1996
      for products with sell-by-dates.
      Can be tested with the Coffee class main program. */

  Batch (double k, Date d) {
    inStock = k;
    sellByDate = d;
  }

  double available ( ) {
    return inStock;
  }

  void sell (double k) {
    inStock -= k;
  }

  String shortDate(Date d) {
    // removes the time from the date.
    String s = d.toString();
    return s.substring(0,11) + s.substring(21,25);
  }

  void display () {
    System.out.println("\t\t"+shortDate(sellByDate) +
        " : " + inStock + "kg");
  }

  boolean equals (Batch b) {
    return (this.sellByDate.equals(b.sellByDate));
  }
    private double inStock;
    private Date sellByDate;

}

//=====================================================


import java.io.*;
import java.util.*;
```

```
class Coffee {
  /* The Coffee class by J M Bishop Oct 1996
     keeps an inventory of batches of coffee of a
     particular kind or blend */

  Coffee ( ) {
    // empty constructor, because all the values
    // are read in via prepareToStock }
  }

  void prepareToStock (DataInputStream in) throws IOException {
    name = Text.readString(in);
    price = Text.readDouble(in);
    reorder = Text.readInt(in);
    batches = 0;
    stock = 0;
    newBatchIn (in);
  }

  private boolean newBatchIn (DataInputStream in) throws IOException {
    int a = Text.readInt(in);
    if (a == 0)
      return false;
    else {
      stock += a;
      String s = Text.readString(in);
      Date d = new Date (Date.parse(s));
      B[batches] = new Batch ((double) a,d);
      batches ++;
      return true;
    }
  }

  void display () {
    System.out.println(name+" @ G"+price);
    for (int i = 0; i < batches; i++)
      B[i].display ();
    System.out.println("\t" + stock + "kg in stock. " +
                "Reorder level is" +reorder+"kg\n");
  }

  private String name;
  private double price; // per kg
  private double stock; // kgs
  private double reorder; // kgs;
  private Batch B [ ] = new Batch [10];
  private int batches;
}

// =====================================================

import java.io.*;
import java.util.Date;

class CoffeeShop {
```

```
 // A test Coffee Shop program        by J M Bishop Oct 1996
    checks that data can be read into the
    Coffee and Batch classes, and printed out again.
    Uses an array to store several objects of each. */

  public static void main (String [] args) throws IOException {

     DataInputStream in = new DataInputStream
                          (new FileInputStream("coffee.dat"));

     // Introductory messages
     Coffee C [ ] = new Coffee [10];
     int blend;
     System.out.println("Nelson's Coffee Shop");
     System.out.println("Inventory control");
     System.out.println("Stocking from coffee.data");

     // Read in the data for the coffees or blends
     for (blend=0; blend<10; blend++) {
       try {
         C[blend] = new Coffee ();
         C[blend].prepareToStock (in);
         boolean morebatches = true;
         while (morebatches)
           morebatches = C[blend].newBatchIn (in);
       }
       catch (EOFException e) {
         System.out.println("That's the shop stocked " +
             "for today\n");
         break;
       }
     }

     // Display all the details
     System.out.println("The contents on " + new Date ());
     for (int i = 0; i<blend; i++)
       C[i].display();
  }
}
```

Testing   For the data above, the output would be:

```
Nelson's Coffee Shop
Inventory control
Stocking from coffee.data
That's the shop stocked for today


The contents on Fri Dec 13 14:43:56 1996
Columbian @ G60
        Tue Apr 15 1997 : 10kg
        Sat May 31 1997 : 25kg
  35kg in stock. Reorder level is 10kg
```

```
Java @ G64
        Fri May 23 1997 : 20kg
        Sat Jul 12 1997 : 100kg
        Fri Aug 01 1997 : 12kg
  132kg in stock. Reorder level is 30kg

Kenyan @ G59
        Tue May 20 1997 : 15kg
   15kg in stock. Reorder level is 10kg
```

7.2   Properties of objects

We now look at more of the properties of objects, and how they can be manipulated in a program.

Null objects

Objects that have not been through a construction process are given the special value null by the Java virtual machine. We can test if an object is null, for example

```
if (s == null)
```

If we try to access members of a null object, then Java will raise an exception, called a `nullPointerException`.[1]

Objects versus variables

How do objects differ from variables? The obvious distinction is based on storage.

- A **variable** has storage for a single value and has available a predefined set of operations, based on its type.

- An **object** has storage for a group of several values, together with a coherent set of user-defined methods that operate on them, all encapsulated in the class from which the object is instantiated.

Apart from the number of items stored, there is another very important distinction. Variables are stored as actual **values**, whereas objects are given **references** to the group of values they represent. A reference is an indirect way of getting to where the actual value is stored. Arrays are, like objects, stored via references.

Consider the declarations from the `Coffee` class, namely

---

[1]It should of course be a `nullObjectException`, but Java shows its C roots here.

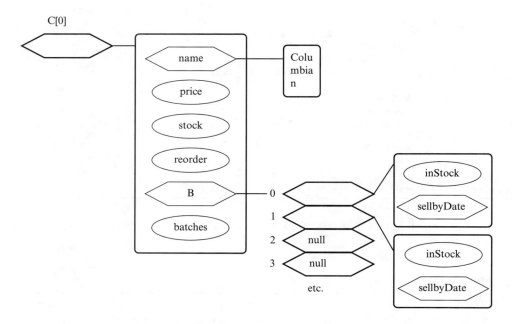

Figure 7.3 *The relationship between variables and objects.*

```
private String name;
private double price;   // per kg
private double stock;   // kgs
private double reorder; // kgs;
private Batch B [ ] = new Batch [10];
private int batches;
```

For our first coffee, Columbian, the object's storage would be represented as in Figure 7.3; name is an object. It therefore has a reference to where the characters of the string are actually stored. price, stock, reorder and batches are all variables and are stored as values. B is an array, and therefore has a reference to its first element, B[0]. Each element of the array is a Batch, so each is a reference to an object. The first two are created with values, the others are null. The object containing this information is named C[0], within the C array.

The Object superclass

We have already been introduced to the superclass Object in the previous chapter (Section 6.5). Object is central to the theory of classes in Java. Java achieves generality by using objects of different classes in the same parts of the program, while just calling them all Objects. This principle is important in cloning, which is the next topic for discussion.

Object equality and cloning

There are two implications of storing objects as references. The first concerns EQUALITY. A straight comparison such as

```
B[i].sellByDate == B[j].sellByDate
```

will compare the *references* of the two dates: that is, do they refer to the same storage? It will not compare the values, which is probably what we intended. To compare the values themselves (all together as a group) we use an `equals` method which we must define for each new class of objects. For example, in the `Batch` class there is:

```
boolean equals (Batch b) {
    return (this.sellByDate.equals(b.sellByDate));
}
```

which defines two batches as being equal if their sell-by dates are equal. Because dates are also objects, we had to use the `Date`'s class equals method to perform the comparison.

The second implication is for **assignment**. If we wish to assign two objects,

```
tempBatch = b[i];
```

will copy the *references*. To copy the values, we need to **clone**[2] the object using a method that once again must be defined for each new class. Using Figure 7.3 as a starting point, Figure 7.4 illustrates the difference between the assignment and cloning of objects.

For assignment, `temp1`'s reference becomes the same as `b[0]`'s. Any changes made to `B[0]` are reflected in `temp1`. With cloning, a copy of the object is made, and `temp2` refers to the copy. Now `temp2` and `B[0]` can change independently.

As mentioned, the class is responsible for defining what is meant by equals and clone. For our example, a clone for `Batch` could be:

```
public Object clone () {
    // create a new Batch with
    // the first value in it
    Batch x = new Batch (inStock, null);

    // Using strings as an intermediary, create
    // a new Date with the same value as the current one.
    String s = new String (sellByDate.toString());
    x.sellByDate = new Date (Date.parse(s));
    // return the new object, having copied
    // all the data over.
    return x;
}
```

Cloning a batch involves copying both data items, the stock and the date. `inStock` is a variable so it can be assigned or supplied in the constructor, as is done here. The only

---

[2]For clone, read copy if you like – a much easier word.

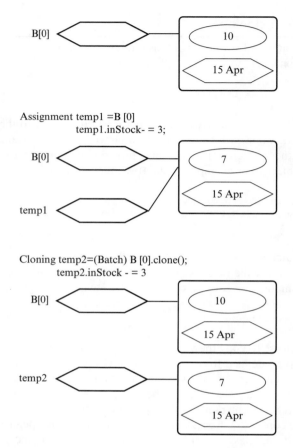

Figure 7.4 *Example of assignment and cloning.*

additional point is that cloning is a special operation in Java, and therefore any class that wants to clone must implement the `Clonable` interface. Interfaces are discussed in Chapter 8. Meanwhile, we can give the general form for a clone declaration:

```
Clone declaration

modifier class classname implements Clonable {

  public Object clone ( ) {
    classname obj = new classname (parameters);
    statements to copy the fields to obj
    return obj;
  }
}
```

Put altogether, Table 7.5 sums up the differences between variables and objects.

Table 7.5   *Variables and objects compared.*

	Created from a	Stored as	Copied with	Compared with
Variable	Type	Value	Assignment =	Equality ==
Object	Class	Reference	Clone method	Equals method

Class conversions

We saw that variables of different types can be converted into each other if this is meaningful. The same applies to objects. In particular, there are methods defined for the Java superclass, `Object`, which can be used by other objects. However before the results are assigned, an explicit type cast must be made. `clone` is one of these methods. Thus to clone a `Batch` and print it out would require:

```
Batch tempBatch = (Batch) B[0].clone();
System.out.println(tempBatch);
```

Calling the clone method on `B[0]` will return an `Object`. It must return an object because that is what the `Clonable` interface requires. But we can convert it to a `Batch` by mentioning the class name. You can insert the clone method into `Batch` and the above statement into `Coffee` and check that it all works.

7.3   Lists of objects

One of the problems with arrays is that they are rigid, both in size and arrangement. One cannot remove an element without pushing all the later elements up, and this takes time and effort. Hashtables, also discussed in Chapter 6, get away from both of these restrictions, but they store the data in a somewhat unconventional way ('hashed'). The classical alternative to an array is the **linked list**, and we shall spend this section looking at how one can be defined in Java, and how it integrates with the example in Section 7.1.

The important problem posed earlier was: how to collect together multiple objects of the same kind, without using a rigid array. The answer is to **link** the objects together, and the result is a **linked list**. These links can be made and broken, and thus we can have a structure that can grow and shrink at will while the program is executing, unlike an array.

Suppose we have some string objects already created in a linked list as in Figure 7.5. If the object with 'Columbia' in it needs to be removed, then we can just arrange to redirect the links as in Figure 7.6. Java will then **garbage collect** the space that the unwanted object occupied and it will be no more.

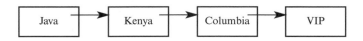

Figure 7.5   *A simple linked list of coffees.*

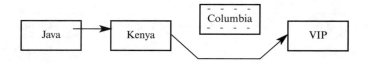

Figure 7.6 *A linked list after deleting a node.*

The question is: what are the links? They are nothing more complicated than the references that we introduced in the previous section. So in order to establish a chain of objects like this, we just need to declare an object inside itself and space for the link will reserved. We shall call the objects forming a linked list **nodes**.

Creating a list

The Java for a general sort of node is:

```
class Node {
  /* The Node class for storing objects that are linked
     together. */

  // The constructor copies in the data
  // and the link to the given node
  // (which may be null).
  Node (Object d, Node n)) {
    link = n;
    data = d;
  }

  Node link;
  Object data;
}
```

To create such a node, we must supply a value for its data and the node it is going to be linked to. Initially, the list will have nowhere to link to, so the following will work:

```
Node list = new Node ("VIP",null);
```

which gives us Figure 7.7.

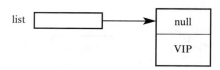

Figure 7.7 *A list with one node.*

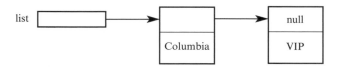

Figure 7.8 *A list after a second node has been added.*

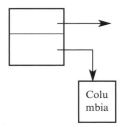

Figure 7.9 *A node with a string item.*

To link the next node on, the statements will be:

```
list = new Node ("Columbia", list);
```

Consider this statement a step at a time. `new Node` creates the space for a node. The data item is filled with `"Columbia"`. The `link` item is filled with a reference to where `list` is currently referring. Then the `list` object is made to refer to this new one, shown in Figure 7.8.

And so the creation of the list can continue. To add the next two nodes, we could use:

```
list = new Node ("Kenya", list);
list = new Node ("Java", list);
```

Notice that we have taken the short cut of drawing the strings inside the nodes themselves. As objects in their own rights, they should of course be represented with references, so that the Columbia node, for instance, would actually look as shown in Figure 7.9.

Removing from a list

Having created a list which has nice dynamic properties, we must consider the Java for removing an item from it. Let us start with the list shown in Figure 7.10. Assume that x, referring to Columbia, has been identified as the object to be removed. What we want to do is take the link that is referring to Columbia – that is, Kenya – and make it refer to what Columbia is presently referring to – VIP. The assignment should be:

```
Kenya's link = x.link;
```

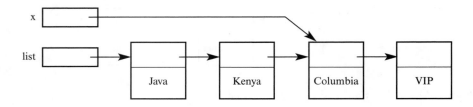

Figure 7.10 *A list before removing a node.*

However, there is a problem with the left-hand side of this assignment. We do not have a name or reference for the Kenyan node. Objects in a linked list are essentially anonymous, except for the first one, unless we travel through the list and establish temporary names for nodes. That is of course exactly what we did in order to find Columbia and have x refer to it. The answer to the problem is to keep *two* objects as we look for something, one running behind the other. Let us assume that this has been done, and that xPrevious refers to Kenya. The assignment then can be:

```
xPrevious.link = x.link;
```

and the resulting diagram is shown in Figure 7.11. It does not matter that Columbia is still referring to VIP as it is no longer linked into the list. However, since another object, x, is still referring to Columbia, it is not garbage collected[3] yet.

However, there is a problem: if x refers to the first node, Java, then what is the meaning of xPrevious? It will start at null. If xPrevious is null, it will not be possible to use the assignment above. This possibility must therefore be taken care of in the remove method as follows:

```
if (xPrevious == null)
  list = x.link;
else
  xPrevious.link = x.link;
```

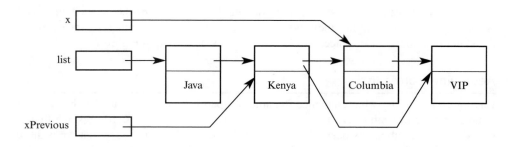

Figure 7.11 *A list after node x has been removed.*

[3]Garbage collection is the process of reclaiming storage. Java does it automatically when objects are no longer in use.

Searching a list

Finally, we consider how x was found in the first place. Now that we know we have to keep track of the previous node as well as the current one, we can devise the general loop for finding a sought-after value in a list as follows:

```
Node x = list;
Node xprev = null;
do {
  if (x.data.equals(soughtAfter)) break;
  xprev = x;
  x = x.link
  }
while (x != null);
```

We assume that data is an object, rather than a variable, and will therefore need to be compared using its equals method.

A class for lists

Given that lists are going to be useful in many circumstances, it makes sense to define them as a class. The classic list class is somewhat more sophisticated than the one we are proposing here, and we shall investigate it in Chapter 12. Meanwhile, in keeping with our 'Gently' approach, we will look at how to define a list from first principles.

What are the members of such a class? The data will be three objects referring to the start of the list and the items we are at now and previously. We shall declare them private to prevent untoward access, and provide all legitimate access to the list through methods.

What methods should the class include? We have already explored add and remove. In addition to these, a list must be able to return its current element – that is, where the user is currently in the list – and also to indicate whether the list is empty or not.

In order to scan through the list for various reasons, such as searching or displaying the items, we provide a trio of methods which mirror the parts of a for-loop. These are reset, succ (for successor) and eol (for end-of-list).

The proposed List class makes use of the Node class, as defined above. Armed with it, we can proceed to rewrite the Coffee Shop program to avoid using arrays.

```
class List {

  List () {now=null; start=null; prev=null;}

  public void add (Object x) {
  if (start == null) {
    start = new Node (x,null);
    now = start;}
  else{
    Node T = new Node (x,now.link);
    now.link = T;
```

```
        now = T;}
     // in both cases, prev remains the same
     }

  public void remove () {
    if (isempty() || eol()) return; else {
      if (prev == null)
        start = now.link;
      else {
        prev.link = now.link;
        now = now.link;
      }
    }
  }

  public boolean isempty ()   {return start == null;}
  public Object current ()    {return now.data; }
  public void reset ()        {now = start; prev=null;}
  public boolean eol ()       {return now == null;}
  public void succ ()         {now = now.link;
                               if (prev == null) prev = start;
                               else prev = prev.link;}

  private Node start, now, prev;
}
```

7.4   Case study 3: Nelson's Coffee Shop

Opportunity

Nelson's Coffee Shop wants to take advantage of the List class to make the stock of coffee types and batches dynamic: That is, the number does not have to be set at the start, and batches (and coffees) can be removed when sold out. The solution, of course, is to use the List class just defined.

Algorithms

The algorithmic part of the system relates to handling sales. These will be entered from an orders file with the name of the coffee followed by the number of kg. First of all, the main program must find the relevant coffee in its list, then call the sell method in that Coffee class. Two things can go wrong:

- the type of coffee is not found;

- there is not enough in stock.

In both cases, the program prints out a suitable message.

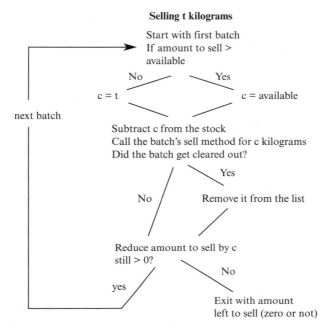

Figure 7.12 *Algorithm to sell coffee.*

Moving now to selling, this algorithm is more complex than one would first imagine. It has to check each batch in turn, using it up and then moving to the next one if there are still kilograms outstanding on the order. The algorithm reduces to that shown in Figure 7.12. The rest of the program follows in similar vein or is fairly simple.

Converting the program

In the `Coffee` class where there is an array, replace it with

```
private List BatchStock = new List ();
```

This has the effect of creating an object with three node references, all initialized to null. The counter, `batches`, can go as well. Adding a new batch becomes a call to add:

```
BatchStock.add(new Batch ((double) a,d));
```

The loop at the end to print all the batches uses the iteration methods we defined: that is,

```
for (BatchStock.reset(); !BatchStock.eol(); BatchStock.succ()) {
  Batch b = (Batch) BatchStock.current();
  b.display ();
}
```

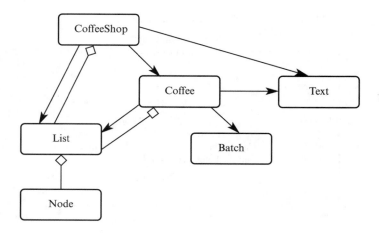

Figure 7.13   *Classes in the dynamic Coffee Shop.*

The reason why the extra local object, b, is necessary is as follows. BatchStock is a List, and it has access to all the List methods. But they are all defined in terms of Objects. There is nothing that ties the List in Coffee to the Batch class. We do put batches in it, but to get batches out, we must convert objects to batches. Then the assignment can take place. We now have a local reference to the current object, and can call Batch's display method on it.

Another place where care must be taken over precisely which objects we are dealing with is in the section of the main program which finds a coffee:

```
String s = Text.readString (orders);
Coffee blend = new Coffee (s);

while (!CoffeeStock.eol()) {
  Coffee b = (Coffee) CoffeeStock.current ();
  if (b.equals(blend)) {found = true; break;}
  else CoffeeStock.succ();
}
```

We cannot of course use == to compare the name of the required coffee with each of the coffees in stock. In the first place, the name is a string, and the coffees are of class Coffee. That is why we must create a temporary coffee. Secondly, we must make sure as before that the item that comes off the list is designated as a Coffee, so that the equals method defined for Coffee is called. This method looks only at the names. Notice that we have caused a new Coffee constructor to be implemented because we must get a name into the temporary coffee object without bothering about all the other fields.

The list of Coffee objects is created in exactly the same way, using List. The only other change to the program as we had it before is that we remove the final 0 from the data in order to trigger the EOFException at the right point.

A diagram showing the main classes in the system is given in Figure 7.13. The arrowed lines indicate 'uses' in the sense of method calls. The diamond lines indicate composition. Thus CoffeeShop has a List, as does Coffee. List has several nodes. Notice that CoffeeShop is not indicated as having any instances of the Coffee class nor does Coffee have any batches. This is not strictly true as they each have a temporary variable respectively. But they do not form a direct composition: the composition is done through the List class.

From the diagram we can deduce that only List knows about nodes and that Batch does not do any input. The other named class in the system is Date (not shown), and it is used by the three main classes.

Program

The program is now split into five compiled files. List and Node are as above. The other three are as follows:

```
/**** The Batch class ****/

import java.io.*;
import java.util.*;

class Batch {
/* The Batch class        by J M Bishop Oct 1996
      for products with sell-by-dates.
      can be tested with the Coffee class main program. */

  Batch (double k, Date d) {
    inStock = k;
    sellByDate = d;
  }

  double available ( ) {
    return inStock;
  }

  boolean sell (double k) {
    inStock -= k;
    System.out.println("Sold "+k+" from batch "+sellByDate);
    if (inStock <= 0) return true; else return false; // sold out
  }

  String shortDate(Date d) {
    // removes the time from the date.
    String s = d.toString();
    return s.substring(0,11) + s.substring(21,25);
  }

  void display () {
    System.out.println("\t\t"+shortDate(sellByDate) +
        " : " + inStock + "kg");
  }
```

```
    boolean equals (Batch b) {
      return (this.sellByDate.equals(b.sellByDate));
    }

    private double inStock;
    private Date sellByDate;

}
```

/**** The Coffee class ****/

```
import java.io.*;
import java.util.*;

class Coffee {
  /* The Coffee class        by J M Bishop Oct 1996
     keeps an inventory of batches of coffee of a
     particular kind or blend */

  Coffee ( ) {
    // empty construction, because all values
    // are read in via prepareStock
  }

  Coffee (String s) {name = new String (s);}   ;

  void prepareToStock (DataInputStream in) throws IOException {
    name = Text.readString(in);
    price = Text.readDouble(in);
    reorder = Text.readInt(in);
    stock = 0;
    newBatchIn (in);
  }

  boolean newBatchIn (DataInputStream in) throws IOException {
    int a = Text.readInt(in);
    if (a == 0)
      return false;
    else {
      stock += a;
      String s = Text.readString(in);
      Date d = new Date (Date.parse(s));
      BatchStock.add(new Batch ((double) a,d));
      return true;
    }
  }

  double sell (double toSell) {
    double fromBatch;
    Batch b;

    display();
    for (BatchStock.reset(); !BatchStock.eol(); BatchStock.succ()) {
      b = (Batch) BatchStock.current();
      if (toSell > b.available())
        fromBatch = b.available();
```

```
        else fromBatch = toSell;
        stock -= fromBatch;
        boolean soldOut = b.sell(fromBatch);
        if (soldOut) {
          System.out.println("Batch now empty");
          BatchStock.remove();
        }
        toSell -= fromBatch;
        if (toSell <= 0) break;
      }
      display ();
      return toSell;
    }

    boolean equals (Coffee c) {
      return (name.equals(c.name));
    }

    void display () {
      System.out.println(name+" @ G"+price);
      for (BatchStock.reset(); !BatchStock.eol(); BatchStock.succ()) {
        Batch b = (Batch) BatchStock.current();
        b.display ();
      }
      System.out.println(stock + "kg in stock. Reorder level is "
                 +reorder+"kg");
    }
    private String name;
    private double price; // per kg
    private double stock; // kgs
    private double reorder; // kgs;
    private List BatchStock = new List ();
}

/* The Coffee Shop class and program ****/

import java.io.*;
import java.util.*;

class CoffeeShop {

/* Coffee Shop Test Program      by J M Bishop Oct 1996
   Includes the ability to sell catches of a blend,
   starting at the oldest. */

  public static void main (String [] args) throws IOException {

    DataInputStream in = new DataInputStream (
                    new FileInputStream("coffee.data"));
    DataInputStream orders = new DataInputStream (
                    new FileInputStream("orders.data"));

    List CoffeeStock = new List ();
    System.out.println("Nelson's Coffee Shop");
    System.out.println("Inventory control");
    System.out.println("Stocking from coffee.data");
```

```
// Read in the data
  while (true) {
    try {
      Coffee c = new Coffee();
      c.prepareToStock (in);
      CoffeeStock.add(c);
      boolean morebatches = true;
      while (morebatches)
        morebatches = c.newBatchIn (in);
    }
    catch (EOFException e) {
      System.out.println("That's the shop stocked for today\n");
      break;
    }
  }


// Display the stock
    System.out.println("The contents on " + new Date ());
    for (CoffeeStock.reset(); !CoffeeStock.eol(); CoffeeStock.succ()) {
      Coffee c = (Coffee) CoffeeStock.current();
      c.display();
    }


// Handle sales
  System.out.println("Coffee sales");
  while (true) {
    try {
      String s = Text.readString (orders);
      Coffee blend = new Coffee (s);
      double amount = Text.readDouble(orders);
      System.out.println("Order for " + s + " " + amount);


      boolean found = false;
      CoffeeStock.reset();
      while (!CoffeeStock.eol()) {
        Coffee b = (Coffee) CoffeeStock.current ();
        if (b.equals(blend)) {found = true; break;}
        else CoffeeStock.succ();
      }
      if (found) {
        Coffee b = (Coffee) CoffeeStock.current();
        double remainder = b.sell(amount);
        if (remainder > 0)
          System.out.println ("Could not match "+ remainder + "kg");{
      }
      else System.out.println("Sorry, we're out of that blend.");
    }
    catch (EOFException e) {
      System.out.println("\n Shop closed"); break;
    }
    }
  }
}
```

Testing

Let us now add the following orders file:

```
VIP 2
Kenyan 15
Kenyan 2
Java 30
Columbian 25
Columbian 5
```

The intention is that the first order's name will not be found. Then all the Kenyan will go in the second order and the third order will not be able to be processed. The Java order will need to take coffee from two batches, as will the first Columbian. The last order is a straightforward one. The detailed output is as follows:

```
Nelson's Coffee Shop
Inventory control
Stocking from coffee.data
That's the shop stocked for today

The contents on Fri Dec 13 18:55:12 1996
Columbian @ G60
      Fri Nov 15 1996 : 10kg
      Fri Jan 31 1997 : 25kg
35kg in stock. Reorder level is 10kg


Java @ G64
      Wed Dec 10 1997 : 20kg
      Thu Jan 16 1997 : 100kg
      Wed Feb 05 1997 : 12kg
132kg in stock. Reorder level is 30kg


Kenyan @ G59
      Fri Jun 20 1997 : 15kg
15kg in stock. Reorder level is 10kg


Coffee sales
Order for VIP 2
Sorry, we're out of that blend.
Order for Kenyan 15
Sold 15 from batch Fri Jun 20 1997
Batch now empty
Kenyan @ G59
0kg in stock. Reorder level is 10kg


Order for Kenyan 2
Kenyan @ G59
0kg in stock. Reorder level is 10kg


Could not match 2kg
Order for Java 30
Sold 20 from batch Wed Dec 10 1997
```

```
Batch now empty
Sold 10 from batch Thu Jan 16 1997
Java @ G64
     Thu Jan 16 1997 : 90kg
     Wed Feb 05 1997 : 12kg
102kg in stock. Reorder level is 30kg


Order for Columbian 25
Sold 10 from batch Fri Nov 15 1996
Batch now empty
Sold 15 from batch Fri Jan 31 1997
Columbian @ G60
     Fri Jan 31 1997 : 10kg
10kg in stock. Reorder level is 10kg


Order for Columbian 5
Sold 5 from batch Fri Jan 31 1997
Columbian @ G60
     Fri Jan 31 1997 : 5kg
5kg in stock. Reorder level is 10kg


Shop closed
```

Other `List` classes

We have explained in detail how to create a simple `List` class. In Chapter 12 we look at the wealth of similar classes Java provides, as well as a more powerful list class. The mission of this book is to teach you more than just the syntax. It aims to teach you the fundamental principles of programming as well. Knowing how to program a list class is one of those principles. You may not use it hereafter, but at least you will have understood how one works, and will be able to apply this knowledge in other circumstances later on in your programming career.

SUMMARY

This has been a crucial chapter in the development of programming skills. It has included specific details about objects, how to use them in a grand plan, and the model of a linked list as the alternative data structure to an array.

Developing a class involves looking at the data items and methods required. Interaction with other classes must be considered at the start, as must the constructors. Empty constructors are possible, especially for classes dealing with input data. The declarations of objects results in a reference to storage, whereas the values of variables are stored directly. The implications of this model are that equality and copying of objects have to be done via the `equals` and `clone` methods. `Clone` relies on the superclass, `Object`, and therefore class conversions become necessary.

Lists are a prime alternative to arrays for storing sequences of data. They have the advantage that ihey can grow and shrink dynamically as items are added and removed. All programmers should know how to set one up.

QUIZ

7.1 If c is a `Coffee` object, why would the compiler reject the following statement in the main `CoffeeStock` program:

```
System.out.println (c.name);
```

7.2 Would it have been possible to have defined the `prepareToStock` method, which reads in values for the particular coffee's batches, so that it could be called thus:

```
prepareToStock (C[blend]);
```

7.3 In the Coffee class there is a reference in `sell` to

```
display ();
```

and in `display` to

```
b.display ();
```

What is the difference between the two calls?

7.4 Define a clone method for `Coffee`.

7.5 Given a declaration for today as a `Date`, how would you clone it?

7.6 Draw a diagram showing how the list in Figure 7.5 would look if another coffee, say `Kona`, was added. Use the `add` method of the `List` class.

7.7 Consider the output at the end of Section 7.4. What would happen if an order for 100 kg of Java came in?

7.8 Why will the following statement not give the result expected?

```
System.out.println("s is an empty string is " +
    s==null);
```

7.9 How should the statement in 7.8 be written?

7.10 Draw a class diagram showing all the items and associations in the final `Coffee` class. Use Figures 7.2, 7.3 and 7.13 as guides.

PROBLEMS

7.1 **Batches in order**. The `List` class used by Nelson's Coffee Shop always adds new nodes to the start of the list. The data in the `orders.dat` file was carefully arranged so that for the batches, the oldest batches were listed last and therefore would get sold first. If batches are arriving at different times of day, one could not always ensure that this happened. In the `Batch` class, add a new method which can find the correct position for a new batch, based on its sell-by date (use the `reset`, `eol` and `succ` methods). Then write another adding method in `List` – say, `insert` – which will add the new batch in the correct position.

7.2 **Coffees in order**. Using the same philosophy as in problem 7.1, we would like to keep the coffee types in alphabetical order. Write a method for the `Coffee` class which will find the correct position for a new coffee, and then use the same `addbefore` method to insert it.

7.3 **Club database.** Choose an activity with which you are familiar and design a class and object structure to store information about the people, equipment or events associated with the activity. Add methods to access the information.

CHAPTER 8

Abstraction and inheritance

8.1　Class power

Object-oriented programming has several ways in which the use of classes is made more powerful. We have already been using classes extensively for what is known as **composition**, in other words, creating an object in a class based on another class. An example of this would be the array of batches kept in the coffee class. Two other techniques that we shall now study are **abstraction** and **inheritance**.

Abstraction

Abstraction enables a class or method to concentrate on the essentials of what it is doing – its behaviour and interface to the world – and to rely on the details being filled in at a later stage. In a way, we can think of it as a more elaborate form of parameter passing, but this time at the class level. Java has two ways of providing abstraction – interfaces and abstract classes – and we will discuss both of them below.

For example, so far, all our classes have related to concrete descriptions of natural items, such as tickets, marks, coffee and so on. If we wanted to perform an operation on all these classes, such as sorting arrays of tickets, arrays of marks or arrays of coffee, then up until now we would need to have three different sort methods. Abstraction is obviously going to cut down on repetition and aid reuse – two of our goals right from the start.

Inheritance

With **inheritance**, we concentrate on defining a class that we know about, and leave open an option to define additional versions of it later. These versions will inherit the properties and characteristics of the original class, and therefore can be smaller in themselves, and neater. In this way we build up hierarchies of classes and can focus changes and additions at the right level. Because all the classes in the hierarchy belong to the family, they have the same type in Java's typing mechanism, and one can be used where the other might be required.

Consider the diagram in Figure 8.1. In chapter 1, we saw that the `Nature` class consisted of animals, trees and birds. Animals could be herbivores or carnivores. Possible herbivores are elephants and rhinos. Now the data item holding the name of the animal could be right in the top class, in `Nature` itself, since all animals, trees and birds will need a name. Similarly a method to write the name would also be placed here. If we had an elephant object and wanted to write the name, the method that would be called would be the one up in `Nature`. However, peculiar to an elephant would be its tusk length. This data item and a method to display it would be kept in `Elephant` itself. Along the way in the

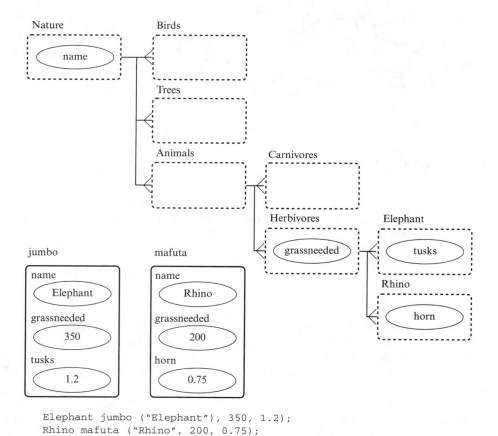

```
Elephant jumbo ("Elephant"), 350, 1.2);
Rhino mafuta ("Rhino", 200, 0.75);
```

Figure 8.1 *An hierarchy in* `Nature`.

hierarchy, there could be a tally of how much grass a herbivore eats a day. Since this applies to all herbivores, we store the information in the `Herbivore` class. All of these decisions are illustrated in Figure 8.1.

jumbo and mafuta are two objects defined as instantiations of classes at the lowest level of the hierarchy. Assuming that only those data items illustrated in Figure 8.1 have been declared, then they will each have three variables, but the last one will be different. Inheritance is covered in detail in Section 8.3.

8.2   Abstraction through interfaces

We have suggested that abstraction will cut down on repetition and aid the generality and reuse of the classes we write. Java provides two ways of obtaining abstraction: **interfaces** and **abstract classes**. Let us start with interfaces and then move on to abstract classes. An interface is a class which defines the specification of a set of methods, and that is all. The methods together encapsulate a guarantee: any class which implements this interface is guaranteed to provide these methods. We can think of an interface as defining a set of standards, and a class that implements them gets a 'stamp of approval' as having conformed to those standards. Objects of the class can therefore gain access to any methods that need an object with those standards.

The form for an interface and for a class that implements it is:

Interface declaration and implementation

```
interface interfacename {
  method specifications
}
```

```
class classname implements interfacename {
  bodies for the interface methods
  own data and methods
}
```

As an example, consider typical operations used on machines that move:

```
interface Movable {
  boolean   start ();
  void      stop ();
  boolean   turn (int degrees);
  double    fuelRemaining ();
  boolean   changeSpeed (double kmperhour);
}
```

Movable defines what all movable machines must be able to do. They may do more, but this is a minimum. Now one way to implement the interface for a plane as a movable machine would be to declare a class as follows:

```
class Planes implements Movable {
  boolean      start () {
```

```
            // do whatever is necessary to start
            // a plane and return true if it worked.
          }

      void    stop () {
          // do whatever is necessary to stop
          // the plane. It had better work!
        }

      boolean turn (int degrees) {
          // do whatever is necessary to turn a plane
        }

      double  fuelRemaining () {
          // return the amount of plane fuel remaining
        }

      boolean changeSpeed (double kmperhour) {
          // accelerate or decelerate if kmperhour is negative
        }
      }
```

A car is also a movable machine, as is a train and a ship. In fact, a lowly lawnmower is also a movable machine and could implement the interface.

How does having the interface help us? Well, it helps when we want to use the abstract concept of movable machines. Suppose we are setting up a handheld remote control device for scale models. It will have buttons and a display corresponding to the operations we have set up in the `Movable` interface. If we do all our development of the remote control based solely on `Movable`, then we can use it at any later date with any of the actual machines mentioned. The remote control will use composition to include the `Movable` interface as follows:

```
      class RemoteControl {

        private Movable machine;

        RemoteControl (Movable m) {
          machine = m;
        }
        ...
        // when the start knob is pressed on the device
        Boolean okay = machine.start();
        if (!okay) display ("No response on start");
        ...
      }
```

The remote control's constructor is given an object which is of class `Movable`. It could be a plane, a car, a ship, a lawnmower or any other valid implementation of `Movable`: they are all guaranteed to have the properties of `Movable`. This object is then stored as part of the controller's private data, and whenever it calls any of `Movable`'s methods, it will be sent to the particular implementation for that class. So, for example, we could set up:

```
RemoteControl (plane);
RemoteControl (ship);
```

and each will operate correctly for its own implementation of the `Movable` interface.

EXAMPLE 8.1   Sorting anything

Problem   The sort we developed in Chapter 6 is obviously extremely useful and we would like to adapt it so that it is independent of what we are sorting.

Solution   We consider what makes a class of objects sortable, and encapsulate this operation (or operations) in an interface called `Sortable`. Then we change the `selectionSort` method so that it works with sortable objects only. Thereafter any class that needs sorting must just implement the `Sortable` interface, and it can call the methods of the `Sort` class. This is summed up in Figure 8.2.

Now what is this `x` method referred to in the diagram? What makes sorting one class different from another? It is not the assignment of the objects, since this is defined for all types and classes. The answer is that it is the comparison between two items. The comparison triggers the interchange of items, which is how all sorts work. How this comparison is done will differ from class to class.

Algorithm   We set up the sortable interface as follows:

```
interface Sortable {
  boolean lessThan (Sortable a);
}
```

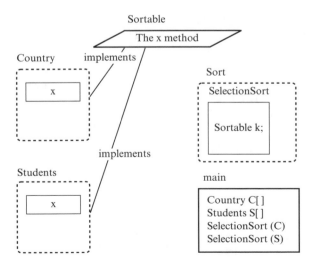

Figure 8.2   *The class involved in abstract sorting.*

Next we include in the class of objects to be sorted an implementation of the `lessThan` method. Let us test the program with a simple class of country names. It would be defined as:

```
class Country implements Sortable {
  /* The country class by J M Bishop Dec 1996
     stores country names and is sortable */

  Country (String s) {
    name = s;
  }

  public boolean lessThan (Sortable a) {
    Country b = (Country) a;
    return (name.compareTo(b.name) < 0);
  }

  public String toString () {
    return name;
  }

  private String name;
}
```

In the implementation of `lessThan` we must first type cast the `Sortable` object passed as a parameter to a `Country`. The `compareTo` method (part of the `String` class) then operates on the current object's `name` and the `name` of the parameter. `compareTo` returns negative if the result is less, positive if it is more and 0 if it is equal.

The `Sort` class defined in Section 6.4 must also be changed slightly as follows:

```
class Sort {
  static void selectionSort (Sortable [ ] a) {
    Sortable temp;
    int chosen;
    int n = a.length;

    for (int leftmost = 0; leftmost < n-1; leftmost++) {
      chosen = leftmost;
      for (int j = leftmost+1; j < n; j++)
        if (a[j].lessThan(a[chosen])) chosen = j;
      temp = a[chosen];
      a[chosen] = a[leftmost];
      a[leftmost] = temp;
    }
  }
}
```

Instead of sorting an array of a specific class, it now sorts an array of any `Sortable` class. Similarly, its local `temp` variable is declared of this same class. Then the comparison which used to use the boolean relation < now calls the `lessThan` method on one of the objects, giving the other as the parameters.

Program Now Country, Sortable and Sort can be used in a test program as
follows:

```
import java.io.*;

class Table {
  /* The Table program      by J M Bishop Dec 1996
     for sorting a table, of countries in this case.
     Illustrates linking up to an independent sorter. */

  public static void main (String [] args) throws IOException {
    Country [ ] T = new Country [10];
    String s;

    DataInputStream in = new DataInputStream
            (new FileInputStream ("Countries"));
    for (int i=0; i< T.length; i++) {
      s = Text.readString(in);
      T[i] = new Country (s);
    }

    System.out.println ("Original");
    System.out.println ("========");
    for (int i=0; i<T.length; i++)
      System.out.println(T[i]);

    Sort.selectionSort (T);

    System.out.println ("");
    System.out.println ("======");
    for (int i=0; i< T.length; i++)
      System.out.println(T[i]);
  }
}
```

Notice that there is actually no mention of Sortable in the program. In other words, this
program could have run with the old sort. The change was effected between the object and
sort. What we have gained is the flexibility to sort other classes.

Testing   Just to be sure of the sort process, we give the data and output for the program:

```
Japan
Russia
Argentina
Finland
Ukraine
Zimbabwe
Algeria
France
Iceland
Israel
```

```
Original
========
Japan
Russia
Argentina
Finland
Ukraine
Zimbabwe
Algeria
France
Iceland
Israel


Sorted
======
Algeria
Argentina
Finland
France
Iceland
Israel
Japan
Russia
Ukraine
Zimbabwe
```

Extension What we really want to test is whether we have achieved the objective of independence. A quick way of doing this is to change Table to sort integers. However, remember that Sortable is dealing with objects, so we must put the integer in a class. This class can be in the same file as the program, which becomes:

```java
import java.io.*;

class TableInt {
   /* The TableInt program       by J M Bishop Dec 1996
      for sorting a table, of integers in this case.
      Illustrates linking up to an independent sorter. */

    public static void main (String [] args) throws IOException {
    OurInteger [ ] T = new OurInteger [10];
    DataInputStream in = new DataInputStream (System.in);

    for (int i=0; i< 10; i++) {
      T[i] = new OurInteger(Text.readInt(in));
    }

    System.out.println ("Original");
    System.out.println ("========");
    for (int i=0; i<T.length; i++)
      System.out.print(T[i].val+" ");
    System.out.println();

    Sort.selectionSort (T);
```

```
      System.out.println ("Sorted");
      System.out.println ("======");
      for (int i=0; i< T.length; i++)
        System.out.print(T[i].val+" ");
      System.out.println();
    }
}

class OurInteger implements Sortable {
  // This local class encapsulates an integer
  // as an object and implements Sortable
  // for integers.

  OurInteger (int i) {
    val = i;
  }
  public boolean lessThan (Sortable a) {
    OurInteger I = (OurInteger) a;
    return (val < I.val);
  }
  int val;
}
```

A run of the program would produce (using data typed in):

```
Original
========
5 8 1 2 0 4 3 7 9 6

Sorted
======
0 1 2 3 4 5 6 7 8 9
```

Before we leave interfaces, we stress that they can only have method specifications in them – no completed methods or variables. However, they can include constants if necessary.

8.3 Inheritance

Following the informal description of inheritance in Section 8.1, let us look at inheritance in practice in Java. Each new level of class is said to **extend** the class above it. The term conveys the impression that the new class can have more variables and methods than the original. The terms for the different class are **superclass** or **parent** (the original) and **subclass** or **child** class.

Inheritance is also transitive: that means that if *a* is a class and *b* extends it, with *c* extending *b*, then *c* is also related by inheritance to *a*. The same would be true in a family, in this case *a* being the grandparent, *b* the parent, and *c* the child. Figure 8.1 shows this kind of hierarchy of inheritance clearly.

The process of inheriting is also sometimes referred to as deriving, but in fact Java's term – **extending** – is the most evocative of what is actually happening.

The example in Figure 8.1 can now be expressed in Java. In outline the important classes are:

```
class Nature {
  private String name;
  // much more here
}


class Animals extends Nature {
  // All sorts of things here
}


class Herbivores extends Animals {
  private protected int grassneeded;
  // plus more about herbivores
}


class Elephant extends Herbivores {
  Elephant (String n, int w, double l) {
    name = n;
    grassneeded = w;
    tusks = l;
  }
  private double tusks; // their length
  // and more on elephants
}


class Rhino extends Herbivores {
  Rhino (String n, int w, double l) {
    name = n;
    grassneeded = w;
    horn = l;
  }
  private double horn; // its length
  // and more on rhinos
}
```

The grassneeded variable in the Herbivores class has an extra modifier – protected. Protected widens the visibility of a private item to include subclasses. Thus Elephant can access grassneeded, but users of Herbivore objects cannot.

As we can see already from the constructors for Elephant and Rhino, subclasses inherit all the declarations of their superclasses and can access them directly. The same applies to methods. Suppose a method is included to play the sound of an animal. We would put this in the Animals class thus:

```
class Animals extends Nature {
  // All sorts of things here
```

```
    void makeNoise (String audioclip) {
      // see Section 10.3 on how to do this
    }
  }
```

Then the declaration:

```
Elephant jumbo ("Elephant", 350, 1.2);
```

would enable us to make the call

```
jumbo.makeNoise ("elephant.au");
```

Working within a hierarchy

The purpose of setting up a hierarchy of classes is to enable us to deal at different levels. At the top level, we just need to know about names of natural beings. At each level below that, we have more information and can perform in appropriate ways. The key to this multi-level operation is being able to assign objects freely within a hierarchy. Put formally:

- any object of a subclass can be assigned to an object of its superclass;

- any object of a superclass can be assigned to a subclass with an appropriate **cast**.

When these assignments are done, the object does not change at all: only the compiler's view of it, for typing purposes, is changed. As an example, if we have:

```
Animals a;

a = jumbo;              // okay
mafuta = a;             // not okay: compiler error
mafuta = jumbo;         // not okay: compiler error
mafuta = (Rhino) a;     // okay
```

The example shows that we cannot assign variables across levels. jumbo and mafuta are of quite different classes and it would never make sense to assign them. But of course, we can work with them together under the Herbivore's banner, or one of the higher ones. The following example shows this:

```
Herbivores greedier;

if (jumbo.grassneeded > mafuta.grassneeded)
  greedier = jumbo;
else
  greedier = mafuta;
```

Notice that a restriction in Java is that a class may only extend one other class: there is no provision for multiple inheritance. However, classes can implement several interfaces, thereby getting much the same effect.

Super constructing

A useful technique in a hierarchy of classes is **super constructing**. A subclass can call the constructor of a parent to perform initialization on those variables for which the parent is responsible. This divides the work up in a cleaner way. Let us rewrite the classes as follows:

```
class Nature {
  private String name;
  Nature (String n); {
    name = n;
  }
  // much more here
}

class Animals extends Nature {
  Animals (String n) {
    super (n);
  }
  // All sorts of things here
}

class Herbivores extends Animals {
  private protected int grassneeded;

  Herbivores (String n, int g) {
    super (n);
    grassland = g;
  }
  // plus more about herbivores
}

class Elephant extends Herbivores {
  Elephant (String n, int w, double l) {
    super (n, w);
    tusks = l;
  }

  private double tusks; // their length
  // and more on elephants
}

class Rhino extends Herbivores {
  Rhino (String n, int w, double l) {
    super (n, w);
    horn = l;
  }
  private double horn; // its length
  // and more on rhinos
}
```

Both `Elephant` and `Rhino` are sent all three initial parameters as before, but they defer to their parent classes as to what should be done with the ones they do not themselves define. The process bubbles up: `Herbivore` takes care of `w`. It passes `n` up to `Animals`. `Animals` at present does nothing other than pass its parameter up to `Nature`.

Note that the call to the super constructor must be the first statement in a constructor.

Shadowing variables

In addition to adding to any inherited data, a subclass can decide to replace data with its own version. It does this by declaring a variable with the same name as one higher up. Mostly we do this to change the type to something more suitable. When the object is created, all the variables still exist, but the higher one is masked out. This is called **shadowing**. For example, supposing the zoologists working with elephants want to be more precise about what they eat, they could decide to record the grass as a real number. Therefore we would add to `Elephant`:

```
double grassneeded;
```

When dealing with elephants, we shall get this version of the variable. Other classes will get the original integer version from the `Herbivore` class.

It is also possible to get at a masked variable by using the **super** prefix. Thus from `Elephant`,

```
super.grassneeded;
```

would refer to the original variable in `Herbivores`.

Overriding methods

Similar to shadowing (but not exactly the same) is **overriding**. A subclass can decide to supply its own version of a method already supplied by a superclass. We would use this facility when we start off defining a general or default method in a superclass, and as we get down the hierarchy we can provide more specialized versions.

For example, all animals sleep, so in the `Animals` class we could add a sleep method:

```
class Animals extends Nature {
  // All sorts of things here

  void sleep () {
    // describes the sleeping habits of animals in general
  }

  void makeNoise (String audioclip) {
    // see Section 10.3 on how to do this
  }
}
```

Then once we have researched how elephants sleep, we would add in the specialized method as follows:

```
class Elephant extends Herbivores {

  Elephant (String n, int w, double l) {
    name = n;
    grassneeded = w;
    tusks = l;
  }

  void sleep () {
    // how elephants sleep
  }

  private double tusks; // their length
  // and more on elephants
}
```

Overriden methods are more powerful than shadowed variables in the following way. When there are several instances of a method in a hierarchy, the one in the closest subclass is always used. This is true even if an object of the subclass is assigned to an object of the superclass and called from there. Consider the following, using jumbo as an example:

```
Animals a;

a.sleep();      // calls Animals version of sleep
jumbo.sleep();  // calls Elephant version of sleep
a = jumbo;
a.sleep();      // still calls Elephant version of sleep
```

Overriding therefore uses **dynamic binding** to find the correct method. Each object has a table of its methods and Java searches for the correct versions of any overridden methods at run time. The default is that methods will need dynamic binding, and this can incur a performance overhead. If we know that a method will not be overidden, we can declare it with the modifier final, and save on speed.

Notice that overriding is not the same as **overloading**. Overloading involves providing several methods with the same name, but with different parameter lists, so that Java sees them as distinct entities. In overriding, the parameter lists are the same. We shall now look at an example of inheritance in a small system. There will be many more examples in the next chapter as inheritance is used extensively in Java's own packages.

Example 8.2 Veterinary tags

Problem The Savanna Veterinary Association several years ago developed a system of tagging pets so that if they were found straying, they could be tracked back to their owners. The tags were small and simple and had the animal's name and owner's phone

Vet

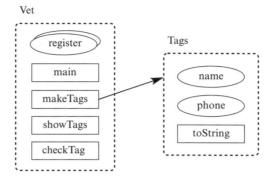

Figure 8.3   *Class diagram for the original veterinary tags system.*

number on them. If a pet was found by a member of the public, he or she could try to phone the owner in order to return it. However, the S.V.A. found that when owners moved, they did not always update their tags, and so tracking owners was more difficult.

It then started to keep a central register of all tags, so that people could phone in and check whether a pet was recorded missing or not. In addition, it wants to introduce an improved XTag which has the vet's name on it as well. Obviously, the old system must continue to run, and the new system along with it. The register is being built up over several months, and will consist of old and new tags together.

Solution   The solution is to use inheritance. The old program already exists and runs with the old tags. What we do is define a new tag, called an XTag, which extends the old tag and has the new data item in it. But both can be stored as tags – the 'family' name – in the register.

Class design   The diagram of the original system (Figure 8.3) uses technique one in class–array interaction. `main` calls the three other methods in `Vet`, and they do the processing as required. `makeTags` will be the method that actually creates the `Tags` objects and puts them in the array, declared as:

```
static Tags register [] = new Tags [100];
```

Program   The original `Tags` class looks like this:

```
class Tags {

  Tags (String n, String p) {
    name = n;
    phone = p;
  }

  public String toString () {
    return name + " tel: " + phone;
  }

  String name, phone;
}
```

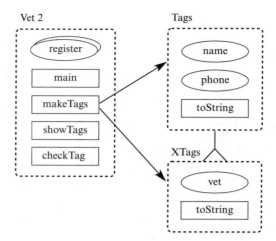

Figure 8.4 *Class diagram for the new veterinary tags system.*

It has a constructor and one method – the standard `toString` method – which enables tags to be concatenated with other strings and used in `println` and other statements where strings are required. The part of `makeTags` which adds a tag to the register is:

```
Tags tag = new Tags (petsName, ownersPhone);
register[index] = tag;
```

In `inventoryReport` it is printed out with:

```
System.out.println("Pet No. "+i+" "+ register[i]);
```

Class design 2 Now we want to add the `XTags` to the system. Their class is given by:

```
class XTags extends Tags {
  XTags (String n, String p, String v) {
    super(n,p);
    vet = v;
  }

  public String toString () {
    return name + " tel: " + phone + " Vet's tel: "+ vet;
  }

  String vet;
}
```

Notice several points here. `XTags` has access to the `name` and `phone` variables in `Tags`. It overrides the `toString` method in `Tags`. It declares its own new data item, `vet`. Now, armed with this new class, we can extend the class diagram shown earlier giving Figure 8.4. Notice the inheritance symbol: a line with an open 'scoop' at the child class. `Xtags` extends `Tags`, so the scoop indicates that it draws in all that `Tags` has.

Program   Before we consider the full Vet2 program, let us look at the important section related to inheritance.

```
1.   Text.prompt("\nPet's name:");
2.   petsName = Text.readString (in);
3.   if (petsName.equals("ZZZ")) break;
4.   Text.prompt("Owner's phone:");
5.   ownersPhone = Text.readString (in);

6.   Text.prompt("Do you want an Xtag? (y or n)");
7.   char ans = Text.readChar(in);
8.   switch (ans) {

9.     case 'n' : case 'N':{
10.      Tags tag = new Tags (petsName, ownersPhone);
11.      register[index] = tag;
12.      break;
13.    }

14.    default :
15.    case 'y' : case 'Y' :{
16.      Text.prompt("Vet's phone?");
17.      String vetsPhone = Text.readString(in);
18.      XTags xtag = new XTags
                (petsName, ownersPhone, vetsPhone);
19.      register[index] = xtag;
20.    }
21.  }
```

Lines 1–5 are concerned with getting in the common information of pet's name and owner's phone number. Then we ask a question: is this going to be an ordinary tag or an XTag? The answer is a single 'y' or 'n', but by using a switch statement, we can easily accommodate both capital and lower-case letters (lines 9 and 15). Lines 10 and 11 come from the old program. A new Tag object is created and is stored in the next position in the array. However, if one of the new tags is requested, then we ask for more information and create an XTag object. The XTag option is also the default because we would like to move the public towards the new version.

Now notice that line 19 assigns the new xtag to the register, while line 11 assigned a tag to the register. The register is declared to consist of class Tag. Because XTag inherits from Tag, in other words comes from the same family, it is accepted wherever a Tag would be welcome. In this way inheritance aids significantly in keeping programs reusable and maintainable.

Now here is the full updated program.

```
import java.io.*;

class Vet2 {

   /* The updated Vet tagging program by J M Bishop Jan 1997
      keeps a register of pets' tags and enables a tag to be
      checked if a stray pet is found.
      Illustrates inheritance. */
```

```
static int index;
static Tags register [] = new Tags [100];

public static void main (String [] args) throws IOException {

  DataInputStream in = new DataInputStream(System.in);

  makeTags (in);
  showTags ();
  try {
    while (true)
      checkTag (in);
  }
  catch (EOFException e) { }
}

static void makeTags (DataInputStream in) throws IOException {

  String petsName, ownersPhone;

  System.out.println("Setting up the Tag Register "+
    "of Pets.data with ZZZ");
  while (true) {
    Text.prompt("\n Pet's name:");
    petsName = Text.readString (in);
    if (petsName.equals("ZZZ")) break;
    Text.prompt("Owner's phone:");
    ownersPhone = Text.readString (in);

    Text.prompt("Do you want an Xtag? (y or n)");
    char ans = Text.readChar(in);
    switch (ans) {

      case 'n' : case 'N' :{
        Tags tag = new Tags (petsName, ownersPhone);
        register[index] = tag;
        break;
      }

      default :
      case 'y' : case 'Y' :{
        Text.prompt("Vet's phone?");
        String vetsPhone = Text.readString(in);
        XTags xtag = new XTags (petsName, ownersPhone, vetsPhone);
        register[index] = xtag;
      }

    }
    index ++;
  }
  System.out.println("/n All"+index+" pets read in.");
}

static void showTags () {
  System.out.println("\n The register is: ");
```

```
    for (int i=0; i<index; i++)
      System.out.println("Pet No. "+i+" "+register[i]);
}

  static void checkTag (DataInputStream in) throws IOException {

    try {
    Text.prompt("\n Found pet's name as on tag:");
    String info = Text.readString (in);
    boolean found = false;
    for (int i=0; i<index; i++)
      if (register[i].name.equals(info)) {
        System.out.println("The pet called "+info+
                           " is registered no. "+i);
        System.out.println("Full info should be "+register[i]);
        found = true;
        break;
      }
    if (!found) System.out.println("The pet called "
                +info+" is not registered.");
    }

    // After the last check has been made, an EOF is
    // entered, which can be thrown straight back at the
    // main program so that it can stop its loop.
    catch (EOFException e) {
    throw new EOFException();
    }
  }
}
```

Testing   The following is a sample run of the program.

```
Setting up the Tag Register of pets.
End data with ZZZ

Pet's name: Fluffy
Owner's phone: 466683
Do you want an Xtag? (y or n) n

Pet's name: Frisbee
Owner's phone: 567345
Do you want an Xtag? (y or n) y
Vet's phone? 333401

Pet's name: Java
Owner's phone: 9980211
Do you want an Xtag? (y or n) y
Vet's phone? 509876

Pet's name: Seza
Owner's phone: 466683
Do you want an Xtag? (y or n) y
Vet's phone? 333401
```

```
Pet's name: ZZZ

All 4 pets read in

The register is:
Pet No. 0 Fluffy tel: 466683
Pet No. 1 Frisbee tel: 567345 Vet's tel: 333401
Pet No. 2 Java tel: 9980211 Vet's tel: 509876
Pet No. 3 Seza tel: 466683 Vet's tel: 333401

Found pet's name as on tag: Java
The pet called Java is registered no. 2
Full info should be Java tel: 9980211 Vet's tel: 509876

Found pet's name as on tag: Puma
The pet called Puma is not registered.

Found pet's name as on tag: Fluffy
The pet called Fluffy is registered no. 0
Full info should be Fluffy tel: 466683

Found pet's name as on tag:
```

8.4   Abstract methods and classes

The final member of the class power trio is abstract methods and abstract classes. When used together with interfaces and inheritance, they provide for a clear and understandable way of putting together large systems.

Abstract methods

Abstract methods provide 'place holders' for methods that can sensibly be mentioned at one level, but which are going to be implemented in a variety of ways lower down. Take for example the sleep method in the Nature example. It probably does not make sense to have a general method to describe sleep patterns of all animals. But we do know that all kinds of animals have sleep patterns, and when we are dealing with objects at the Animals class level, it would be useful to be able to call the different methods supplied for the different classes at the bottom. What we are looking for is the concept of an abstract method. Thus we declare:

```
abstract void sleep ();
```

in Animals. The effect of such an inclusion in Animals is to turn it into an abstract class.

Abstract classes

An abstract class is any class with at least one abstract method. An abstract class cannot be used to declare objects any more: the presence of the abstract method means that it is incomplete. It must first be subclassed and the abstract method(s) filled in. In the above example, `Animals` becomes:

```
abstract class Animals extends Nature {
  // All sorts of things here

  abstract void sleep ();

  void makeNoise (String audioclip) {
    // see Section 10.3 on how to do this
  }
}
```

Now each of the bottom level of classes, such as `Elephant` and `Rhino`, can complete the definition of sleep. If `Herbivore` mentions nothing about sleeping, then by implication it must also be declared as abstract.

How would we use the hierarchy now? Well, all declarations will take place at the bottom, concrete level, for example:

```
Elephant [] E = new Elephants [10];
Rhino [] R = new Rhino [5];
```

But now we cannot declare any `Herbivores` or `Animals` as such (they are abstract) and we have lost the ability to use the hierarchy at various levels. For this reason it is more appropriate to make use of interfaces rather than abstract classes in many cases. The combination of inheritance and interfaces in Java is a winning one.

Abstract classes are not a useless concept, however. There are several examples in the standard classes of the language, some of which are discussed in Chapter 9.

SUMMARY

Object-oriented programming is much enhanced in power by the use of abstraction and inheritance. Abstraction enables us to concentrate on the essentials of a method or class: what it must guarantee to the user. The details can then be filled in later, and perhaps by more than one implementation of the abstraction. Java provides interfaces and abstract classes and methods as means of achieving abstraction.

Inheritance serves at least two purposes. We can prolong the life of a system by creating new versions of classes which include new features, but which inherit the old. The two classes are regarded as being of the same family and therefore the child can be used wherever the parent was expected. We can also divide up information into what is essential at any level, creating a hierarchy of classes, all of which can be used together or separately.

QUIZ

8.1 A giraffe is also a herbivore. Give the class definition for a giraffe which records the length of its neck.

8.2 If `car` is going to implement the `Movable` interface, what is the minimum set of methods that it must declare?

8.3   If we want to sort giraffes based on the length of their necks, what interface must we implement?

8.4   The following is an attempt to implement a `lessThan` method for comparing giraffes' neck lengths. It will not compile. What is wrong with it? (Hint: look at the `OurInteger` class in the extension to Example 8.1.)

```
public boolean lessThan (Sortable a) {
   return (neck < a.neck);
}
```

8.5   Would the following be a valid declaration for a companion elephant to jumbo?

```
Elephant dumbo (1);
```

8.6   There is a temporary `Elephant` object called `patient`. Draw class diagrams for the results of the following statements.

```
Elephant patient;
patient = jumbo;
```

8.7   In Example 8.2 (veterinary tags) give an example of a method declaration which illustrates overriding.

8.8   In Example 8.2 the statement

```
System.out.println("Full info should be "+register[i]);
```

sometimes prints out two values (name and phone) and sometimes three (name, phone and vet's phone). Explain carefully how this happens.

8.9   In Example 8.2's main method there is a try-while sequence as follows:

```
try {
  while (true)
    checkTag (in);
  ( )
}
catch (EOFException e) { }
```

How and where does the exception actually get detected and passed on to this handler?

8.10   Based on Figure 8.1 (the hierarchy of `Nature`) which of the following statements are incorrect, and why?

```
Nature n;
Animals a;
Herbivores h;
Elephant e;
Rhino r;

a = n;
e = r;
h = e;
a = h;
```

PROBLEMS

8.1   **Sorting pets**. Using the `Sortable` interface, include a facility in the veterinary system (Example 8.2) to sort pets based on their names and print out a sorted register.

8.2 **Adapting the marker**. Adapt the student marker system (Example 6.7) to include a facility to sort the students based on their final mark, and print a list in this order.

8.3 **Extending the marker**. Savanna University is introducing continuous assessment from 1998 and wants to extend the marker system so that new students will have two sorts of marks: *seen* marks, which relate to assignments and projects, and *unseen* marks which relate to tests and examinations. Decide on how to extend the `Students` class to include this facility and examine carefully what, if anything, of the `Marker` class itself needs to be changed as a result. Get the new system working.

8.4 **Model Club**. The Savanna Models Club is interested in a simulation of its remote control models (planes, trains, cars, boats). Implement the system discussed in Section 8.2, using input from the keyboard to drive a selection of models at the same time. For example, commands might be:

```
P S       // plane start
P C 10    // plane change speed to 10 k/h
P T 15    // plane turn 15 degrees
P P       // plane stop
```

8.5 **Nelson sells ice-creams**. Nelson is contemplating selling ice-creams at his Coffee Shop during a heatwave. Obviously he has to keep track of stock and watch expiry dates and so on, so that much of the programming associated with keeping ice-cream is already part of keeping coffee. Study the Coffee Shop program and its associated classes and investigate how it could be adapted to include ice-cream. Should one use interfaces or inheritance? Is a major rewrite of the `Coffee` class necessary first?

CHAPTER 9

Graphical user interfaces

9.1 Introduction to the awt

The real world has been converted to wysiwyg[1] and GUI[2] interfaces, and Java is fully equipped to provide these soft options. The GUI part is provided inside a package called awt – Abstract Windowing Toolkit. From now on we shall call it the awt (pronounced 'ought') package, and know that it is Java's platform-independent approach to user interfacing.

Awt is also completely driven from within the Java language. That means that any graphical layout tools that allow pointing and selecting of the visual appearance of an application, and generate the code for you, are separate from Java itself. These tools do exist, but running them will need a larger computer and more resources than one at first bargained for.

A complete tour of all the facilities available through awt is beyond the scope of this book. What we aim to do is to reveal the overall structure of the package and then to introduce several of the most used features through examples.

---

[1]What you see is what you get, pronounced 'wizzywig'.
[2]Graphical user interfaces, pronounced 'gooey'.

Overall structure of awt

The classes in the awt package can be classified as:

- graphics;
- components, including windows and menus;
- layout managers;
- event handling;
- image manipulation.

Graphics permits the drawing of shapes, lines and images; the selecting of fonts, colours and so on. **Components** are items such as buttons, dialog boxes, menus and scroll bars. We can put them in **containers** and then choose one of a selection of **layout managers** to arrange them suitably on the screen. The **event** class typically handles external events such as pushing buttons and moving the mouse. Finally, `java.awt.image` is a package on its own which is used by awt to incorporate **images** in a variety of formats. Figure 9.1 gives an overall picture of the awt.

There are four abstract classes – `Component`, `Container`, `MenuComponent` and `Graphics`. `LayoutManager` is an interface, and all the rest are classes, inheriting

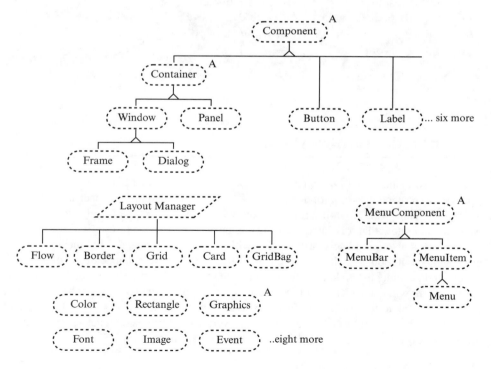

Figure 9.1   *The awt class structure.*

from the classes drawn above them. Thus `Frame` is a `Window`, which is a `Container`, which is a `Component`.

With all these different parts to GUI, it is actually hard to know where to start. We shall use a very simple example – the one in Chapter 2 for drawing a virus warning box on the screen – and introduce the various parts of awt as they are needed. In particular, we shall see that there are several ways of achieving very similar effects, and that awt has quite a rich selection of features from which to choose.

9.2 Putting graphics in a window

Graphical interfaces are presented to the user in **windows**. Java has a `Window` class, but in practice we usually use one of its subclasses, `Frame` or `Dialog`. On the same level as `Window`, implementing the `Container` abstract class, is `Panel`, which is needed by applets but is also useful in ordinary applications. Figure 9.2 gives a representative list of some methods available in each of these classes.

`Frame` – the basic window

We start off with `Frame` as the basic presenter of GUI items. Each application can have several windows and, for each, we declare a class that inherits `Frame` and includes the methods necessary to display information in the window and perform other actions. The first action is to set up the title of the window, which is done through the constructor. Thus the form for defining and constructing a new frame is given below. All user window classes extend `Frame`. In order to position a title on the top window bar, we call the constructor of `Frame`, referred to as the superclass constructor, or just `super`.

```
Defining a new Frame class

public classname extends Frame {

    classname (String title) {
        super (title);
        More constructive actions
    }

    Other methods

}
```

In the main program a frame is declared, created as a new instance of the window class that is to occupy the frame, and then the two `Window` methods – `resize` and `show` – are called to activate the drawing of the frame.

```
Creating a frame

Frame f = new classname ("title");
f.resize (width, height);
f.show ();
```

```
   public abstract class Component
        extends Object implements ImageObserver {
     // the superclass of all GUI components except menus.
     public boolean              action (Event evt, Object what);
     public void                 update (Graphics g);
     public void                 paint (Graphics g);
     public void                 show ( );
     public void                 rsize (int width, int height);
     public synchronized void    hide ( );
     public boolean              handleEvent (Event evt);
     public synchronized void    setBackground (Color c);
     public synchronized void    setForeground (Color c);
     public synchronized void    setFont (Font f);
     public void                 mouseMove (int x, int y);
     public boolean              keyDown (Event evt, int key);
     // and 63 others

   public abstract class Container extends Component {
     public Component            add (Component comp);
     public synchronized void    remove (Component comp)
     public int                  countComponents ( );
     public LayoutManager        getLayout ( );
     public void                 setLayout (LayoutManager mgr);
     // and 18 others
   }

   public class Window extends Container {
     // a top level window with no borders or menu bar
     public                      Window (Frame parent);
     public synchronized void    pack ( );
     public synchronized void    show ( );
     public void                 toBack ( );
     public void                 toFront ( );
     public synchronized void    dispose ( );
     // and 2 others
   }

   public class Frame extends window {
     // an optionally resizable top level window
     public                      Frame ( );
     public                      Frame (String title);
     public boolean              isResizable ( );
     public void                 setResizable ( );
     public void                 setTitle ( );
     public string               getTitle ( );
     // and 8 others plus 14 special cursor constants
   }

   public class Panel extends Container {
     // suitable for holding portions of a GUI within a parent
     // Frame or Dialog or another Panel
     // only 2 methods
   }
```

Figure 9.2   *Some methods of initial awt classes.*

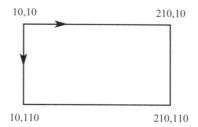

10,10   210,10

10,110   210,110

Figure 9.3 *Drawing a rectangle in the* Graphics *package.*

At this point, control is passed back to the awt which will first look for a paint method, to set up the contents of the window. The form for a paint method is:

Redefining the paint method

```
public void paint (Graphics g) {
    Calls to methods in Graphics, prefixed
    by g.
}
```

The paint method is supplied with a Graphics object customized for the particular platform the program is running on. In this way, Java can take advantage of the good points of any particular platform, and make the awt present a familiar look and feel to the users of different platforms.

The full list of the Graphics class is given in the Java libraries on our website. It includes methods for drawing rectangles, arcs, polygons and so on. For example, to draw a rectangle (as the only output), we would say:

```
public void paint (Graphics g) {
   g.drawRect (10, 10, 200, 100);
}
```

which starts at a point 10 pixels in from the top left corner of the screen, and draws a rectangle 200 wide by 100 deep (Figure 9.3).

Writing in an awt window with drawString

Working with the Graphics package, the equivalent of println in awt is drawString. For example, we could say:

```
g.drawString ("Hello Pierre",30,15);
```

which would write the string 'Hello Pierre' 30 pixels in from the left and 15 pixels down from the top of the screen. The size and number of pixels varies from screen to screen, but typically a screen will have 600 × 400.

The difference between `println` and `drawString` is that `drawString` gives a choice of fonts, font styles and font sizes, and these affect the dimension of each letter. Consequently the positioning of the start of a string can be difficult. Most books on Java and programs on the Web use actual numbers to fix the x, y coordinates of the start of a piece of text (as we did above). When trying to get a program to work to one's satisfaction, these numbers can change many times, so it is better to base everything on the relative size of letters. `FontMetrics` is an awt class which has methods for finding out the size of letters, but for the time being we shall just assume that a letter is five pixels wide and a pleasing line spacing is 15. In other words, if we declare the following constants at the start of a program:

```
static private final int letter = 5;
static private final int line = 15;
```

an equivalent call to `drawString` to the one above would be:

```
g.drawString ("Hello Pierre", 6*letter, line);
```

meaning six letters in from the left and one line down.

Closing a window

A program that runs in a window needs some way of stopping. One of the accepted methods is to click on the window close box in a top corner. Clicking is an event and can be detected by the `Event` class in the awt. The `Event` class has a method called `handleEvent`, which we can redefine, or **override**. The correct action is to find out if the event is the close window one, and if so, call `System.exit()`. Otherwise, we return to event's version of `handleEvent`. This sequence is summarized in the following form:

```
Closing a window

public boolean handleEvent (Event e) {
   if (e.id == Event.WINDOW_DESTROY)
      System.exit (0);
   return super.handleEvent (e);
}
```

Although not everything in this form is a Java keyword, it is all compulsory, and forms a little mantra that can be put in all GUI programs. We are now ready for our first example, a very simple one indeed.

EXAMPLE 9.1   Virus warning using graphics

Problem   The virus warning of Exercise 2.1 should appear in its own window and be more striking.

Solution Use the awt windows and the drawString and rectangle facilities as described above. To make the rectangle striking, we need colour. Colour is provided by the setForeground and setBackground methods in the Component interface, using the colour constants defined in the Color[3] class. We will use a cyan background, Color.cyan.

Program We set up letter and line constants and base the text writing on multiples of these. To enhance readability, the parameters are nicely lined up in the paint method. The drawRect and resize methods also use suitable multiples of letter and line.

```java
import java.awt.*;

class graphicWarning extends Frame {
  /* The Graphic warning Program      by J M Bishop Oct 1996
     produces a warning message on the screen in cyan
     and black.
     Illustrates setting up a window, painting in it
     and enabling the close box. */

  static private final int line = 15;
  static private final int letter = 5;

  public graphicWarning (String title) {
    super (title);
  }

  public void paint (Graphics g) {
    setBackGround (Color.cyan);
    g.drawRect (2*letter, 2*line, 33*letter, 6*line);
    g.drawString("W A R N I N G",            9*letter, 4*line);
    g.drawString("Possible virus detected", 4*letter, 5*line);
    g.drawString("Reboot and run virus",    5*letter, 6*line);
    g.drawString("remover software",        7*letter, 7*line);
  }

  public boolean handleEvent (Event e) {
    if (e.id == Event.WINDOW_DESTROY)
      System.exit (0);
    return super.handleEvent (e);
  }

  public static void main (String [] args) {
    Frame f = new graphicWarning ("graphicWarning");
    f.resize (50*letter,10*line);
    f.show ();
  }
}
```

Testing Figure 9.4 shows the output of the program (reduced to black and white, unfortunately). To stop the program, we click on the close button on the left.[4] The window closes, and the final statement is a call to System.exit(0).

---

[3]Notice that it is Color without a 'u', American-style.
[4]This picture shows Unix output: on a Windows 95 or NT system, the close box will be on the right.

Figure 9.4 *Graphic output for the virus warning program.*

9.3 Laying out buttons and labels

Although very versatile, the `Graphics` class is not all that convenient for handling text. Java's awt provides a different range of classes for this purpose. Two components that provide for limited text output are `Label` and `Button`. As shown in Figure 9.1, there are more such components, some of which are studied in later sections. There is a summary of all of them at the end of this section.

The two classes `Label` and `Button` provide for the output of simple text, and for the creation of reactive buttons. Both take strings as parameters to their constructors, though `Button` does not have to, so the forms are:

Creating a Label or Button
new Label ("*Text*")
new Button ("*Text*")
new Button ()

Why are there no parameters indicating *x,y* positions on the screen? The reason is that these components (unlike graphics drawings) work with **layout managers**.

Layout managers

Layout managers take over control of the positioning of components that are added to a window, and arrange them sensibly. If the window is resized by the user, the layout manager endeavours to adjust the components in the new area so that they are all still visible.

Java has five such managers, but we shall look at only the first three: flow, border and grid. They all implement the interface `LayoutManager`, as shown in Figure 9.1. The form for incorporating a layout manager is:

Incorporating a layout manager
setLayout (**new** *Manager(parameters)*);

where `setLayout` is a call to a method in `Container`, the abstract class from which `Window` and hence `Frame` inherit (see Figure 9.1). The default layout manager is `BorderLayout`, but `FlowLayout` is actually more useful for our purposes. It also has the desirable property that it is the default manager for applets. An example layout set up is:

```
setLayout (new FlowLayout(FlowLayout.CENTER,horigap,vertigap));
```

The first parameter indicates that the items added to the frame should be centred: they could also have been left or right justified. The horigap and vertigap parameters are constants that indicate the minimum distance (in pixels once again) between items in the frame. All three parameters are optional. Examples of flow layout are given in the sample programs later on.

Reacting to buttons

In addition to having an event handler for closing the window, we now also have to react to the buttons being pressed. In `Component`, which is the top level awt class, there is a method called `action`. `action` is called whenever any event such as a mouse click or user input takes place. However, since `Component` is an abstract class, there is no implementation of `action`: we have to supply it. Fortunately, this is exactly what we want.

The `action` method has two parameters, an `Event` and an `Object`, which in the case of buttons is a `String`. The parameters can be examined to decide what to do next. A full discussion on events is given in Section 9.6, but for buttons the event reported is `ACTION_EVENT` and the string is the label originally supplied for the button.

If there are several buttons, all with different string labels, then the only way to distinguish between them is to have a sequence of if–else statements, checking for each possibility. Figure 9.5 shows a diagram for such an algorithm.

A button press is just one kind of event, so a diagram such as this one will become very useful when the logic of handling events is more complicated, as discussed in Section 9.6.

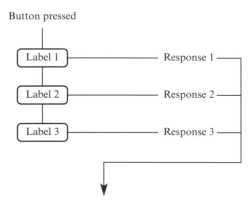

Figure 9.5 *Algorithm for responding to a button press.*

EXAMPLE 9.2 Warning with two responses

Problem Improve the warning notice by including two buttons. One should enable the user to acknowledge the message, but wait. In this case, the whole window should turn red. The other button should force a reboot.

Algorithm Use the flow layout manager, labels and buttons to achieve the necessary effect. Select background and foreground colours from the Color class. For the actions, the Reboot button being pressed causes a simulated reboot in a similar way to closing the window. Pressing the Wait button changes colours as specified. Figure 9.6 shows the algorithm in diagrammatic form.

Program The program is quite simple, and illustrates the essential sequential nature of GUI programming. The message to be displayed is passed to the new extension of the Frame as an array of strings. Each line is displayed through adding it as a label.

```
import java.awt.*;

public class ButtonTest extends Frame {
   /* The Button test Program       by J M Bishop Sept 1996
       prints a warning message, but when a Wait
       button is pressed, it turns the window red.
       Illustrates Buttons and the action method for
       handling events. */

   private static final int horigap = 15;
   private static final int vertigap = 10;

     public ButtonTest (String title, String [] message, int n) {
        // The constructor is responsible for setting
        // up the initial buttons and colour background.
        super(title);
        setBackground(Color.cyan);
        setForeground(Color.black);
        setLayout (new FlowLayout(FlowLayout.CENTER,horigap,vertigap));
```

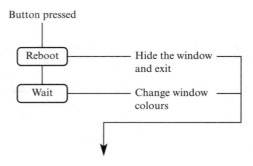

Figure 9.6 *Algorithm for responding to Reboot or Wait buttons.*

```
        for (int i=0; i<n; i++)
          add(new Label (message[i]));
        add (new Button ("Wait"));
        add (new Button ("Reboot"));
      }

    public boolean action (Event e, Object arg) {
        // Two events to handle:
        // the Reboot and Wait buttons

        if (arg.equals("Reboot")) {
        this.hide ();
        this.dispose ();
        System.exit (0);
      }
      else if (arg.equals("Wait")) {
        setForeground(Color.white);
        setBackground(Color.red);
        return true;
      }
      return false;
    }

    public boolean handleEvent (Event e) {
      if (e.id == Event.WINDOW_DESTROY)
        System.exit (0);
      return super.handleEvent (e);
    }

    public static void main (String [] args) {

      String message [] =
        {"W A R N I N G",
         "Possible virus detected.",
         "Reboot and run virus",
         "remover software"} ;

      Frame f = new ButtonTest ("Button Test", message, 4);
      f.resize (200,200);
      f.show ();
    }
  }
```

Testing   The first display from this program will be as shown in Figure 9.7.

Other layout managers

In addition to flow, the other four layout managers and their features are:

- **Border**. Allows positioning of items (scroll bars, menus, buttons, etc.) in fixed size borders indicated by a parameter which can nominate the North, South, East or West of the window, with the remainder of the space being the Center.[5]

---

[5]Note the American spelling once again for Center.

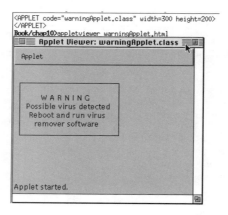

Figure 9.7 *Output from the Button Test program.*

- **Card**. Overlapping panels of information can be selected by clicking on tabs on the top of each panel.

- **Grid**. The frame is divided into a specified number of rows and columns which can be selected by number.

- **Grid bag**. Fine-grained layout where each component is given exact pixel constraints. Although complex to use, it is the most versatile and portable.

Since `LayoutManager` is an interface, it is possible to define your own layout manager, with customized (and sometimes very pleasing) results.

Other component options

Labels and buttons are components, and we indicated that were another six similar classes. To round things off, we name them and indicate their main functions here.

- **TextComponent**, together with its two subclasses `TextArea` and `TextField`, handles multiple lined text, text selecting and editing.

- **Scrollbar** is useful with text and enables the contents of the container to move in the window.

- **Canvas** is an additional window area which can be used for drawing in, so as not to interfere with buttons.

- **Checkbox** provides for yes/no or on/off selection. An example would be selecting bold on a tool bar in a text processor.

- **Choice** provides dropdown lists from which choices can be made, similar to the ones provided for fonts in a text processor. One choice can be made.

- **List** is similar to choice except that the items are always on screen, and multiple selections can be made.

Some of these are used in the case study at the end of the chapter.

9.4   Panels and canvases for grouping

Java provides higher-level groupings of components, which can then be moved around together in a window and are protected from overwriting each other. The first is a panel, which is used to keep groups of like components such as buttons. The panel is then passed to the layout manager as an entity.

For example, the two buttons above could be grouped as follows:

```
Panel p = new Panel ( );
p.setLayout (new FlowLayout());
p.add (new Button ("Wait"));
p.add (new Button ("Reboot"));
```

The panel can then be added to the frame in its constructor. In order to get the buttons always at the bottom of the screen, we can use BorderLayout and position the panel in the South area. BorderLayout is already the default manager for frames, while FlowLayout is the default for panels. Thus we can leave out calls to set them up, unless we wish to alter the gaps and so on. When adding to the BorderLayout, the first parameter selects one of five areas, as shown in Figure 9.8.

The borders are narrow, being deep enough for one component only. Thus a couple of buttons will fit, or a heading, or a scroll bar but no more. An equivalent to the constructor in Example 9.2 is:

```
public ButtonTest (String title, String [] message, int n) {
   // default BorderLayout
   super(title);
   setBackground(Color.cyan);
   setForeground(Color.black);
   Panel m = new Panel ( ) // default FlowLayout
   for (int i=0; i<n; i++)
     m.add(new Label (message[i]));
   add ("Center", m);
   Panel p = new Panel ( ); // default FlowLayout
   p.add (new Button ("Wait"));
```

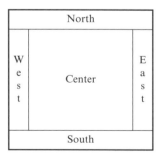

Figure 9.8 *Areas recognized by Border Layout.*

```
    p.add (new Button ("Reboot"));
    add ("South", p);
}
```

Canvases

The function of a canvas is to provide an area where drawing can take place. The drawing could be controlled and initiated by the program (for example, designs, logos, ticking clocks) or user-supplied drawing with a mouse. The next example explores both panels and canvases.

EXAMPLE 9.3 Traffic lights

Problem The traffic department would like to simulate traffic light times, and watch how pedestrian button requests affect the changing of the lights.

Solution Design a screen along the lines of Figure 9.9. Then handle the interaction of the lights and buttons as required. Such interaction needs event-based programming, so we shall take it up in Section 9.6 and complete the example there. Meanwhile we shall work on setting up the window ready for action.

Figure 9.9

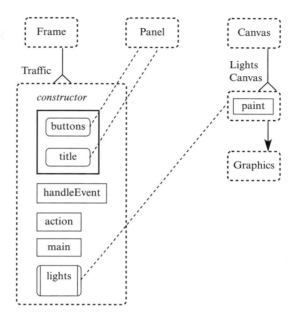

Figure 9.10   *Class diagram for initial Traffic Light Simulation.*

Class design   Put the traffic light in a canvas, with the circles, and so on, drawn using methods from Graphics. Put the buttons in one panel and the title in another. The class diagram for the program is shown in Figure 9.10.

Traffic extends Frame, as it must in order to display graphics. The buttons and title objects are both instances of the Panel class. Lights is a private object which is an instance of a separate small class called LightsCanvas. LightsCanvas inherits from Canvas and has a single method, paint, which calls methods in Graphics.

Program

```
import java.awt.*;

public class Traffic extends Frame {
  /* The Traffic light program      by J M Bishop Oct 1996
     Displays a representation of traffic lights,
     in preparation for a simulation.
     Illustrates panels and canvases and the
     BorderLayout manager.*/
  public Traffic ( ) {
    setTitle("Traffic Lights");

    lights = new LightsCanvas ();
    add("Center", lights);

    Panel buttons = new Panel ();
    buttons.add(new Button("WALK"));
```

```
      buttons.add(new Button("CANCEL"));
      add ("South", buttons);

      Panel title = new Panel ();
      title.add(new Label("Savanna Traffic Light Simulation"));
      add ("North", title);
    }

    public boolean handleEvent(Event evt) {
      if (evt.id == Event.WINDOW_DESTROY) System.exit(0);
      return super.handleEvent(evt);
    }

    public boolean action(Event evt, Object arg) {
      boolean reply = true;
      if (arg.equals("CANCEL")) {
        this.hide();
        this.dispose();
        System.exit(0);
      }  else
      if (arg.equals "WALK"))
        {// not implemented yet }
      return false;
    }

    public static void main(String[] args) {
      Frame f = new Traffic ( );
      f.resize(300, 200);
      f.show();
    }

    private LightsCanvas lights;
  }

class LightsCanvas extends Canvas {
  public void paint (Graphics g) {
    g.drawOval (97, 10, 30, 68);
    g.setColor (Color.red);
    g.fillOval (105, 15, 15, 15);
    g.setColor (Color.yellow);
    g.fillOval (105, 35, 15, 15);
    g.setColor (Color.green);
    g.fillOval (105, 55, 15, 15);
    g.fillOval (105, 85, 15, 15);
    g.setColor (Color.black);
    g.drawString ("RED",    15, 28);
    g.drawString ("YELLOW", 15, 48);
    g.drawString ("GREEN",  15, 68);
    g.drawString ("WALK",   15, 98);
  }
}
```

Testing   See Figure 9.11. In colour, the three lights show up well; in black and white they are somewhat invisible, except for red! To ensure at least an outline for each light, we

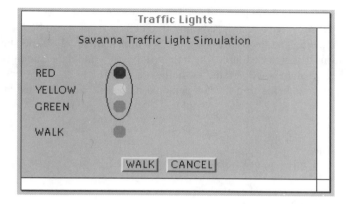

Figure 9.11 *The screen drawn for the Traffic Light Simulation.*

should add `drawOval` with the same centre to the corresponding `fillOval`, using one pixel more in each direction, and drawn in black. For example:

```
g.setColor (Color.red);
g.fillOval (105, 15, 15, 15);
setColor (Color.black);
g.drawOval (105, 15, 16, 16);
```

9.5   Interaction with text fields

To get text into a GUI program, Java provides a component `TextComponent` with two subclasses, `TextField` and `TextArea`. `TextArea` is for multi-line text and works in conjunction with scroll bars. We shall just consider the single-line text fields. To declare a component as a `TextField`, we use the form:

Creating a text field
`TextField t = new TextField("initial value",n);`

n is the number of characters one expects in the field, but will not fully define its width, since the width is also influenced by the font chosen and the layout manager used. However, the field will scroll if the user enters more than *n* characters, so there is no problem in guessing *n* incorrectly. The methods available on a `TextField` are:

Using a text field
`astring = atextfield.getText ();`
`atextfield.setText ("value");`
`atextfield.setEditable (boolean);`
`booleanvar = atextfield.isEditable ();`

`getText` and `setText` are the read and write equivalents for a `TextField`. Each field can also be open for input – that is, editable (the default) – or it can be locked. In the first state, it will be white, and the user must move the mouse there, click and start typing, ending with a return. If it is not editable, the field will be grey and data cannot be entered. The need for these two states is illustrated in the next section.

To set up text fields to collect a person's name and age together in a `Panel` we would use:

```
Panel p = new Panel ();
p.add (new Label ("Name"));
TextField name = new TextField("",40);
p.add (name);
p.add (new Label ("Age"));
TextField age = new TextField("",5);
p.add (age);
```

which would give:

Name	I

Age | I |

Inputting numbers

You may have noticed that there is only one get method for `Text`, and it returns a `String`. Thus we are faced once again with translating the contents of the string to a number, if that is what we want. We discussed this process in Section 6.3, where the following key statement was used:

Translating a string to an integer
`i = Integer.valueOf (s.trim()).intValue();`

Exactly the same technique can be used in GUI programming. However, a simple statement like this assumes that nothing will go wrong in the conversion, such as a non-numeric character in the string. The `Text` class took care of these problems, and one could envisage a similar class being written, called say `GUIText`, which would perform exactly the same function, but with input from a `TextField` instead of a `DataInputStream`. For now we shall live dangerously, and leave the development of `GUIText` as a worthwhile exercise for the reader.

Avoiding input

We mentioned at the end of Section 9.3 that there were several other components in the awt, some of which provide for selections from lists or choices. Essentially, these save the user from typing in a lot of data, and also create a more secure environment because there is no opportunity for unexpected input. Take a simple example. If we want the user to give us a day of the week, we do not ask for text to be typed into a text field, with all its accompanying checking. Instead we provide a `Choice` list, which gives the seven choices, and the user simply selects one with the mouse. `CheckBox` and `List` have similar uses. An example of the use of a `Choice` is given in the next development of the traffic light program.

EXAMPLE 9.4 Traffic light calibration

Problem   Continuing the traffic light example, the simulation is going to look at the effectiveness of different timings for the lights. For example, should red be on for longer than green, and so on.

Solution   For an easy-to-use simulation, we must have the ability to change the time each light is on. In other words, we must read in new values. Doing so requires

- the selection of one of the four lights;
- the entering of the new duration.

Algorithm   The necessary components can be added to the buttons panel and appear at the bottom of the screen.

Program   The full constructor for such a frame is now:

```
public Traffic ( ) {
   setTitle("Traffic Lights");

   Panel title = new Panel ();
   title.add(new Label("Savanna Traffic Light Simulation"));
   add ("North", title);

   lights = new LightsCanvas ();
   add("Center", lights);

   Panel buttons = new Panel ();
   buttons.add(new Button("WALK"));
   buttons.add(new Button("CANCEL"));
   Choice c = new Choice ();
   c.addItem ("Red");
   c.addItem ("Yellow");
   c.addItem ("Green");
   c.addItem ("Walk");
   buttons.add (c);
   buttons.add (new Label ("Duration"));
   duration = new TextField ("",3);
   duration.setEditable(false);
   buttons.add (duration);
   add ("South",buttons);
}
```

Testing   The output of the new constructor is shown in Figure 9.12.

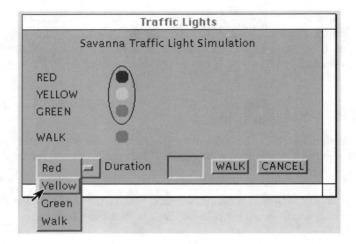

Figure 9.12 *Output of the Traffic Light Simulation with a choice.*

9.6 Event-driven programming

Clearly, responding to events is an important part of GUI programming. The Event class of Java's awt records information about events that occur. There is a list of nearly 30 events, but for the components we are using, only those given in Table 9.1 are relevant right now.

In terms of interaction with the user, events are single happenings, but together they can form a chain of events. In other words, causing a certain event to happen need not always elicit the same response. There may be two or three responses, depending on the events that have gone before.

How do we record what has gone before? In most cases, we use suitably named Boolean variables which indicate whether or not a previous event happened.

For example, in the panel in Example 9.4 which enabled the selection of a light, and then the entering of a new duration, we could force these two to happen in this order. We may also like to disable both of these components until a Change button has been pressed. We indicate the flow of this logic in Figure 9.13.

Notice some interesting consequences of this logic. The Change button acts as an on–off button, so that no matter what progress had been made with selecting a choice, if change is then pressed, the choice will be cancelled. Also, choice can be called over and

Table 9.1 *Details of some common events.*

Component	Event Type	What happened	Argument
Button	ACTION_EVENT	User clicked button	String: button label
Choice	ACTION_EVENT	User selected item	String: label of item
TextField	ACTION_EVENT	User pressed <Return>	String: user's text
Window	WINDOW_DESTROY	Window was destroyed	–

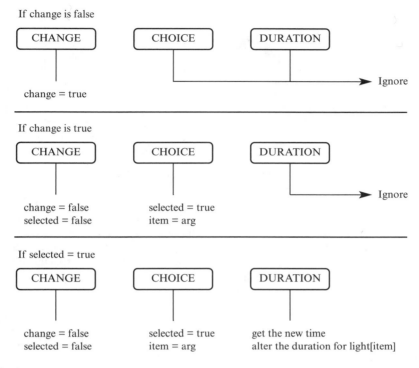

Figure 9.13

over, with new selections being made until one is satisfied. Finally, once a duration is selected, both choice and change go back to their original states so that the process must begin again. The logic did not have to be so: one could have said that having selected a duration, we can leave change on and leave the choice where it is, thus enabling a new duration to be entered immediately for the same item.

The point is that whatever logic we choose, we must be clear about it and it must contain no dead ends. It is also unnecessary to provide a guide to the user about what to do, since just clicking the buttons will soon make the sequence clear.

The formulation of the traffic light simulation has been deliberately vague on the question of how the lights actually count down and change. In order to make this kind of animation work, we shall need some of the threaded facilities available in the `java.net` package. Networks are covered in Chapter 11, when the example is picked up again. The case study, however, puts into practice the ideas regarding event handling which we have developed in this section.

9.7   Case study 4: Supermarket till

The solution to the following problem exploits different components of a GUI interface as well as event handling.

3kg Strawberries @ G12 = G36

Figure 9.14 *A model for the grocery till.*

Problem

Savanna Grocers wishes to computerize the weighing of fruit and vegetables at its tills. It envisages a display with buttons for the different produce and a space to enter the mass. At present the scales are not directly linked to the till, and there is not a special unit to print a price sticker, but the price of each item should be entered on the usual till slip.

Solution

The sequence of events required is shown in Figure 9.14. Thus if the strawberries weigh 3 kg, we enter 3 in the mass field. The cost per unit is given in graz, let us say G12 per kilogram. The mass times unit cost, which is G36, will appear in the cost field, and a line is printed for the complete transaction.

The solution devolves nicely into two parts: the design of the screen, and the organization of the event handler.

The design of the screen

Apart from the mass and cost text fields with their accompanying labels, there must be a button for each type of produce. These can be laid out in rows and columns like calculator buttons. In this case, the best layout manager is not flow, but grid. With `GridLayout` we specify the expected number of rows and columns, and Java will line the components up in these boxes as they are added. The result is more symmetric and fixed than with `FlowLayout`.

All in all, we have three panels on the screen, which fit into a `BorderLayout` as follows:

Cost panel
Buttons panel
Mass panel

The buttons panel contains a button for each item of produce, plus three others for controlling the till, WEIGH, PRINT and CLOSE. CLOSE is not really needed since the system stops when we close the window, but it could be used to cause the printing of a running total or something like that.

Event handling

We start by listing the possible events:

> WEIGH pressed
> produce button pressed (e.g. peas)
> mass entered
> PRINT pressed
> CLOSE pressed
> window close

Not all of these are always valid. We want to force an ordering of events for weighing produce so that everything is entered before PRINT is pressed, that is:

these three in any order { press WEIGH
press a produce button
click on mass field, enter mass, press RETURN

press PRINT

Now we tabulate the events and indicate their effect:

WEIGH	opens up mass field
a produce button	sets unit cost and sets chosen
text in weigh field	sets mass and sets weighed
PRINT	prints the cost and resets everything

However, these effects cannot be achieved if the sequence of events is not correct. So we need to build that in too with the help of a couple of Boolean variables (Figure 9.15).

Data entry

There remains the question as to how to get the basic data into the program: that is, the produce names and their unit costs. Since the items could vary from day to day, and their prices certainly will, it would make sense to have this information stored in a file. For ease of getting the program up, though, we shall embed a few items in the program for now, and leave the extension to a file as an exercise.

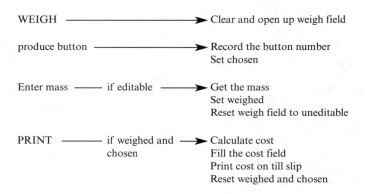

Set chosen and weighted to false
Set the weigh field to uneditable

WEIGH ────────────────────► Clear and open up weigh field

produce button ─────────────► Record the button number
Set chosen

Enter mass ───── if editable ────► Get the mass
Set weighed
Reset weigh field to uneditable

PRINT ─────── if weighed and ───► Calculate cost
chosen   Fill the cost field
Print cost on till slip
Reset weighed and chosen

Figure 9.15   *Algorithm for handling events in the grocery till.*

Program

The program is as follows:

```java
import java.awt.*;

public class Till extends Frame {
    /* The Grocery Till program       by J M Bishop Oct 1996
       Simulates the operation of a grocery till for
       up to 12 products, together with the costs per
       kilogram.
       Illustrates Panels, different layout managers,
       (including grid) and the handling of events that
       can occur in any order. */

    public Till ( ) {
    // Set up the initial screen with textfields
    // to the north and south and the twelve
    // products but three action buttons in the
    // centre panel.
    // The mass is initially editable.
    // The cost is always not editable.

        setTitle("Grocer");

        Panel q = new Panel ();
        q.add(new Label ("MASS: "));
        weighField = new TextField ("",4);
        weighField.setEditable(false);
        q.add (weighField);
        add ("South", q);
```

```
        Panel p = new Panel();
        p.setLayout(new GridLayout(5, 3));
        for (int i = 0; i <= 11; i++)
          p.add(new Button(items[i]));
        p.add(new Button("WEIGH"));
        p.add(new Button("PRINT"));
        p.add(new Button("CLOSE"));
        add("Center", p);

        Panel r = new Panel ();
        r.add(new Label ("COST: "));
        totalField = new TextField ("0",6);
        totalField.setEditable(false);
        r.add (totalField);
        add("North", r);
}

public boolean action(Event evt, Object arg) {
  // The main control of the program.
  // There are five possible events:
  // Weigh, Print and Close buttons,
  // Mass textfield data and the product buttons.

  // Always allow a close.
  boolean reply = true;
  if (arg.equals("CLOSE")) {
    this.hide();
    this.dispose();
    System.exit(0);
  } else

  // Allow a mass to be typed in after Weigh has
  // been pressed.
  if (evt.target == weighField & weighField.isEditable()) {
    kg = (double) Integer.valueOf
        (weighField.getText().trim()).intValue();
    weighed = true;
    weighField.setEditable(false);
  } else

  // Always allow Weigh to be pressed
  if (arg.equals("WEIGH")) {
    weighField.setText("");
    weighField.setEditable(true);
  } else

  // Only allow a print after a mass is in and
  // a product has been chosen.
  if (arg.equals("PRINT")) {
    if (weighed & chosen) {
      total = kg*unitCosts[select];
      totalField.setText("G " + total);
      System.out.println(kg + " kg " + items[select]
      + " @ G " + unitCosts[select] + " = G " +
      total);
      kg = 0;
```

```
                     weighed = false;
                     chosen = false;
                     total = 0;
             }   // else ignore PRINT
           }  else

        // Always allow a product to be chosen
        if (arg instanceof String) {
          chosen = true;
          select = 0;
          while (!arg.equals(items[select])) select++;
        }
        // event not identified, so
        else reply = false;
        return reply;
    }

public boolean handleEvent(Event evt) {
    if (evt.id == Event.WINDOW_DESTROY) System.exit(0);
       return super.handleEvent(evt);
  }

public static void main(String[] args) {
  Frame f = new Till( );
  f.resize(300, 200);
  f.show();
}

private TextField weighField,totalField;
private double total;
private boolean chosen = false;
private boolean weighed = false;
private int select;
private double kg;

// Set up the products and the unit costs per kilogram.
private String items [ ] = {"Apples","Pears","Oranges",
                     "Potatoes","Lemons","Squash",
                     "Onions","Garlic","Avocados",
                     "",  "",""} ;
private double unitCosts [ ]= {6.00,5.00,7.00,
                     3.00,10.00,4.00,
                     4.00,12.00,15.00,
                     0, 0, 0} ;
}
```

Examining the action method, we see that there are five if-statements. These correspond to the five events, excluding closing a window which is handled separately in the handleEvent method. Three of the events are unconditional: CLOSE, WEIGH and pressing a produce button. They always cause the action as given. The other two rely on previous events, so that the weighField can get input only if it is editable, and the PRINT button causes a reaction only if weighed and chosen have already been set.

Figure 9.16 *Output from the grocery till program.*

Testing

The screen looks like Figure 9.16 after a few items have been entered.

SUMMARY

Graphics programming is fun but time-consuming. The graphics methods of Java are contained in the `Graphics` class and accessed by defining versions of the `paint` and `repaint` methods. All drawing takes place in a `Frame`, which is a subclass of the abstract class `Container`. Other containers are Buttons, Labels, Textfields and so on, all of which can be used to construct interactive user interfaces. The layout of containers on the screen can be left up to default flow managers, or can be controlled in a number of ways, such as grids and borders. Java provides the full range of check buttons, menus, choices, scrollbars and so on that one needs.

Once a screen has been laid out and displayed, interaction with the user begins. Moving the mouse, clicking a button or entering text constitutes an event, and the action method must be programmed to handle these. Event-driven programming requires careful algorithm development, especially for events that have to be forced into a certain order, for example weighing before printing.

QUIZ

9.1   The following declaration is not valid. Why not?

```
Component area = new Component ();
```

9.2   Given a panel p, write awt calls to create a textfield with 'NAME' to its left.

9.3   What is the default layout manager for a `Frame`?

9.4   Write awt calls to set up a choice list for the days of the week.

9.5   What is the effect of `setEditable(false)` on a `TextField`?

9.6   Create a typed method for reading in a double value from a `TextField` and show how it could be called in the action method of the `Till` class, line 16.

9.7   Is there space in the `Till` class to add another three products? What would happen if we added another six?

9.8   The Olympic Rings in Figure 2.3 are rather thin. Write graphics calls to draw thicker rings.

9.9   If you wanted to force the user to choose a product before pressing weigh, what would you have to do?

9.10   In the alternative `ButtonTest` constructor (Section 9.4) the last two statements are:

```
p.add (new Button ("Reboot"));
add ("South", p);
```

Why does the last statement not have an object before the add? Explain what the statements do.

PROBLEMS

9.1   **Shape selector**. A teacher wishes to let toddlers draw shapes (circle, square, triangle) in three colours (red, blue, yellow). The children cannot read. Provide a suitable GUI interface for selecting a shape and colour and drawing the object at a position given by a mouse click.

9.2   **Two traffic lights**. Improve the lights system to display two identical traffic lights on the screen.

9.3   **GUI Text**. Implement a companion class to `Text` (Sections 4.2 and 6.3) for input from `TextFields`.

9.4   **Improving the grocery range**. Alter the Till program so as to have the items and costs stored on a file and read in at the start of the main program before the window is activated. Will the `GridLayout` size be affected or will it automatically accommodate more buttons?

9.5   **Till slip**. Create a proper till slip for a weighed item in a separate window, using a pleasing design similar to that of your local supermarket.

9.6   **Digital watch**. Design the display and knobs of a digital watch to appear in a window. Link up with Problem 11.9 to make it work.

9.7   **Several tills**. Experiment with the Till program to bring up several Till windows at once by creating several `Frames` objects. Can you work with them alternately?

9.8   **Remote control**. Implement a user interface for the remote control device described in Section 8.2.

9.9   **GUI Coffee Shop**. Create a design for a full screen version of Nelson's inventory control program. Rewrite the classes so as to access the screen effectively. Find out what events may occur, and set up a suitable event handler.

CHAPTER 10

Applets in action

A great deal of the excitement surrounding Java has had to do with its integration into the World Wide Web. As we shall see, once the mechanics of accessing Java through the web have been sorted out, and we have looked at the facilities available in the standard Java packages, it will be very easy for you to branch off on your own and create applets bounded only by your imagination.

10.1 From applications to applets

So what is an applet? An applet is a Java program that operates within a browser, and hence can appear in a web page. The applet runs on the user's computer, even though it may have been fetched from far away. This is possible through a combination of Java being interpreted (on the user's machine) and Java being enabled on the web browser being used (for example Netscape). The advantages of having applets in a web page are that:

- the calculations are done on the site where they are needed, so there is less traffic on the network;

- the user's machine is dedicated to the applet and can run the applet much faster than could a share of a server where the web page resides;

- the full facilities of the Java programming language are available,[1] especially the graphical user interface package, awt.

The last point is important: Java applets actually rely on the awt interface for communication. To get an idea of how an applet differs from an application, let us go back to the first awt example in Chapter 9 and convert it to an applet.

Converting an application to an applet

The steps to achieve the conversion are as follows:

1. Check that all **input/output** relevant to the user goes through the awt interface. For example, replace

    ```
    System.out.println("=====================");
    ```

    with

    ```
    g.drawString("=====================");
    ```

2. Check that there is a means for **stopping** the applet (e.g. by closing the window).

3. Import the `applet` package and in the main **window**, extend `Applet`[2] instead of `Frame`, with the consequences listed below. For example, replace

    ```
    class graphicWarning extends Frame {
    ```

    with

    ```
    class appletWarning extends Applet {
    ```

4. Remove the **main** method from the program, as the applet package will take over its functions.

5. Create an **html** file which refers to the applet's class file or include html instructions (called **tags**) in a web page (see form below).

6. **Run** the html file through an applet viewer or through a web browser such as Netscape.

    The possible consequences of point 3 are:

    (a) A call to `setTitle` must be removed: `Applet` has its own way of handling the title of a window.

---

[1]Barring some safety restrictions discussed below.

[2]applet with a small a is the name of the package that is imported; `Applet` with a capital A is the name of the class that is extended.

(b) The class's constructor is replaced by an redefinition of the `init` method, which is called by `Applet` to make any one-off initializations. For example,

```
graphicWarning {
```

becomes

```
void init {
```

(c) `Applet`'s default layout is flow, so if the frame was relying on border layout by default, add a call to make it specific, thereby overriding flow layout: for example, add

```
setLayout (new BorderLayout ());
```

(d) Replace any other `Frame`-specific calls by `Applet` ones: for example, `dispose` becomes `destroy`.

Html stands for Hypertext Markup Language. We need to know only the bare basics of it to run applets. In fact, the form for activating an applet consists of one tag as follows:

Html tags for an applet

```
<APPLET code="name" width=n height=m>
</APPLET>
```

Points 5 and 6 above indicate that there are two ways of running an applet. Let us first consider how to do this through the applet viewer supplied with Java. In the next sections we shall consider how to integrate applets with a browser.

EXAMPLE 10.1 Virus warning applet

Opportunity   The warning program has become popular, and others would like to use it.

Response   Following the steps above, we can convert the application of Example 9.1 into an applet. The html file that must be created contains the following:

```
<APPLET code="warningApplet.class" width=300 height=200>
</APPLET>
```

Program   The program was pretty simple to start with, so it does not require much conversion. Points 1, 2, 3a, 3c and 3d above do not apply in this case. Notice that as an applet, it is shorter than the original because the main program has gone.

```
import java.awt.*;
import java.applet.*;

public class warningApplet extends Applet {

   static private final int line = 15;
   static private final int letter = 5;
```

Figure 10.1 *Apple output for the Warning program.*

```
public boolean handleEvent (Event e) {
   if (e.id == Event.WINDOW_DESTROY)
   System.exit (0);
   return super.handleEvent (e);
}

public void paint (Graphics g) {
   g.drawRect (2*letter, 2*line,        33*letter, 6*line);
   g.drawString("W A R N I N G",        9*letter, 4*line);
   g.drawString("Possible virus detected", 4*letter, 5*line);
   g.drawString("Reboot and run virus",   5*letter, 6*line);
   g.drawString("remover software",       7*letter, 7*line);
}
}
```

Testing

The output from the applet (Figure 10.1) looks exactly the same as that from an application, except that the title bar of the window is set up by the applet viewer as the file's name and there is a clear indication that the window is created by an applet.

10.2 Applets in browsers

Before Java, web browsers were mainly static, presenting information to the viewer exactly as it was stored at the original site. There were facilities for returning data to the host via form collecting and mailing, but Java's idea of having calculations at the host site is novel. With applets being able to be included in web pages, what comes down the link can now present a dynamic interface to the user (refer back to Figure 1.1).

Work can be done and results can be returned back to the host machine. Without Java, the same sequence of events as in Figure 1.1 occurs, except that this time, the display includes only text and images.

Where are the applets?

If an applet is stored on a host machine, then it is accessible to any other machine on the internet via its World Wide Web protocol and name or URL.[3] The `warningApplet`'s URL would be something like:

```
http://www.cs.up.ac.za/javagently/warningApplet.html
```

where the html file is stored on a web accessible directory. The class file it refers to can be in another directory, but then the html CODE tag must specify its path.

Consider now an example of an applet that actually interacts with the user, and compare its operation locally through applet viewer and remotely via Netscape.

EXAMPLE 10.2   Supermarket till applet

Opportunity The directors of Savanna Grocers see the opportunity of keeping the master version of the supermarket till program in one place, and letting the various tills download it as required. There could well be advantages for updating, for franchising and for changing computers.

Response Convert the program into an applet as per the instructions. Create an html file and access it via a browser loaded onto each till.

Program The changes occur in the constructor – which becomes `init` – and in the `action` method. The `main` method is removed, but everything else stays the same.

```
import java.awt.*;
import java.applet.*;

public class tillApplet extends Applet {
  public void init ( ) {
    setLayout (new BorderLayout ());

    … as before
  }
}
```

[3]URL stands for Universal Resource Locator.

Figure 10.2 *Applet output from the Till program via a viewer.*

```
public boolean action(Event evt, Object arg) {
    boolean reply = true;
    if (arg.equals("CLOSE")) {
        destroy ();
        System.exit(0);
    }
}
```

Testing   If we run the applet via the applet viewer, then the till applet's output (Figure 10.2) is the same as that of the original application. It responds in the same way and is closed either by pressing CLOSE or clicking the window's close square (top left).

Now if we store the html file in a location which is accessible on the web, then we can run a browser and move to the location specified. The result is shown in Figure 10.3. There are two differences between what the user sees of the applet in the two environments:

• The applet viewer still gives access to the DataStreams and the screen for printing. Under Netscape, open up the Java Console window to see the output.

• The applet viewer responds to stopping events, whereas under a browser, the applet ends only when the page it is running in is closed.

In all other respects applets behave the same under either environment.

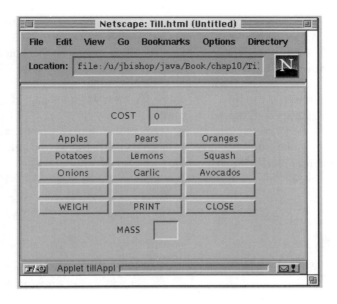

Figure 10.3   *The Till applet running under Netscape.*

Applet security

A danger of using the web is that a program you download could be corrupt, and cause damage to your system. In every possible way, Java guards against this happening. In the first place, there is a validity check on the bytecode that arrives at your computer. If it had been tampered with en route, your Java Virtual Machine will not run it. Secondly, the JVM itself will not perform any operation that could potentially harm your machine. For example, an applet from far away cannot find out your password, nor can it delete your files. The full set of rules is summarized in Table 10.1.

Table 10.1   *Applet security.*

Operation	Java application	Applet in an applet viewer	Netscape and local applet	Netscape and URL applet
Access local files	√	√		
Delete a local file	√			
Run another program	√	√		
Find out your name	√	√	√	
Connect back to the host	√	√	√	√
Connect to another host	√	√	√	
Load the Java library	√	√	√	
Call exit	√	√		
Create a pop-up window	√	√	√	√

A Java application is a full program and as such can do anything that is required on your computer. An applet is quite different, and is subject to scrutiny and the rules above. Applets running in the applet viewer can do everything that an application can, except for deleting files. However, once they run within Netscape, their activities are curtailed somewhat.

Within a browser, an applet does not end: it ends when the page it is in is replaced by another page. Thus it does not call exit, nor is there any close box. Applets in web pages are **seamless**, as shown in the case study. The fact that applets cannot read or write the local file system can be a disadvantage. In fact, this restriction is true only of Netscape at present. It is not part of the definition of Java, and could well be relaxed in later versions of browsers. Finally, additional restrictions apply to remotely loaded applets, and these are all to the good.

EXAMPLE 10.3   The newspaper competition

Problem   The *Savanna News* runs an annual competition based on readers' names. A value is assigned to each letter of the alphabet and there is a winning score. If you are one of the readers whose name adds up to the winning score, then you can enter for a prize. To even things out, every name is expanded or contracted to 20 letters. The competition is repeated for four weeks with different letter values and a different winning score each week.

Example

```
Alphabet  A B C D E F G H I J K L M N O P Q R S T U V W X Y Z
Values    5 1 3 6 7 9 2 3 7 5 4 1 3 8 9 7 5 4 3 2 1 3 2 4 5 4
Winning score 100
Names  JudyBishopJudyBishop   94
       JohnSmithJohnSmithJo  100
       RoelfvandenHeeverRoe  118
       TimothyFoxFoxRobinso  116
```

So John Smith can enter the competition this week. The others can try again when the values change next week.

Now the editor would like the competition to be available on the Web so that people can try out their names and get an up-to-date immediate response.

Solution   Write a Java applet, of course! This competition is ideal for an applet because it contains information which is maintained centrally (the letter values) and which must be protected, but we want everyone to be able to do the calculation. Moreover, doing it by hand is actually quite tedious, so the calculation facility offered by applets is valuable.

Algorithm   The competition applet splits into two parts. The first one handles the setting up of the screen and the data; the second one handles the input of names and the calculation of the result through a GUI interface (Figure 10.4).

Figure 10.4   *The Competition applet running via a viewer.*

To set up an interface, we have to have some idea of the layout. Having been through this process several times now, we shall just present a final layout which covers most of what we need. The awt calls to create the buttons, text fields and labels in border and grid layouts are standard.

Setting up the data requires more thought. We want to associate values with characters. In other words, we want an array indexed by characters. Unfortunately, as we discovered in Section 6.5, Java does not allow this. Instead, we have to use a hash table, where the characters and corresponding integers are both stored using put, and extracted using get.

One could create a GUI way of altering the scores each week, but a simple text file is by far the best way. To access it and read from it in an applet, we have to be careful of IOExceptions: they cannot be thrown outside of the init method. Therefore, we catch them immediately within init. Since we do not seriously anticipate an error, we make null catches, as in:

```
try {
  in = new DataInputStream
      (new FileInputStream ("letter.data"));
} catch (FileNotFoundException e) {}
```

The interface has three display fields – the magic score, your score and a message – and two input fields – the name and an Again button. Thus the action method must handle events on these two fields.

Clicking Again will set the fields to their original state, which is easy. Handling the name is more complex. The algorithm required is shown below. To work on the name, we can use several of the methods supplied with the String class, such as trim, toLowerCase and toCharArray. The last converts a string into an equivalent array of characters, which is more convenient for our purposes.

Get the text
Trim it of trailing blanks
Convert it to lower case
Remove all spaces and punctuation
Cut the name to 20 chars max or repeat the name to 20 chars
Consult the hash table for the values for each letter and compute the Total
Total is wining score?

                      no

  yes

Good Luck message   Bad Luck message

Applet   The Java applet follows. It is not all that long, but is effective. It can be tested with the names above, or with a variety.

```
import java.awt.*;
import java.applet.*;
import java.util.*;
import java.io.*;

public class Competition extends Applet {

  /* The competition applet       by J M Bishop Oct 1996
     Runs a competition screening mechanism.
     Illustrates Text input and other awt features.
     Needs a file called letters.data. */

  public void init () {
    // Sets up the applet interface

    // First, read in the letter values
    try {
      in = new DataInputStream(new FileInputStream ("letter.data"));
    } catch (FileNotFoundException e) {}

    // Create the hash table of letter and number values
    char ch; int l;
    try {
      winningScore = Text.readString(in);
      for (int i = 0; i<26; i++) {
        ch = Text.readChar(in);
        l = Text.readInt(in);
        values.put(new Character(ch),new Integer(l));
      }
    } catch (IOException e ) {}   ;

    // draw the user interface
    setLayout (new BorderLayout ());
    add ("North", new Label
        ("Savanna News Competition",Label.CENTER));
```

```
      Panel p = new Panel ();
      p.setLayout(new GridLayout(3,2));
      p.add (new Label ("Today's score"));
      target = new TextField (winningScore,4);
      target.setEditable(false);
      p.add (target);
      p.add (new Label ("Type in your name"));
      name = new TextField ("",30);
      p.add (name);
      p.add (new Label ("Your score"));
      score = new TextField ("",4);
      score.setEditable(false);
      p.add (score);
      add ("Center", p);

      Panel q = new Panel ();
      result = new TextField (openingMessage);
      result.setEditable(false);
      q.add (result);
      q.add (new Button ("Again"));
      add ("South", q);
   }

   public boolean action (Event evt, Object arg) {

      // Again resets everything. It is always available
      if (arg.equals("Again")) {
        name.setText("");
        score.setText("");
        result.setText(openingMessage);
      }
      else {

      // Otherwise, insist on getting a name
      char [] c;
      char d [] = new char [40];

      c = name.getText().trim().toLowerCase().toCharArray();
      int n=0;
      for (int i=0; i<c.length & n<lettersCounted; i++) {
        if (Character.isLowerCase(c[i])) {
          d[n] = c[i];
          n++;
        }
        if (i==c.length-1) i=-1;
      }

      // the stripped down array is now in d[0] to d[n].
      int total = 0;
      for (int i=0; i<n; i++) {
         Integer I = (Integer) values.get(new Character(d[i]));
         total += I.intValue();
      }

      // Calculate the score. Compare and display a message.
      score.setText(Integer.toString(total));
```

```
            if (total == Integer.valueOf(target.getText().trim()).intValue())
               result.setText("Good luck in the lucky draw");
            else
               result.setText("Bad luck! Try again next week");
         }
         return true;
      }

      private static DataInputStream in;
      private static String winningScore;
      private static TextField target, name, score, result;
      private Hashtable values = new Hashtable ();
      private static final int lettersCounted = 20;
      private static final String
              openingMessage = "See if your name is a winner!";
   }
```

10.3   Sound and images

One of the joys of Java is being able pull in sound and images easily and effectively into a program.

Sound

The `Applet` package has an interface called `AudioClip` which has three methods: `play`, `stop` and `loop`. The `Applet` method `getAudioClip` will return an object which implements this interface, and then we can play that object. The form is:

Audio clip declaration and play

```
AudioClip name;
name = getAudioClip (getCodeBase (), filename);
name.play();
```

The `getCodeBase` method in `Applet` finds out where the applet is running, so that the sound can be played there. The file, at the moment, must be an .au file, not a .wav file, but see below for future developments..

Suppose we have a file called 'ouch.au' and want to play it. The following statements will set this up:

```
AudioClip ouch;
ouch = getAudioClip (getCodeBase (), "ouch.au");
ouch.play();
```

There is also a shorthand version of the above which uses anonymous clips as follows:

```
play(getCodeBase (), "ouch.au");
```

The first form is preferable if you are going to use the clip more than once in a program. Sound is used in Example 10.4.

Images

Images are pixel data that is stored in a file, is brought over the network or is being created in realtime by a graphics engine or video camera. Java has extensive facilities for handling all these, and in particular for addressing the problems of working in a distributed, networked environment. You will have already experienced the varying speeds at which images are downloaded within a browser. One of the more useful options in a browser is to set autoloading of images, meaning that the text will continue to come in while the image is also being displayed. Thus we are not held up just for a picture we may have already seen and do not particularly want.

Java can perform the same kind of control through objects called `Observers`. We can also animate images, control flickering and filtering and run through videos at varying speeds. All of this is a topic on its own. In this chapter, we shall look at a simple fetch of a single image, and the usual way of moving it around on the screen.

Like audio clips, Java has a class for images, and the form for getting one is exactly the same as above, with `AudioClip` replaced by `Image`. Thus an example of fetching an image would be:

```
Image me;
me = getImage (getCodeBase (), "bishop.gif");
```

To display the image, we access the `drawImage` method within the `Graphics` class of the awt. The form for displaying an image is:

Display an image
g.drawImage (*name*, *x*, *y*, *observer*);

The *x* and *y* coordinates specify the top left corner of the spot where the image should be drawn on the screen. In most cases our applet is the observer and therefore we use this as the fourth parameter. For example:

```
g.drawImage (me, 0, 0, this);
```

Moving images

The technique for moving an image around on the screen is a well-known one. Java just makes it easier. In many other systems, when you take an image and draw it somewhere else, you also have to take care to wipe out the old one. In Java, the use of the paint method means that the screen is written correctly as we want it each time. What we have to do is make sure that we specify the coordinates for moving objects in a relative way: that is, using variables rather than constants for their coordinates. Example 10.4 shows how this is done.

EXAMPLE 10.4 Catching the duke

Problem We would like to have a little game where an image moves around the screen, and we move the mouse to try to catch it. The game should have sound as well.

Solution First we need to get hold of a gif file and two au files – one for a hit and one for a miss. In my experience, the gif files should not be larger than 10K and the au files should be at least 6K to be playable. These are guidelines: your computer could possibly handle different sizes. Then we shall draw the image and let the user track it with the mouse. Hits will be rewarded by one sound, and misses by another. In order to reinforce the sounds, we shall also print out corresponding messages.

Algorithm The applet method for moving the image works like this. Once the image has been fetched and drawn, we can obtain its width and height. When the user clicks the mouse, a mouseDown event occurs and we can then check if the current mouse coordinates are within those of the image. After reacting with a win or lose sound and message, we repaint the screen, having moved the image.

Moving the image is done by adding a random amount onto the coordinates that we pass to drawImage.

Now consider carefully the dynamics of the system. When do things actually move? Well nothing happens in the applet, unless we activate an event. So the image will remain stationary until we start to move the mouse. Every time the applet detects a mouseMove event (as opposed to a mouseDown event) it can repaint the screen. Repainting includes changing the x, y coordinates, so the image will seem to move randomly as we move the mouse, and we shall have to 'chase' it. In order to make the game realistic, we move the image only if a current position coordinate is a multiple of 3. Thus the x can change without the y coordinate changing.

Program The program follows the algorithm and forms described above.

```
import java.awt.*;
import java.applet.*;

public class CatchM extends Applet {
   /* The Catching the Duke program     by J M Bishop Dec 1996
      Try to catch the duke and hit it by pressing the left
      mouse button.
      Illustrates sound, images and movement. */

   int x, y, limitx, limity ;
   int wins;
   int d;
   int change;
   Image duke;

   public void init() {
      wins = 0;
      d = size().width - 1; // the size of the window
      change = = d - d/10;
```

```
        duke= getImage(getCodeBase(),"duke.gif");
    }

    public void paint(Graphics g) {
        // wait till the image is in before getting the
        // size. Can't put these statements in init
        limitx = duke.getWidth(this);
        limity = duke.getHeight(this);

        // draw a boundary
        g.drawRect(0, 0, d, d);

        // calculate a new place for the duke
        // and draw it.
        x = (int)(Math.random()*1000) % change;
        y = (int)(Math.random()*1000) % change;
        g.drawImage(duke, x, y, this);
    }

    public boolean mouseDown(Event evt, int mx, int my) {
      requestFocus();
      if((x < mx && mx < x+limitx) &&
         (y < my && my < y+limity)) {
           wins++;
           getAppletContext().showStatus
               ("Caught it! Total " + wins);
           play(getCodeBase(), "sounds/ouch.au");
      } else {
           getAppletContext().showStatus("Missed again.");
           play(getCodeBase(), "sounds/haha.au");
      }
      repaint();
      return true;
    }

    public boolean mouseMove(Event evt, int mx, int my) {
      if((mx % 3 == 0) && (my % 3 == 0))
      repaint();
      return true;
    }
}
```

Testing   Unfortunately, it is very difficult to show a test of the program in the book. This is one case where you are going to have to get onto the web and see and hear it!

Sound, images and the future

The worlds of graphics and audio have produced a great variety of file formats. One needs only bring to mind a few graphics file formats to see this: GIF87, GIF89a, JFIF (often called JPEG), PNG, PBM/PGM/PPM, TIFF, TARGA, PDS/VICAR Sun Rasterfile, BMP, ILBM, PCX, PICT, at almost at any colour depth from 1 to 32 bits. To support every file format is clearly not feasible and Sun made an obvious statement in favour of portability in their decision to support only a few formats in Java.

The essence is that if you want to support exotic formats of whatever nature, then it is incumbent upon you to make the necessary conversions to and from the formats which Java supports. As network bandwidth becomes more freely available, so the formats used for graphics and sound will evolve.

Sound uses far less resources than does graphics. Compare a 72 minute music CD with 650MB of 800×600, 32-bit colour, 55-frames-per-second animation. In the case of the sound, the human ear cannot discern the fact that the music is stored discretely, whereas given a 22 inch monitor, the pixels are visible at a normal viewing distance to most people. This brings home the fact that in order to store sound and especially high-quality graphics, we need high compression ratios if we are not to exhaust even the high-est density storage media at our disposal. These high compression ratios, in turn, imply complicated code (with attendant bloat in program size) and, depending on the algorithms, even some loss in data (as in JFIF).

As if the above were not enough, the law has been an impediment to progress. Reflect upon the amount of time, energy and money poured into creating new formats, merely in order to obviate the need for licensing fees to some patent holder. A case in point is the GIF (Graphics Interchange File) format. It had been used free of charge by devel-opers since its inception in 1987. It appears that CompuServe developed the format, but used LZW (Lempel-Ziv-Welch) compression, which is covered by US patent 4,558,302, held by Unisys Corporation. Unisys decided to enforce this patent, thus forcing all devel-opers of code which use GIF in any way to pay royalties to Unisys or sublicensing fees to CompuServe. That this happened on 29 December 1994, once GIF had become a *de facto* standard, is food for thought. Since then, a new format, called the PNG (Portable Network Graphic) format, has appeared. PNG is essentially a better GIF, but is free and portable.[4]

From the above it should be clear that in order to keep the code small, Java supports as few formats as it does. This begs the question of how to convert existing files. There are free and shareware utilities for almost every conceivable format available. A good place to start would be at ftp://sunsite.unc.edu or one of its mirrors, as well as the Usenet new-groups and their FAQs (Frequently Asked Questions), the canonical site of which is ftp://rtfm.mit.edu.

10.4 Case study 5: The Nature Conservation Project

The project to create a web site related to the animals, birds and trees of Savanna was pos-tulated and described in Chapter 1. Now we have sufficient knowledge to examine how such a system is put together, and what the relationship is between the html scripts, the Java applets and the images that will illustrate the site.

Web pages

Referring to Figure 1.3, which is the first page of the site, we see that it is a simple display consisting of a heading, some text, an image and two links – to animals and trees. A third

---

[4]Refer to Dr. Dobb's Journal of July 1995 for in-depth information on PNG.

link – to birds – is promised but not yet implemented. To create such a page, one can use the interactive editor in a browser such as Netscape 3.0 Gold, or one can write html. Either way, there will be an html document which looks like this:

```
<!DOCTYPE HTML PUBLIC "-//W3C//DTD HTML 3.2//EN">
<HTML>
<HEAD>
  <TITLE></TITLE>
  <META NAME="Author" CONTENT="">
  <META NAME="GENERATOR"
    CONTENT="Mozilla/3.0Gold (X11; I; SunOS 5.4 sun4m) [Netscape]">
</HEAD>
<BODY>

<CENTER<>P><FONT COLOR="#0000FF"><FONT SIZE=+2>Savanna Nature
Conservation</FONT></FONT></P></CENTER>

<CENTER><P>IMG SRC="Elephant.jpg" HSPACEnb=20 HEIGHT=117 WIDTH-178
ALIGN=LEFT></P></CENTER>

<P>FONT COLOR="#000000">Savanna's Nature Conservation Department
aims to help you find out about animals that inhabit the Grasslands
of Africa.
</FONT></P>

<P><FONT COLOR=#000000"> You can also interact with us, register
sightings and add to our data interactively.</FONT></P>

<P><FONT COLOR="#000000"> Version 1 of our homepage has sections on
<A HREF="Animals.html">animals</A>,
birds and <A HREF="Trees.html">trees</A>.</FONT></P>

</BODY>
</HTML>
```

The document starts off with some header information. Thereafter the heading is printed in a larger than normal font. The image of the elephant is expected to be in the same directory as the html file itself, and it is in JPG format. Various dimensions are specified, and it is indicated that the image will go to the left of any text that follows. The next three paragraphs have the text with the last one including two links to other pages with file names Animals.html and Trees.html.

Animals.html follows a similar pattern, except that it has six images to display. At this stage, a schematic diagram of the system can be built up, as in Figure 10.5. The arrows indicate html links and the plain lines indicate images and applets that are included.

Including an applet

The Trees.html document presents the page shown in Figure 1.5. An abbreviated version of the html code for it is:

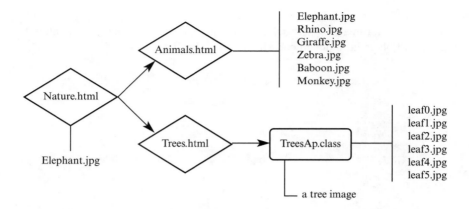

Figure 10.5 *Schematic of the Nature Conservation System.*

```
>!DOCTYPE HTML PUBLIC "-//W3C//DTD HTML 3.2//EN">

>HTML>

<HEAD>
  <TITLE></TITLE>
  <META NAME="Author" CONTENT="Judith Bishop">
  <META NAME="GENERATOR"
  CONTENT="Mozilla/3.0Gold (Win95; I) [Netscape]">
</HEAD>

<BODY>

<CENTER><P><FONT COLOR="#008000"><FONT SIZE=+2>Trees of
Savanna</FONT></FONT></P></CENTER>

<P>With a twig in hand, find out what your tree is by selecting the
leaf type and giving the leaf measurements in millimetres. Some of the
trees we can identify so far are:</P>

<TABLE BORDER=1 WIDTH="100%">

<TR>

<TD><APPLET CODE="TreesAp.class" WIDTH=350 HEIGHT=300><PARAM
NAME="entries" VALUE="19"><PARAM NAME="tree-1" VALUE="Protea"><PARAM
NAME="Codes-1" VALUE="165 175 176"><PARAM NAME="tree-2"
VALUE="Milkplum"><PARAM NAME="codes-2" VALUE="156 166">

… and more parameters

NAME="tree-19" VALUE="Candle acacia"><PARAM NAME="codes-19"
VALUE="666"></APPLET></TD>

<TD ALIGN=RIGHT><FONT COLOR="#0080FF"><FONT SIZE=-1>Protea<BR>
Milkplum <BR>
Wild fig<BR>
```

...   and more trees

```
Fever tree<BR>
Camel thorn<BR>
Umbrella thorn<BR>
Candle acacia</FONT></FONT></TD>
</TR>
</TABLE>
<FONT COLOR="#0080FF"></FONT>
</BODY>
</HTML>
```

Once again, we start with a heading and a short piece of text. Then we want to have an applet next to a list of tree names. An easy way to accomplish this is to set up a table and put the applet in one of the cells and the text in the other. A side effect of using a table is that a nice border is drawn for free.

The applet tag specifies that the applet comes from TreesAp.class, and occupies a certain height and width. Thereafter there is a long list of names of trees and values. These are discussed below. The list of 19 trees is given as part of the html as well, and it is this list which is displayed in blue on the right of the table

Passing data to an applet

Consider once again the Trees applet, the output of which we repeat in Figure 10.6, as run from the appletviewer. The purpose of the applet is to receive three pieces of data – a leaf width, a leaf length and a matching leaf pattern – and to display an image of the tree that

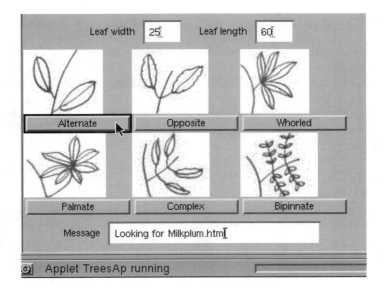

Figure 10.6   *Trees applet output.*

might have been found as a result. Figure 10.6 shows the entering of particulars related to the Milkplum tree, and Figure 1.6 shows the result. This is the one way in which we pass data to an applet – by entering values in fields and clicking buttons.

However, this applet also needs to keep a complete list of trees and their associated particulars. How should this be done? There are three ways:

- Initialize an array with the data, as was done for the till example

- Read the data off a file – but this is not possible via a browser

- Use the browser's PARAM facility.

The PARAM facility operates by having named parameters listed in the html document that the applet can read using a method called `getParameter`. Each parameter must be of the form:

Html PARAM
`<PARAM NAME="formal" VALUE="actual">`

NAME indicates that the string that follows is the name of the parameter that is being sought, so that there can be more than one parameter. If we want to have parameters which form an array (such as our 19 trees) then there must be 19 different strings, such as tree-1, tree-2 and so on. Then within the same set of angle brackets, forming a pair, there is the VALUE to be assigned to that parameter. This is also a string, but obviously can be decoded into a number or whatever other type is required. An example from the applet's html of a parameter is:

```
<PARAM NAME="tree-2" VALUE="Milkplum">
```

The applet constructs a three digit code from the data entered by the user. Each tree could have several (up to four, say) of these codes, since there is a range of leaf sizes that might apply. So for each tree we need its name, as described above, and we also need a set of codes that can be used to identify it. For example, the milkplum has alternate leaves of between 40 and 80 cm long and a width between 20 and 30 cm. This reduces to two codes (in a coding system adapted from Moll, Moll and Page[5]), namely 156 and 166. Therefore matching the tree-2 parameter shown above, we need to have a codes-2 parameter like this:

```
<PARAM NAME="codes-2" VALUE="156 166">
```

Of course, nature is notoriously difficult to code, and in reality there are possibly other trees which would fit a 156 or 166 code as well. But in the main, the Molls' system works and so we can proceed to choose a list of curious-sounding trees, enter them in the html with their codes, and activate the applet.

[5]Eugene and Glen Moll and Nicci Page, *Common Trees*, Struik, 1989

Inside the applet

In order to conclude this example, we should look at the details of the applet:

- how the layout is achieved;

- how the tree names and codes are stored and accessed in a hash table; and

- the event handling necessary collect the user input and return an image.

These are all explained in the comments associated with the Java that follows.

```java
import java.applet.*;
import java.awt.*;
import java.net.*;
import java.util.*;

public class TreesAp extends Applet {

  /* The Trees applet       by J M Bishop  January 1997
     Asks for information about the leaves of a tree.
     Codes the information and brings up an image of
     a possible real tree with that kind of leaf structure.
     Uses tree information from an HTML page.

     Illustrates interaction with a browser,
     nested panel layouts and string tokenisers.
  */

  public void init () {
    // First read in the parameters from the HTML page
    setUpTable();

    // Create the applet screen with two text fields above
    // and one below. In the centre is the grid of nine
    // leaf patterns, each a border panel in its own right
    // with a button in the south and a canvas occupying
    // the rest. The canvas is painted by the leafPattern
    // class.

    setLayout (new BorderLayout());
    Panel p = new Panel ();
    p.add (new Label ("Leaf width",Label.RIGHT));
    width = new TextField (8);
    p.add (width);
    p.add (new Label ("Leaf length",Label.RIGHT));
    length = new TextField (8);
    p.add (length);
    add ("North",p);
    Panel q = new Panel ();
    q.setLayout (new GridLayout (3,3));
    for (int b = 0; b<patterns.length; b++) {
      Panel s = new Panel ();
      s.setLayout (new BorderLayout());
      leafPattern c = new leafPattern (this,b);
      s.add ("Center",c);
```

```
            s.add ("South",new Button(patterns[b]));
            q.add (s);
        }
        add ("Center",q);
        Panel r = new Panel ();
        r.add (new Label ("Message",Label.RIGHT));
        message = new TextField (50);
        r.add (message);
        add ("South",r);

        gotChoice = false;
        gotWidth = false;
        gotLength = false;

    }


    private void setUpTable () {
        String s, item;
        StringTokenizer t;
        int code;
        s = getParameter("entries");
        int n = Integer.parseInt(s);
        for (int I = 0; i<n; I++) {

          // extract a tree name from the html
          String tree = getParameter("tree-"+(i+1));

            // read all its codes
            s = getParameter ("codes-"+(i+1));
            t = new StringTokenizer (s);

            // store each code-tree pair in the table.
            while (true) {
              try {
                item = t.nextToken();
                code = Integer.valueOf (item,trim()).intValue();
                table.put (new Integer(code),tree);
              }
              catch (NoSuchElementException e) {
                break;
              }
            }
        }
    }


    Hashtable table = new Hashtable (100);

    private String patterns [] = {

      "Alternate",
      "Opposite",
      "Whorled",
      "Palmate",
```

```
      "Complex",
      "Bipinnate"};

// A TextField, boolean and integer for each leaf part.
private TextField choice, width, length, message;
private boolean gotChoice, gotWidth, gotLength;
private int c, w, l;

private int readValue (TextField t) {
    int x = Intger.valueOf (t.getText().trim()).intValue();
    t.setEditable (false);
    return x;
}

public boolean action (Event evt, Object arg) {
  if (evt.target == width) {
    w = readValue (width);
    gotWidth = true; }
  else if (evt.target == length) {
    l = readValue (length);
    gotLength = true; }
  else if (arg instanceof String) {
    c = 0;
    while (!arg.equals(patterns[c])) C++;
    gotChoice = true; }
  if (gotChoice & gotLength & gotWidth)
    findTree ();
  return true;
}

private void findTree () {
  int part2=convertLength ();
  int part3=convertWidth ();
  int code = 100*(c+1)+10*part2+part3;
  String tree = (String) table.get (new Integer (code));
  if (tree == null)
    message.setText("No information of that yet"+" Code "+code);
  else
    fetch (tree);
  gotChoice = false;
  gotWidth = false; width.setEditable(true);
  gotLength = false; length.setEditable(true);
}

private void fetch (String treeName) {
  try {
    AppletContext context = getAppletContext ();
     String s = treeName+".html";
     message.setText("Looking for"+s);
     URL u = new URL (getCodeBase(),s);
     context.showDocument (u,"_self");
     }
     catch (MalformedURLException e) {
      showStatus ("No picture for that tree yet");
  }
}
```

```
    private int convertLength () {
    // returns a code based on the leaf length supplied
      if (1<=25) return 4; else
      if (1<=50) return 5; else
      if (1<100)return 6; else
      if (1<=200)      return 7; else
          return 8;
    }

    private int convertWidth () {
    // returns a code based on the leaf width supplied
      if (w<=10)return 4; else
      if (w<=20)return 5; else
      if (w<=40)return 6; else
      if (w<=80)return 7; else
          return 8;
    }
  }
```

Restrictions

While writing applets which pull in images seems a great idea, it has a serious restriction: other people's pictures are usually copyrighted. The implication is that we cannot use them freely in our own web pages, even experimental ones. We must use our own pictures, ones that we own. For this reason, the photographs in Chapter 1 were taken by myself, and the diagrams drawn especially for this book.

The infrastructure provided by Java's multimedia facilities is so powerful and easy to use that one tends to forget that the content required to fill an applet or web page also has to be created. Look out for shareware images, and when in doubt, ask permission from the author, artist, originator or publisher.

SUMMARY

Applets are similar to applications, but because they run within the context of the `Applet` class, they do not need a main method, and all input–output must be through the awt. An applet must have an accompanying html file which calls it. This html file can be supplied to an applet viewer or to a browser, or can be called from within a web page. Applets run in browsers stop only when the page they are in is discarded. Java provides a considerable amount of security surrounding applets so that they cannot cause damage after coming over the network.

Applets, as well as applications, can make use of sound and images. Both can be simply set up in Java using objects to connect to au and gif or jpeg files respectively. The images can be made to move on the screen by repainting the screen with new coordinates.

QUIZ

10.1   What is the method to be used instead of `println` in applets?

10.2   Compared with awt applications, why do applets not have `main` methods?

10.3   Applets usually have an `init` method: what is its counterpart in an application?

10.4 Give the html tag for running an applet in Orange.class with a width and length of 200 pixels.

10.5 What does the `getCodeBase` method do?

10.6 What are the two image formats supported by Java?

10.7 What does the `getAppletContext` method do?

10.8 Given the html parameter tag

```
<PARAM NAME="yenexchange" VALUE="6.578">
```

what would be the corresponding Java statement to get the yen exchange rate read in?

10.9 In Example 10.4, what happens each time we call `repaint()` from the `mouseMove` method?

10.10 On average, which requires more storage space: sound or images?

PROBLEMS

10.1 **Your trees**. The Nature Project is in its infancy and still needs to be considerably extended to fulfill its mandate of allowing visitors to the site the ablity to add new specimens that they identify. If you watch the *Java Gently* web site, you may see new versions of the system as they become available. One improvement you could make on your own is to change the list of trees to reflect your own environment. You should be able to do this by altering only the html.

10.2 **Till user's guide**. How to use the till applet is not really intuitive. Set up an html page which has some instructions on the left and includes the till applet on the right.

10.3 **Savanna News Competition Rules**. Create a set of rules for the name competition and embed the competition applet in an html document. If you have a scanner, scan in the masthead from your local newspaper and put it on top. Otherwise create a big heading with a new and interesting font.

10.4 **Lots of dukes**. Add more dukes to the catching applet. Have each move at a different rate.

10.5 **Better competition interface**. Alter the competition applet so that letter values come in from the html document.

10.6 **Letter value update**. Create a separate applet with a password which can be selected from the Competition html page and will enable one of the newspaper employees to change the letter values interactively.

10.7 **Nelson's applet**. Referring to exercise 9.9, put the GUI version of Nelson's coffee shop in an applet and html document.

10.8 **Banking rates**. Consider example 5.2 on exchange rates. Create an applet and html document to provide an interactive version of the program for buying foreign currency.

CHAPTER 11

Networking

11.1 Connecting via URLs

Java was built to access the network. It has extensive features for network programming at various levels from connecting via URLs or sockets to common gateway interfaces (CGI) and database connecting (JDBC), as well the means for controlling multiple threads within a single program. We shall examine most these in this chapter by using examples in the usual *Java Gently* way. The chapter stops short of looking at CGI and JDBC, leaving these to a later course.

The `java.net` package contains the features described in this chapter, unless otherwise specified.

URL contents

Java has a class called URL which enables the data referred to by a URL to be downloaded, and some interaction with the resource to be achieved. Given a string, Java will create an appropriate URL which can then be used in one of two ways:

- get the complete contents in one go using `getContent`;

- establish a `URLConnection` to enable interaction as defined by the resource's protocol, perhaps via I/O streams.

The form for creating a URL is

URL creation

```
URL name = new URL (String);
URL name = new URL (base, String);
getDocumentBase ();
getCodeBase ();
```

For example,

```
URL info = new
("file:/u/jbishop/java/Book/chap11/Walkmen/Museum.java");
```

will find the resource indicated and set up a reference to it from the Java program. The second form of the URL constructor enables us to have relative URLs. The above declaration can be split into two as follows:

```
URL info = new
   ("file:/u/jbishop/java/Book/chap11/Walkmen/");
museumURL = new (info, "Museum.java");
```

URLs can also be relative to the applet that is running. `getDocumentBase` returns the URL of the page from where the applet was loaded. `getCodeBase` returns the URL of the applet itself. Examples of the use of `getCodeBase` were shown in Section 10.3 and Example 10.4. The catching the duke applet refers to its own location and to files and subdirectories to display its image and sound files:

```
duke = getImage (getCodeBase(), "duke.gif");
play (getCodeBase(), "sounds/ouch.au");
```

Both constructors make sure that you have the correct syntax for forming a URL. If not, a `malformedURLException` is thrown. It is therefore usual to put the declaration in a try-statement and catch the exception.

Our first example uses a URL very simply to get a whole text file and print it out.

EXAMPLE 11.1   Fetching a file

Problem   A file known by its URL needs to be printed out.

Solution   Connect to the URL and use the `getContent` method.

Program   The program is very simple:

```
import java.io.*;
import java.net.*;

class Fetch {
  /* Fetching a file       by J M Bishop January 1997

     Illustrates the URL.getContent() method.
     Must be called with an argument which is a URL
     e.g. file:/ ... or file:\*/

  public static void main(String[] args)
              throws MalformedURLException, IOException {
    URL filename = new URL(args[0]);
    System.out.println((String) filename.getContent());
  }
}
```

We first import the network package. Then we pick up the name of a file from a run-time parameter, given by `args[0]`. Applying the `getContent` method, the whole file is converted to a Java string, which is then printed.

Testing A typical call of the program from a command line would be:

```
java Fetch file:/u/jbishop/java/Book/chap11/Walkmen/Museum.java
```

which will display the contents of the file.

Fetching images

Will `getContent` work with other forms as well as text? Certainly we can fetch and display images using only slight modifications to the above program. The first is that the program must pull in the services of the awt, and in particular of the `awt.image` package. Therefore it must have a `paint` method and pass the fetched image to be drawn there.

It would be nice if we could simply replace `String` by `Image` as the type cast, but Java needs to treat images with a bit more care. If `f is` the frame we are in, then

```
f.createImage ((ImageProducer) imagename.getContent());
```

will return an image. `ImageProducer` is an interface, so we type cast the contents of the file into a class that conforms to the requirements of this interface. In the `Component` class, which `Frame` inherits, we call the `createImage` method which will convert an `ImageProducer` interface object to an `Image` object.

EXAMPLE 11.2   Fetching an image

Illustration   The following program illustrates the fetching of an image from a URL.

```
import java.awt.*;
import java.awt.image.*;
import java.net.*;
import java.io.*;

public class FetchImage extends Frame {

   /* Fetch an image program by J M Bishop Jan 1997
      fetches a jpg or gif image into a window.

      Illustrates use of awt.image. */

   private Image i;

   public void paint(Graphics g) {
     g.drawImage(i, 50, 50, this);
   }

   public static void main(String[] args) throws Exception {

     // Create the window
     FetchImage f = new FetchImage();

     // Get the image
     URL imagename = new URL(args[0]);
     f.i = f.createImage((ImageProducer) imagename.getContent());

     // Activate the awt to display the image
     f.resize(300, 300);
     f.show();
   }

   public boolean handleEvent (Event e) {
     if (e.id == Event.WINDOW_DESTROY)
        System.exit (0);
     return super.handleEvent(e);
   }

}
```

Testing   To test out the program, we run it with a known image file name, as in:

```
java FetchImage file:/u/jbishop/java/Book/chap1/elephant.jpg
```

A window will open up (as is usual with awt programs) and the elephant image will be displayed therein. The window can be closed by clicking the close box, because we have included a `handleEvent` method for this purpose.

URL connections

`getContent` is powerful and rather nice to have. But suppose we wish to look at each line of the file as it comes over. In this case, we shall have to set up a connection to the resource and create an input stream.

The relevant form for achieving this is:

Creating a URL connection

```
URLConnection connection = URLname.openConnection ();
DataInputStream streamname =
    new DataInputStream (connection.getInputStream());
```

The stream now acts as any normal input source. Its use is illustrated in the following example.

EXAMPLE 11.3   Listing a file

Problem   It is useful to be able to list files together with line numbers. Assuming the information is coming over the Internet via a URL, how can we produce such a listing?

Solution   Connect into the resource and read each line at a time, printing a line number with it.

Program   The program uses a local static method, list, just to separate the two operations of making the connection and printing the file.

```
import java.io.*;
import java.net.*;
import java.util.*;

class Lister {
  /* Listing a file      by J M Bishop January 1997

     Illustrates a URL connection.
     Must be called with an argument which is a URL
     e.g. file:/ ... or file:\*/

   static void list (URLConnection c, URL u) throws IOException {

      // print a heading of the file name and date
      String s = u.toExternalForm();
      System.out.println(s+" on "+new Date());

      // underline the file name and date (which takes 32 chars)
      for (int i=0; i<s.length()+32; i++) System.out.print('-');
      System.out.println("\n");

      // list each line with a line number
      DataInputStream in = new DataInputStream (c.getInputStream());
      for (int i=1; ; i++) {
        String line = in.readLine ();
        if (line == null) break;
        System.out.println(i+" "+line);
      }
   }
}
```

```
    public static void main(String[] args)
                throws MalformedURLException, IOException {
        URL resource = new URL(args[0]);
        URLConnection connection = resource.openConnection();
        list (connection, resource);
    }
}
```

Testing If we ran the program thus:

```
java Lister file:/u/jbishop/java/Book/chap11/List/Lister.java
```

we would get the same file out as follows:

```
file:/u/jbishop/java/Book/chap11/List/Lister.java on Thu Jan 16
                                                13:24:38 GMT 1997
-----------------------------------------------------------------------

1 import java.io.*;
2 import java.net.*;
3 import java.util.*;
4
5 class Lister {
6    /* Listing a file by J M Bishop January 1997
7
8       Illustrates the URL connections.
9       Must be called with an argument which is a URL
10       e.g. file:/ ... or file:\*/
11
12      static void list (URLConnection c, String s) throws
                                                    IOException {
13
14        // print a heading of the file name and date
15        System.out.println(s+" on "+new Date());
16
17        // underline the file name and date (which takes 32 chars)
18        for (int i=0; i<s.length()+32; i++) System.out.print('-');
19        System.out.println("\n");
20
21        // list each line with a line number
22        DataInputStream in = new DataInputStream
                                        (c.getInputStream());
23        for (int i=1; ; i++) {
24          String line = in.readLine ();
25          if (line == null) break;
26          System.out.println(i+" "+line);
27        }
28      }
29
30      public static void main(String[] args)
31                  throws MalformedURLException, IOException {
32        URL resource = new URL(args[0]);
33        URLConnection connection = resource.openConnection();
```

```
34          list (connection, args[0]);
35      }
36 }
```

From the listing we can see that the connection is opened on line 33. It is then passed to the `list` method for processing, together with the original argument from the command line. `list` needs this string in order to print the name of the file, which is done on line 15. The input stream is set up on line 22 and thereafter the loop takes care of the printing. The loop ends when `readLine` returns a null object (line 25). Notice that a null object is quite different from an empty line: lines 7, 11, 13 and so on are empty, but exist as strings and therefore are printed.

URLs are useful when we are dealing with applets and web pages. The above examples show that Java can integrate well into this environment. In Section 11.4 we shall look at connections at one level lower down: that of ports and sockets. But first we need to tackle multi-threading.

11.2 Multi-threading

In operating system terms, a program that is running is known as a **process**. An operating system can be running several processes for different users at any one time. Not all of these need be active: they could be awaiting their share of processor time, or they could be waiting for some information, such as user input.

Now within a single process, the same division into separately runnable tasks can be made. In Java these are known as **threads** and a program with threads is called **multi-threaded**. Each thread looks like it is running on its own. It can communicate with other threads in the same process, though care must be taken when this is done through changing the value of variables.

In the same way that the operating system must share time between processes, so it must share time between threads. The fairest way to share is to give each thread a time slice, at the end of which it is suspended and the next thread ready to run is given a chance. The Windows NT and 95 operating systems follow this approach. A less attractive method is for a thread to run until it needs information from elsewhere (another thread, or the user, say), and only then to relinquish control of the processor. The problem with this approach is that a single thread can hog the processor. At the moment, the Sun operating systems still support multi-threading in this way.

Why threads?

Why do we actually need threads? Two particular situations illustrate their value:

1. **User interfacing.** If an applet or graphics application is busy drawing or displaying text, the user may wish to stop it. If a button is provided, we can press the

Compute thread Button thread

Time

Work

Work

Wait for button press

Work

Wait for button press

Detect button pressed

Work

Throw exeption across

Handle exception
and stop

Figure 11.1 *Multi-threading for a user interface.*

button, *but* the program will only detect the button press, once it has reached a passive state: that is, it has finished computing or outputting and is waiting for events. However, if the button is being handled by a separate thread, the opportunity to react will come around regularly, even while the other computation is proceeding. Figure 11.1 illustrates the time line associated with two such threads.

2. **Many instances.** Sometimes one wants identical copies of a picture, multiple windows or different versions of a computation to be available simultaneously. For example, the set of traffic lights of Example 9.4 could be duplicated and we could watch two or three sets working at once. Each would be handled by a separate thread. In the simple case, the threads will be straight copies of each other and will run independently. Java will also allow the threads to communicate and synchronize their activities, as discussed in Section 11.3.

From the user's point of view, the presence of multiple threads should be transparent. From the programmer's side, though, work has to be done to set up the threads in the first place, to keep them running and to detect when they should finish. During the lifetime of a process, threads can be created and destroyed at will. They are a cost-effective way of handling processor power and memory for non-trivial programs.

Setting up threads

To 'thread' a program, we first have to identify those methods that can run independently. Usually, these are already in a class and it is the class that becomes a thread, possibly in multiple instantiations.

Thread is a class in the java.lang package. Any class that wishes to be a thread class, must inherit from Thread. In addition, Thread implements the Runnable interface, which has one method, run. Therefore the prospective thread class must implement run as well. Basically, we take all the executable part of the class and put it in a run method (allowing run of course to call methods to assist it as usual).

The main method is by default a thread, and it is from there, or from another active method such as action, that the other threads are set in motion. As we shall see in later examples, threads can spawn their own threads as well.

Let us consider an example of changing a program to have threads. Take Example 9.4, the traffic light calibration. We would like the lights to rotate through their assigned sequence of red–yellow–green, while the buttons and other choices at the bottom of the screen are still active. In the original program, the main method sets up the headings and buttons, and then creates a canvas which has a paint method to draw the lights. Omitting the constructor, handleEvent and action methods, the program looked like this:

```java
import java.awt.*;

public class Traffic extends Frame {
   /* The Traffic light program      by J M Bishop Oct 1996
      Displays a representation of traffic lights,
      in preparation for a simulation.
      Illustrates panels and canvases and the
      BorderLayout manager.

   public Traffic ( ) {
     —
   }

   public boolean action(Event evt, Object arg) {
     —
   }

   public static void main(String[] args) {
     Frame f = new Traffic ( );
     f.resize(300, 200);
     f.show();
   }

   private LightsCanvas lights;
}

class LightsCanvas extends Canvas {
   public void paint (Graphics g) {
     g.drawOval (97, 10, 30, 68);
     g.setColor (Color.red);
```

```
      g.fillOval (105, 15, 15, 15);
      g.setColor (Color.yellow);
      g.fillOval (105, 35, 15, 15);
      g.setColor (Color.green);
      g.fillOval (105, 55, 15, 15);
      g.fillOval (105, 85, 15, 15);
      g.setColor (Color.black);
      g.drawString ("RED", 15 ,28);
      g.drawString ("YELLOW", 15, 48);
      g.drawString ("GREEN", 15, 68);
      g.drawString ("WALK", 15, 98);
    }
  }
```

Now we need to turn `LightsCanvas` into a thread. In other words, it must

- extend `Thread`, and

- have a `run` method which repeatedly executes.

But a class can inherit from only one other class, so we have to adopt the following strategy:

1. Let `LightsCanvas` extend `Thread`.

2. Pass an instance of the canvas to a new `LightsCanvas` constructor.

3. Store the reference to the canvas instance in the thread locally.

4. Call `getGraphics` to establish the canvas in the window with which the thread is dealing.

The `paint` method as it exists above is called automatically via the awt. Since we are now going to have independent drawing going on in a single window, we had better have it more under control. In other words, the `run` method should explicitly cause the drawing to be done.

The simplest run method is:

```
public void run () {
  while (true) {
    draw ();
    try {sleep (500);}  catch (InterruptedException e) {}
  }
}
```

Here we repeatedly draw the picture, waiting at least 500 milliseconds before doing it again. The `InterruptedException` can be thrown by the system to start the thread up if its turn has come round in the meantime.

Putting it all together, the new version of the `LightsCanvas`, with a new name, is:

```
import java.awt.*;

  class SetOfLights extends Thread {

    SetOfLights (Canvas c) {
      area = c;
    }

    public void run () {
      while (true) {
        draw ();
        try {sleep (500);}  catch (InterruptedException e) {}
      }
    }

    void draw ( ) {
      Graphics g = area.getGraphics();
      g.drawOval (97, 10, 30, 68);
      g.setColor(Color.red);
      g.fillOval (105, 15, 15, 15);
      g.setColor(Color.yellow);
      g.fillOval (105, 35, 15, 15);
      g.setColor(Color.green);
      g.fillOval (105, 55, 15, 15);
      g.fillOval (105, 85, 15, 15);
      g.setColor(Color.black);
      g.drawString ("RED",    15, 28);
      g.drawString ("YELLOW",15, 48);
      g.drawString ("GREEN", 15, 68);
      g.drawString ("WALK",  15, 98);
    }

  private Canvas area;
}
```

To create the thread and set it running, we call its constructor and then call `start`:

```
SetOfLights lights = new SetOfLights (area);
lights.start();
```

The `Thread` class

After the above informal introduction to threads, let us consider the `Thread` class more specifically. Among many others, it has the following important methods:

Thread creation and methods
Threadclass threadname = **new** *Threadclass (parameters);* **new** *Threadclass (parameters)*
start (); run (); stop ();
sleep *(milliseconds);* yield ();

A new thread is created in the same way as any other object declaration, as shown in the first line of the form. Alternatively, if there is no need to give the thread a name which its parent knows, we can use the second form, which simply creates a thread of the given class. Threads are dynamically created in Java: we do not need to state in advance how many of a certain kind of thread there will be. Every time a new thread declaration is executed, a new thread object comes into existence.

`start`, `run` and `stop` are the three important thread methods. After a thread has been created via its constructor, the creating method calls `start`, which is defined in the `Thread` class. `Start` will cause `run` to be called, thus causing the thread to join the operating system's list of threads waiting to run. In a while, it will get its chance at the processor and start executing independently.

`run` will usually consist of a loop which continues until some condition is met, in which case the loop ends. At this point the `run` method meets a natural end and the thread dies as a result.

The `stop` method can be called from one thread to another and once received via the `Thread` class will cause the called thread to die. In most cases, the `stop` method is not used, and 'natural death' is more common.

`sleep` and `yield` are class methods. Both cause the thread to relinquish the processor. `sleep` will wait for the specified time, and then the thread will be ready to run again. `yield` is not needed if the operating system is sharing time between procesors, but if it is not, then calling `yield` is a way for a thread to stand back and give others a chance.

Java also supports priorities for threads. These can be set as a value between 1 (low) and 10 (high) and direct the operating system as to which thread to run next, if there is a choice. Higher priority threads that are waiting to run will always go first.

It is now time to put this all together in a working example.

EXAMPLE 11.4 Traffic lights flashing

Problem The static representation of the lights in Example 9.4 needs to be improved to show the lights actually flashing. Furthermore, we would like to have more than one set of lights operational at any one time, so that we can compare changes.

Solution Implementing the flashing is a question of awt graphics programming. Displaying several lights can be done with threads. We create a new class for the lights as discussed above, have it extend `Thread`, and repeatedly draw the full set of lights. The time specified for the sleep will then represent the time that one of the lights is on and the others off. Using a switch-statement, we can implement the required green–yellow–red sequence.

Class design Because we are using threads, the relationship between the classes in awt and those we define is slightly altered. The new class diagram (refer back to Example 9.4) is shown in Figure 11.2.

The differences are those that we have already explained. `setOfLights` inherits `Thread`, and so cannot also inherit `Canvas` as well. Instead, the canvas, called `area`, is passed as a parameter from `Traffic`'s `action` method to `SetofLights`' constructor.

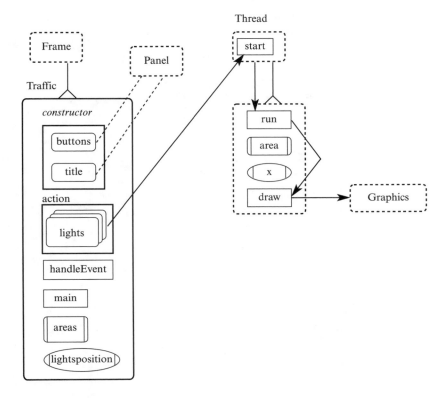

Figure 11.2 *Class diagram for traffic lights with threads.*

The reference to this canvas is used by the `draw` method to access the methods in the `Graphics` class successfully.

Program   The `SetofLights` class is as follows:

```
import java.awt.*;

  class SetOfLights extends Thread {

    SetOfLights (Canvas c, int x) {
      area = c;
      this.x = x;
    }

    public void run () {
      while (true) {
        for (int light = 0; light < 3; light++) {
          draw (light);
          try {sleep (500);}  catch (InterruptedException e) {}
        }
      }
    }
```

```
    void draw (int light) {
      Graphics g = area.getGraphics();
      g.setColor(Color.black);
      g.drawOval (x-8, 10, 30, 68);
      g.drawOval (x, 85, 15, 15);
      g.drawString ("RED",    x-90, 28);
      g.drawString ("YELLOW", x-90, 48);
      g.drawString ("GREEN",  x-90, 68);
      g.drawString ("WALK",   x-90, 98);

      switch (light) {
      case 0: {g.setColor(Color.red);
        g.fillOval (x, 15, 15, 15);
        g.setColor(Color.lightGray);
        g.fillOval (x, 35, 15, 15);
        g.fillOval (x, 55, 15, 15);
        break;}
      case 1: {g.setColor(Color.green);
        g.fillOval (x, 55, 15, 15);
        g.setColor(Color.lightGray);
        g.fillOval (x, 15, 15, 15);
        g.fillOval (x, 35, 15, 15);
        break;}
      case 2: {
        g.setColor(Color.yellow);
        g.fillOval (x, 35, 15, 15);
        g.setColor(Color.lightGray);
        g.fillOval (x, 15, 15, 15);
        g.fillOval (x, 55, 15, 15);
        break;}
      }
    }

  private Canvas area;
  private int x;
}
```

The run method has its own inner loop, going through the three light phases. Depending on which light has to be shown, the switch colours one circle in with the appropriate colour and renders the other two in grey. The program that activates these threads is:

```
import java.awt.*;

public class Traffic extends Frame {
  public Traffic ( ) {

    setTitle("Traffic Lights");
    Panel title = new Panel ();
    title.add(new Label("Savanna Traffic Light Simulation"));
    add ("North", title);
    area = new Canvas ();
    add("Center",area);
    Panel buttons = new Panel ();
```

```
      buttons.add(new Button("Start"));
      Choice c = new Choice ();
      c.addItem ("Red");
      c.addItem ("Yellow");
      c.addItem ("Green");
      c.addItem ("Walk");
      buttons.add (c);
      buttons.add (new Label ("Duration"));
      duration = new TextField ("",3);
      duration.setEditable(false);
      buttons.add (duration);
      buttons.add(new Button("Walk"));
      buttons.add(new Button("Close"));
      add ("South",buttons);
   }

   public boolean action(Event evt, Object arg) {
      if (arg.equals("Start")) {
         SetOfLights lights = new SetOfLights(area, lightsPosition);
         lights.start();
         lightsPosition += 150;
      }
      else if (arg.equals("Close")) {
         this.hide();
         this.dispose();
         System.exit(0);
      }
      else return super.action(evt,arg);
      return true;
   }

   public static void main(String[] args) {
      Frame f = new Traffic ( );
      f.resize(450, 210);
      f.show();
   }

   public boolean handleEvent(Event evt) {
      if (evt.id == Event.WINDOW_DESTROY) System.exit(0);
      return super.handleEvent(evt);
   }

   private Canvas area;
   private int lightsPosition = 105;
   private TextField duration;
}
```

The new addition to the button panel is a Start button. When pressed, this will start up a new thread for another set of lights. In order to have the lights drawn across the window, we supply a new x starting position, which increases by 150 pixels for each light.

Testing   Figure 11.3 shows the screen with three lights at different phases.

Figure 11.3 *Traffic lights in multiple copies using threads.*

Communication between threads

The threads in the above example are quite independent. However, it is often the case that threads need to pass information between each other – results of subcalculations, or signals to change to another mode of working, for example. Because threads are objects, such communication can use the normal object techniques, such as calling methods or updating non-private variables. On the face of it, there would seem to be no problem in threads communicating in either of these ways. However, conflicts can occur which would cause the program as a whole to give incorrect results. This is the subject of Section 11.3. Meanwhile, we can proceed with the traffic example, and show how simple, non-conflicting communication can be handled.

EXAMPLE 11.5 Traffic lights for walking

Problem Right at the beginning of the traffic light simulation (Example 9.3) we mentioned the objective of examining the effect of pedestrians pressing the Walk button. The Walk button is present in the control panel of the simulation as it stands. We would now like it to cause the walk light to flash as soon as a red light phase comes around again.

Solution The first consideration is whether one leaves a single Walk button for all sets of lights on the screen, or whether we alter the screen to have a Walk button under each set. The latter seems more reasonable, but is more difficult to implement because we are using a very simple border layout to keep the lights in the centre panel and the buttons in the south. Therefore we elect to keep the one button, but we select the set of lights we want affected by clicking somewhere in that general area. The mouseDown method in the awt is of assistance here.

The second point is what do we actually do once the Walk button is pressed. Well, we must pass the information over to the particular thread running that set of lights. The thread need not react immediately, because the requirement is that it continues through its cycle until it reaches red, and then starts flashing the walk light. We can therefore achieve the communication by having a Boolean variable called Walk in the lights thread, and setting it to true once Walk is pressed.

How do we know which thread to talk to? Well, each thread will need to be recorded in the main program with a name, and the simplest way is to have an array of threads. Depending on the mouse press on the central canvas, we deduce which set of lights is intended, and can make any subsequent press of Walk refer to that thread in the array.

Class design   The class diagram in Figure 11.4 reflects these changes. Previously, the lights objects were created inside `action`, and the name, `lights`, was reused each time a new one was needed. Now because we need to keep track of the names of the threads throughout the lifetime of the program, we declare an array of threads as private. Each new element of the array is activated via a call to `start`. `action` also affects the `walk` variable of each of the threads, and this is indicated specifically by an additonal arrowed line.

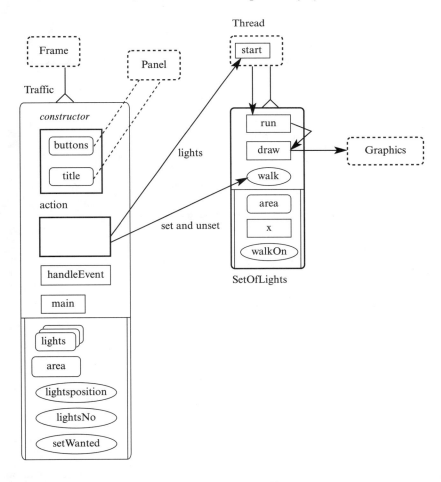

Figure 11.4 *Class diagram for traffic lights with walking.*

Program   The main `Traffic` program is the same as before, except for the addition of a `mouseDown` handler method and the change in the reaction to the Start and Walk buttons being pressed. In fact, in this version of the program, the Start button is deliberately renamed the New Set button, to emphasize the creation of a new thread. Omitting the constructor, `handleEvent` and `main` methods, the class is:

```java
import java.awt.*;

public class Traffic extends Frame {
  public Traffic ( ) {
  … as before
  }

  public boolean mouseDown (Event evt, int x, int y) {
    setWanted = x / lightsWidth;
    return true;
  }

  public boolean action(Event evt, Object arg) {
    if (arg.equals("New Set")) {
      lights[lightsNo] = new SetOfLights(area, lightsPosition);
      lights[lightsNo].start();
      lightsPosition += lightsWidth;
      lightsNo++;
    }
    else if (arg.equals("Walk"))
      lights[setWanted].walk = true;
    else if (arg.equals("Close")) {
      this.hide();
      this.dispose();
      System.exit(0);
    }
    else return super.action(evt,arg);
    return true;
  }

  public static void main(String[] args) {
  … as before
  }

  public handleEvent (Event evt) {
    … as before
  }

  private Canvas area;
  private int lightsPosition = 105;
  private static final int lightsWidth = 150;
  private SetOfLights [] lights = new SetOfLights [3];
  private int lightsNo, setWanted;
  private TextField duration;
}
```

The reaction to the Walk button is to set the `walk` variable in the correct thread to true. The desired thread has been pre-selected by clicking the mouse somewhere on the screen and dividing by the width of a full set of lights, which we have set at 150 pixels.

The logic associated with the lights proceeds as follows. Each time the red light is about to come on, we need to check if the `walk` variable is set. If so, we go into a separate loop for 10 cycles which keeps the red light on, and alternates the walk light between green and grey. The `run` method becomes:

```
public void run () {
   while (true) {
      for (int light = 0; light < 3; light++) {
         if (light==red & walk) {
            walkOn = false;
            for (int i=0; i < 11; i++) {
               draw(light);
               try {sleep (500);}  catch (InterruptedException e) {}
               walkOn = !walkOn;
            }
            walk = false;
         }
         else {
            draw (light);
            try {sleep (500);}  catch (InterruptedException e) {}
         }
      }
   }
}
```

The `walkOn` variable is set and unset to control the flashing of the walk light. After ten iterations, `walk` is reset and the set of lights can proceed to the next normal phase, which would be green. The appropriate change in the `draw` method is at the end where we add:

```
        if (light==red & walk) {
          if (walkOn)
            g.setColor(Color.green);
          else g.setColor(Color.lightGray);
          g.fillOval(x+1, 85, 14, 14);
        }
        else {
            g.setColor(Color.black);
            g.drawOval (x, 85, 15, 15);
        }
      }

   private Canvas area;
   private int x;
   boolean walk = false;
   private static final int red = 0;
   boolean walkOn = false;
}
```

Testing   The program can be run as before, and the Walk button can be pressed for each of the sets of lights at different times. Extensions to the program, including setting the duration that a light is on, are discussed in the problems at the end of the chapter.

11.3 Synchronizing between threads

In the above example, the main program communicated with each thread individually. In other words, we had channels of communication as shown in Figure 11.5.

There was no possibility that `Traffic` calling `lights[0]` could interfere with the communication between `Traffic` and `lights[1]`, say. However, suppose for the sake of illustration that the lights threads have each to alter the same variable in `Traffic` (for example, a count of the number of times yellow lights come on). The calling diagram would be as shown in Figure 11.6.

Now there is a chance that the threads could interfere with each other's operation, leading to corrupted values. The corruption could happen like this. Thread 1 starts to increment a variable with value 52 to 53, say. It gets halfway through before it is interrupted by the operating system and Thread 2 is given the processor. Thread 2 reads the current value of the variable, which is still 52, updates it to 53 and continues. Control is eventually passed back to Thread 1 which is still in the middle of the update. It has already read the variable's value as 52 and so writes 53 back. The correct answer would have been 54 (after two updates), but the interference meant that Thread 1 overwrote the update made by Thread 2.

To avoid such a possibility, Java provides means for threads to **synchronize** their activities. There are two levels of synchronization provided:

- protection of shared resources;

- signalling changes in conditions between threads.

Protecting shared resources

In order to protect resources such as variables that could be accessed by several threads at once, we funnel updates through a method, and mark the method with a special modifier:

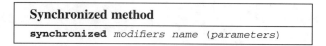

Synchronized method

synchronized *modifiers name (parameters)*

Figure 11.5

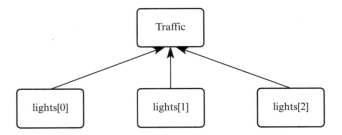

Figure 11.6

Java then guarantees that once a thread has gained access to a synchronized method, it will finish the method before any other thread gains access to that or any other synchronized method in that object. Such threads are placed in a queue, awaiting their turn. The thread therefore has exclusive access to the object from within the synchronized method. An object with one or more synchronized methods acts as a **monitor** on its data.[1]

In order not to delay the other threads unduly, synchronized methods should be kept to a minimum and only contain statements which are genuinely sensitive to interference.

The following small program illustrates the difference between using a synchronized method and not using it.

```
import java.io.*;

class TestSynch {

  /* The Test Synchronize program      J M Bishop  January 1997

     Has two threads altering a common counter.

     Illustrates the need for thread synchronization.
     Counter should remain 0 at all times.
     The program could start to print non-zero values
     unless update is designated synchronized. */

  public static void main (String args []) {
     Updater thread1 = new Updater ();
     thread1.start ();
     Updater thread2 = new Updater ();
     thread2.start();
     Holder h = new Holder ();
  }
}

class Holder {
  static void display () {
     {System.out.print(counter+" ");}
  }
```

[1] **Monitors** are a very important operating system concept invented by Per Brinch Hansen and Tony Hoare in the early 1970s.

```
    static int counter = 0;
    static void update () {
      counter++;
      counter --;
      display();
    }
  }


  class Updater extends Thread {

    public void run () {
      while (true) {
        Holder.update();
        try {sleep(5);}  catch(InterruptedException e) {}
      }
    }
  }
```

The two update threads call the `update` method in the `holder` thread to add and subtract one from a counter. The net result should always be zero. Potentially, though, `thread1` and `thread2` could interfere with each other in updating the counter. We should therefore designate `update` as `synchronized`.

Should `display` also be synchronized? No, `display` is a passive method, merely looking at the value of `counter` and sending it to be printed. But what if both threads start displaying at once: will the output lines become entangled? Fortunately not, because `print` and all similar methods in the `PrintStream` class are declared as `synchronized`. Therefore only one method can be using them to affect the `System.out` object at once.

Signalling between threads

Protecting shared resources is one aspect of synchronization. The other is indicating to a thread when a condition that it is waiting for has been met. The methods involved are:

Synchronization methods
`wait ();` `notify ();`

If a thread finds that it cannot continue because the object it is busy with is not quite in the right state, it calls `wait` from within a synchronized method belonging to that object. The thread will then be placed on a queue associated with the object.

A thread that has altered some relevant data or conditions in an object should call `notify`. This will give all the waiting threads a chance to recheck their conditions for getting on the queue. Some of them may then be able to run at the next opportunity provided by the operating system.

In theory, threads that are waiting should eventually be notified that they can run. In practice, this depends on careful programming, considering all possible combinations. It is quite possible to construct a program where a certain condition does not get set and we find thread one waiting for thread two which is waiting for thread one. This situation is called **deadlock** and means of detecting and preventing it are covered in courses on operating systems and concurrency. Java can detect some logical errors, particularly if `wait` and `notify` are used with unsynchronized methods. In this case an `IllegalMonitorStateException` will be thrown.

The next, rather extensive, example shows how threads of different kinds can be started up at run-time and synchronized to achieve a common goal.

EXAMPLE 11.6 Walkman hire

Problem Savanna Museum is going to introduce a modern system of hiring out Walkman tape players which visitors can listen to instead of having guided tours of the exhibits on display. At the entrance to the museum, there is a counter where a variable number of volunteer helpers is on duty at any one time to hire out the Walkmen. The charge is one graz. Visitors arrive in groups of between 1 and 10 and wait until the correct number of Walkmen is available. We would like to simulate the system in advance, to see how many Walkmen will be needed for a given arrival rate of visitors.

Solution How does one begin to tackle a simulation such as this? The stepping off point is to draw a diagram of the real-life set-up, and to use this to identify the objects and their interactions. Figure 11.7 gives a start.

The day begins with the museum opening with a given number of Walkmen, and then counter threads being created, one for each helper available. The museum is a monitor class with two synchronized methods: hire and replace. The counter helpers call hire, and when their request for a given number of Walkmen is satisfied, they create a new visitor thread, simulating the idea of a visitor group wandering around the museum on their own. The visitors drop their Walkmen directly off at the museum exit, without joining counter queues again. This has the effect of replenishing the number of Walkmen for hire, and may enable a helper who to satisy a request.

For example, suppose there are only two Walkmen left. In the diagram, neither group at the counter can proceed, and must wait. Then suppose the two looking at the Mona Lisa decide to go home. They deposit their two Walkmen, the total becomes four, and one or other of the groups will be satisfied, on a first come, first served basis. The pool will then be down to one or zero again.

Class design This time we shall not draw a detailed class diagram, but rather indicate the interation of the objects of the four classes at a high level. Figure 11.8 gives such a diagram. Synchronized methods are marked with an S in the corner. `WalkmanHire` instantiates the `Museum` class. It also starts up the counters as threads. The counters start up `Visitor` threads as needed. Counters hire Walkmen from the museum object, and visitors replace them.

Program Now consider the synchronization parts of the program in detail. `hire` and `replace` are the two methods that control the number of Walkmen and the amount of

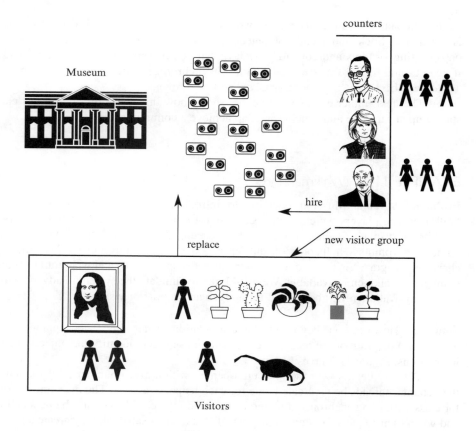

Figure 11.7 *Layout of the museum simulation.*

cash taken as deposits. Obviously, the sum of these two must always be equal to the initial amount. Here is what the class looks like. Read the comments to understand how the `hire` and `replace` interact. `Museum` provides some rudimentary commentary to the user as to how the hiring process is proceeding.

```
import java.io.*;

class Museum {

  Museum (int w) {
    walkmen = w;
    cash = 0;
  }

  synchronized void hire (int c,int n) {
```

WalkmanHire   Counter

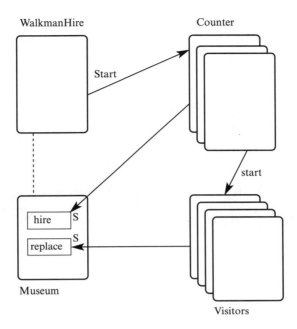

Figure 11.8   *High-level object diagram for the Walkman program.*

```
// If there are not enough Walkmen left,
// wait until someone at another counter returns
// some and notifies us accordingly.
// If the returns are not enough, we'll carry on
// waiting.
System.out.println("Counter "+c+" wants "+n);
while (walkmen < n) {
  try { wait(); }
  catch (InterruptedException e) {}
}

// Hire out the Walkmen and take the deposit.
// Let the customers at this counter "walk away"
// by relinquishing control of the monitor with
// a notify call.
walkmen -= n;
cash += n;
System.out.println("Counter "+c+" acquires "+n);
System.out.println("Pool status:"+
  " Deposits "+cash+" Total "+(walkmen+cash)
  + " Walkmen "+walkmen);
notify ();
}

synchronized void replace (int n) {

  // Always accept replacements immediately.
  // Once the pool and deposits have been updated,
```

```
    // notify any other helper waiting for Walkmen.
    System.out.println("Replacing "+n);
    walkmen +=n;
    cash -= n;
    notify ();
  }

  private static int walkmen;
  private static int cash;
}
```

Calling the `hire` part of `Museum`, we have the `Counter` threads. Once their needs have been satisfied, they create a new `Visitor` thread and then sleep for a while before serving another batch of customers. Both the number of visitors in a group and the time between groups are based on random numbers.

```
class Counter extends Thread {

  Counter (Museum m, int q) {
    museum = m;
    queue = q;
  }

  public void run () {

    // Decide how many Walkmen are needed for a
    // group of visitors and attempt to hire them
    // (waiting until successful). The visitors are
    // sent off on their own to walk around (by
    // starting a new Visitors thread which runs
    // independently.)
    while (true) {
      int w = a(7);
      museum.hire(queue, w);
      new Visitors (museum, w).start();

      // Wait a bit before the next people arrive
      try {sleep(a(100));}  catch(InterruptedException e) {}
    }
  }

  Museum museum;
  int queue;
}
```

The `Visitor` threads simulate the groups walking around for a random time, viewing the exhibits and then returning the Walkmen directly to the `Museum` object. The `replace` method is synchronized so that there may be a small wait if a counter thread is busy completing the hiring out of Walkmen at that precise moment, but otherwise, the visitors can get on their way without queueing.

```
class Visitors extends Thread {

  Visitors (Museum m, int w) {
    museum = m;
    groupSize = w;
  }

  public void run () {

    // The group walks around on its own for 50 time units.
    // You may need to alter this figure to suit your computer.
    // They then replace all their Walkmen and leave.
    // The thread dies with them.
    try {sleep((int) (Math.random()*1000)+1);}
         catch(InterruptedException e) {}
    museum.replace(groupSize);
  }

  Museum museum;
  int groupSize;
}
```

Finally, there is the main program itself. This is responsible for starting the Museum and Counter threads. In order to let the user change the size of the simulation, the numbers of Walkman and counters can be set from the command line. By default they are 50 and 3 respectively.

```
class WalkmanHire {

  /* The Museum Walkman Hire program       J M Bishop  Jan 1997
     simulates the hiring of Walkmen from a fixed pool for G1
     each. There are several helpers at different counters
     handling the hire and replacement of the Walkmen.

     The number of Walkmen in the original pool is 50
     and the number of helpers serving is 3,
     but these can be overridden by parameters at run time
     e.g. java WalkmanHire 100 8.
     The cash float starts at zero.

     Illustrates monitors, with synchronize, wait and notify.
     Shows a main program and two different kinds of threads
     running simultaneously.
  */

  public static void main (String [] args) {

    // Get the number of Walkmen in the pool
    // and open the museum for business.
    if (args.length >= 1)
      pool = Integer.parseInt(args[0]);
    else pool = 50;
    Museum m = new Museum (pool);
```

```
    // Get the number of helpers
    // and open the counters.
    if (args.length >= 2)
      helpers = Integer.parseInt(args[1]);
    else helpers = 3;
    for (int i=0; i<helpers; i++)
      new Counter (m,i).start();
  }
  static int pool;
  static int helpers;
}
```

Testing   The program produces text output. Let us consider just a small part of it, at a point where the number of Walkmen is getting low. We number the lines for reference.

```
1.   Pool status: Deposits 15 Total 20 Walkmen 5
2.   Counter 1 wants 5
3.   Counter 1 acquires 5
4.   Pool status: Deposits 20 Total 20 Walkmen 0
5.   Counter 2 wants 7
6.   Counter 0 wants 2
7.   Counter 1 wants 4
8.   Replacing 1
9.   Replacing 2
10.  Counter 0 acquires 2
11.  Pool status: Deposits 19 Total 20 Walkmen 1
12.  Replacing 6
13.  Counter 2 acquires 7
14.  Pool status: Deposits 20 Total 20 Walkmen 0
15.  Counter 0 wants 5
16.  Counter 2 wants 1
17.  Replacing 1
18.  Replacing 5
19.  Counter 0 acquires 5
20.  Pool status: Deposits 19 Total 20 Walkmen 1
21.  Counter 2 acquires 1
22.  Pool status: Deposits 20 Total 20 Walkmen 0
23.  Counter 2 wants 2
24.  Counter 0 wants 7
25.  Replacing 7
26.  Counter 1 acquires 4
27.  Pool status: Deposits 17 Total 20 Walkmen 3
28.  Counter 2 acquires 2
29.  Pool status: Deposits 19 Total 20 Walkmen 1
```

The program was set running with a pool of 20 Walkmen and with three counters (0, 1 and 2). At the beginning of this extract, there are five Walkmen left. Counter 1 wants 5 and gets them, leaving none. At that point each of the counters puts in a request, and all are blocked until some groups start returning sets. On line 8, one set was returned to the pool, but this was not enough for any of the waiting threads, so they continue to wait. On line 9 another two come back. By line 10, there are three sets in the pool so the thread from counter 0 can continue. Notice that this was not the first one queued: counter 2 requested 7 on line

5, but still has to wait. Fortunately, on line 12, six more Walkmen come back, making seven in all, so that group can now continue. The pool, however, is back to zero again.

Study the rest of the output, and run the program yourself with different parameters to get a feel for the dynamics.

11.4   Ports and sockets

In Section 11.1, we concentrated on connections via high-level URLs. Java provides another level of connection, that of ports and sockets. A **port** is an abstraction of a physical place through which communication can proceed between a server and a client. The server is said to provide the port, and the client links into it.

Operating systems have processes assigned to specific ports, with server software that runs continuously, listening for anticipated messages of particular kinds. Ports are generally known by numbers. For example, under Unix, connecting to port 13 will return the date and time of the computer. Other ports provide for receiving and sending mail, checking the status of the computer, finding out who is logged on, and so on. Most of the time these ports will not be available to mere users, as security could be impaired. However, there are many vacant ports which we can use where we can create our own services.

Such a service will be a multi-threaded Java program which provides sockets on the given port. A **socket** is an abstraction of the network software that enables communication in and out of this program. A Java socket can be created if we have a valid computer Internet address and a valid port number. Several sockets can be created on a single port, enabling many clients to make use of the service provided, as shown in Figure 11.9.

Once a socket has been created, the client and server communicate in whatever way has been arranged. In Java, the simplest method is to establish an ordinary stream from the server to the client. Thereafter, the server can use read and print methods to get and send data.

If the client is a Java program then it will also have a socket and streams which match those of the server. Alternatively, the client could be an existing program such as

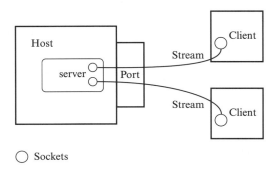

Figure 11.9   *Digrammatic view of ports and sockets.*

telnet, or the server could be an existing service such as the time of day. The forms associated with setting up a sockets and streams are:

Sockets and streams

```
ServerSocket listener = new ServerSocket (port);
Socket name = listener.accept();

Socket name = new Socket (host, port);

DataInputStream instreamname =
    new DataInputStream (name.getInputStream());
DataInputStream outstreamname =
    new DataOutputStream (name.getOutputStream());
```

If we are creating a socket on the server side, we first set up a permanent listening socket on that port, based on the `ServerSocket` class. Then for each client that accesses the port, a separate socket of the `Socket` class is set up via the `accept` method. From the client's side, to create such a socket we instantiate the `Socket` class directly and indicate the host to which it must connect.

A simple program to act as a client accessing an existing server on a host is the following. It uses the second form for creating a socket.

```
import java.io.*;
import java.net.*;

class Ports {
  public static void main(String[] args) {
    String computer;
    int port;

    if (args.length > 0) computer = args[0];
    else computer = "jupiter.cs.up.ac.za";
    if (args.length > 1) port = Integer.parseInt(args[1]);
    else port = 13; // the clock port

    System.out.println("Accessing port "+port+" on "+ computer+"\n");
    try {

      // Create a socket to the given port.
      // Set up an input stream to read what the socket on that
      // side provides.

      Socket t = new Socket(computer, port);
      DataInputStream in = new
          DataInputStream(t.getInputStream());

      // Read from the server until readLine
      // returns no more data
      while (true) {
        String s = in.readLine();
        if (s == null) break;
        else System.out.println(s);
```

```
        }
      }
      catch(IOException e) { System.out.println("Error" + e); }
   }
}
```

If we ran this program without parameters, it would default to the computer called jupiter.cs.up.ac.za and to port 13. The result would be the date and time printed out, such as:

Accessing port 13 on jupiter.cs.up.ac.za

Sun Jan 19 15:57:14 1997

We now consider how to create our own server program on a spare port. Ports above 8000 are usually spare, so we can use one of those.

EXAMPLE 11.7   Creating an echo server

Problem   We would like to set up a server on a vacant port. The service should allow multiple connections from clients, and simply echo anything they say back to them.

Solution   If there are to be multiple clients then it is certain that they will be running at different speeds and will need their own threads within the server. This is no problem, as we have fully investigated how to set up threads in Section 11.2. The question is rather how to test the service. We could set up a client similar to the one discussed above, but actually there is an easier way: we can use another existing client, telnet. Telnet has a simple protocol which, in the absence of any other instructions, will read and write to a host, line by line. Thus we can telnet into our chosen port and type in lines one at a time. Each should be echoed back.

Program   The programs make use of a class called `InetAddress` which represents Internet addresses, as well as their string equivalents. The server follows (with comments to explain what is happening at each stage).

```
import java.io.*;
import java.net.*;

class server {

   /* Server program      J M Bishop Jan 1997
      acts as a server for multiple clients,
      echoing back each line sent.
      Can be called from telnet with the port given.
      Will set up multiple handlers for multiple clients.

      Illustrates port, sockets and serversockets. */

   public static void main(String[] args ) {
```

```
    // default to port 8190 if no argument
    int port = 8190;
    if (args.length > 0)
      port =Integer.parseInt(args[0]);

    // The server must be running on a computer connected
    // to the internet.
    InetAddress serverAddress=null;
    try {
      serverAddress = InetAddress.getLocalHost();
    }  catch (UnknownHostException e) {}

    // Issue some instructions.
    System.out.println("****** The Echo Server ********");
    System.out.println("Telnet in to "+serverAddress.getHostName()+
        " on port "+port);
    System.out.println("from any number of different computers or");
    System.out.println("from different active Windows.\n");

    // Provided the port is not being used by another server
    // program already, proceed.
    try {

      // Set up the listening socket.
      ServerSocket listener = new ServerSocket(port);

      int c = 0;

      // Keep listening until one of the clients tells
      // us to shut down.
      while (!done) {

        // A new client has come in. Set up a new socket.
        // Write an introductory message
        // and create a new handler thread for the client,
        // giving it the socket reference and client number.
        Socket client = listener.accept( );
        c ++;
        System.out.println("From Echo: Connection received from " +
            client.getInetAddress().getHostName());
        System.out.println
            ("From Echo: Starting a new client, numbered "+c);
        new handler(client, c).start();
      }
      listener.close();
    }
    catch (IOException e) {
     System.out.println
        ("Port "+port+" may be busy. Try another.");
    }
  }

private static boolean done = false;

// Called from a handler
```

```
      static void closeDown () {
        done = true;
      }
    }
```

Notice that we do not keep track of the handlers by name or reference: they are simply spawned off to do their own thing. The handler threads look like this:

```
class handler extends Thread {

  private Socket toClient;
  private int id;

  handler(Socket s, int i) {
    toClient = s;
    id = i;
  }

  public void run() {
    try {
      DataInputStream in = new
            DataInputStream(toClient.getInputStream());
      PrintStream out = new PrintStream(toClient.getOutputStream());

      out.println( "From Echo: Hello! Type QUIT to end." );
      String s = in.readLine();
      if (s.trim().equals("SHUTDOWN")) server.closeDown();
      else {
        int lineno = 0;
        while (true) {
          lineno++;
          out.println("From Echo:" + lineno+ ": "+s);
          if (s.trim().equals("QUIT")) break;
          s = in.readLine();
        }
      }
      toClient.close();
    }
    catch (IOException e) {System.out.println("IO Error");}
  }
}
```

Each thread records its socket reference when constructed. It then asks for the input and output streams associated with that socket, which will give it access to the client that is on the other side. There is an introductory message, a chance to stop the server (not generally advertised) and thereafter the handler enters its loop, echoing lines until QUIT is typed. When the loop ends, the socket to the client must be closed and then the thread dies naturally. To make the echoing more interesting, each line is numbered, as we did when we set up the Lister program (Example 11.3).

Testing   To run the server, we simply execute it as a normal Java program. If we want to telnet into the server from the same machine (which is certainly possible) then we should run it in the background. To hook into the server, we use telnet as follows. Bold indicates output, plain type is what we input.

```
Chat/ServerOnly>****** The Echo Server ********
Telnet in to jupiter on port 8191
from any number of different computers or
from different active Windows.

Chat/ServerOnly>telnet jupiter 8191
Trying 137.215.18.16 ...
Connected to jupiter.cs.up.ac.za.
From Echo: Connection received from jupiter.cs.up.ac.za
From Echo: Starting a new client, numbered 1
Escape character is '^]'.
From Echo: Hello! Type QUIT to end.
hi
From Echo:1: hi
me
From Echo:2: me
more
From Echo:3: more
QUIT
From Echo:4: QUIT
Connection closed by foreign host.
```

Notice that we told telnet to look for the host called 'jupiter' and it translated this to a numeric Internet address, 137.215.18.16. The server, once it accepts the client, can get this Internet address and translate it back to its full string equivalent, in this case 'jupiter.cs.up.ac.za'. You can also use the special Internet address '127.0.0.1' to telnet into your own machine.

The echo server is taken further in the case study that follows.

11.5   Case study 6: Chatter system

In Example 11.7, each of the clients was completely independent. It would be nice to extend the system so that the messages typed in by one are relayed to each of the others by the server. Such a server is known as a 'Chat program'.

Keeping track of clients

The first issue is how to keep track of clients within the server. Clients can sign on and leave at will, and the number of clients could be very hard to control or predict. It thus makes sense to envisage a linked list of clients, since we know that we can add and remove from such a list without worrying about the number of elements.

If we declare

```
private static List clientList = new List ();
```

then adding a new client thread's reference to the list is done by:

```
clientList.reset();
clientList.add(client);
```

We have to reset the list, because it may have been left in an unsatisfactory position by some other operation. This way, the new clients are added to the front of the list each time. These statements appear in the main program, just after the launching of a new handler for the client.

Now, how do we remove a client from the list? Clearly, the client must request such removal, once a BYE has been detected. The client knows what its socket reference is, and this is unique among the current clients. Therefore, the server can look through the list, comparing socket references, and when a match is found, delete that object from the list. The extract of code is:

```
Socket t;
for (clientList.reset(); !clientList.eol(); clientList.succ()) {
  t = (Socket) clientList.current();
  if (t.equals(s)) break;
}
clientList.remove();
```

Since this loop is in a method which has been called by a thread which 'owns' an existing socket, the loop will eventually detect a matching socket and reach the break-statement.

Broadcasting to all clients

Broadcasting a message to all clients is even easier than the above removal. Since the message has to be echoed to the originator as well, we do not have to differentiate between that client and the rest and we simply loop through all of them.

```
for (clientList.reset(); !clientList.eol(); clientList.succ()) {
  s = (Socket) clientList.current();
  p = new PrintStream(s.getOutputStream());
  p.println(name + ": "+message+"\r");
}
```

For each client on the list, we get the corresponding output stream and send the message there.

Synchronizing activities

The removal and broadcast operations both access the list of clients kept by the server. Given that the removal operation will make fairly drastic changes to the list, it would not be wise for both operations to be active simultaneously. Therefore they are declared as synchronized and Java will ensure that once one has begun, it will finished before the other is attempted.

A class diagram

This time, let us record a class diagram for the server and its handlers, shown in Figure 11.10.

The server

The code for the chat server therefore looks like this in full:

```
import java.io.*;
import java.net.*;

class ChatServer {

    /* The Chatter program by J M Bishop January 1997
       Sets up a server for multiple conversations.

       Join in by typing
          telnet x y
       where x and y are the computer's name and port as
       given when the Chatter starts.

       Illustrates sockets, streams on sockets,
       threads, synchronization and the use of lists (again).
    */
```

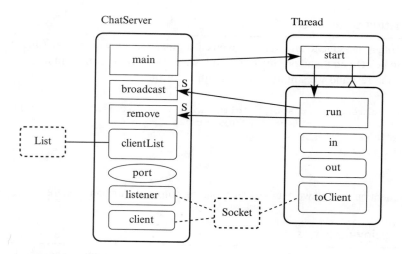

Figure 11.10 *The Chat server class diagram.*

```java
public static void main (String [] args) throws IOException {

  //Get the port and create a socket there.
  int port = 8190;
  if (args.length > 0)
    port = Integer.parseInt(args[0]);
  ServerSocket listener = new ServerSocket(port);
  System.out.println("The Chat Server is running on port " + port);

  // Listen for clients. Start a new handler for each.
  // Add each client to the linked list.
  while (true) {
    Socket client = listener.accept();
    new ChatHandler(client).start();
    System.out.println("New client no."+id+
      //" from "+ listener.getInetAddress()+
      " on client's port "+client.getPort());
    clientList.reset();
    clientList.add(client);
    id++;
  }
}

static synchronized void broadcast (String message, String name)
  throws IOException {

  // Sends the message to every client including the sender.
  Socket s;
  PrintStream p;
  for (clientList.reset(); !clientList.eol(); clientList.succ()) {
    s = (Socket) clientList.current();
    p = new PrintStream(s.getOutputStream());
    p.println(name + ": "+message+"\r");
  }
}

static synchronized void remove (Socket s) {

  // Finds the client on the list (by comparing socket
  // references) and removes it.
  Socket t;
  for (clientList.reset(); !clientList.eol(); clientList.succ()) {
    t = (Socket) clientList.current();
    if (t.equals(s)) break;
  }
  clientList.remove();
  id--;
}

private static List clientList = new List ();
private static int id = 0
}

class ChatHandler extends Thread {
```

```
      // The Chat Handler class is called from the Chat Server:
      // one thread for each client coming in to chat.

      ChatHandler (Socket s) {
        toClient = s;
      }

      public void run () {
        try {

          // Create i-o streams through the socket we were
          // given when the thread was instantiated
          // and welcome the new client.

          in = new DataInputStream (toClient.getInputStream());
          out = new PrintStream (toClient.getOutputStream());
          out.println("*** Welcome to the Chatter ***\r");
          out.println("Type BYE to end\r");
          out.println("What is your name? \r");
          String name = in.readLine();
          ChatServer.broadcast
              (name+" has joined the discussion.","Chatter");

          // Read lines and send them off for broadcasting.
          while (true) {
            String s = in.readLine ().trim();
            // Check first three characters for BYE.
            // Avoids problems with different line end characters.
            if (s.charAt(0)=='B' && s.charAt(1)=='Y' && s.charAt(2)=='E') {
              ChatServer.broadcast
                (name+" has left the discussion.","Chatter");
              break;
            }
            ChatServer.broadcast(s,name);
          }
          ChatServer.remove(toClient);
          toClient.close();
        }
        catch (Exception e) {System.out.println("Chatter error: "+e);}
      }

      private DataInputStream in;
      private PrintStream out;
      private Socket toClient;
      private String name;
    }
```

A sample chat session

Once again. we use telnet for the clients. The following could be a sample chat session, as recorded on the server's display.

```
Chat/Chatter>java ChatServer 8191 &
[2] 5802
```

```
Chat/Chatter>The Chat Server is running on port 8191

Chat/Chatter>telnet jupiter 8191
Trying 137.215.18.16 ...
Connected to jupiter.cs.up.ac.za.
New client no.0 on client's port 57889
Escape character is '^]'.
*** Welcome to the Chatter ***
Type BYE to end
What is your name?
Nelson
Chatter: Nelson has joined the discussion.
Anyone out there?
Nelson: Anyone out there?
New client no.1 on client's port 1026
Chatter: Seagull has joined the discussion.
Hi Seagull
Nelson: Hi Seagull
Seagull: Hi Nelson, how's the coffee shop?
Great. Business is booming.
Nelson: Great. Business is booming.
Seagull: Oh well, bye for now
Seagull - you must type BYE to end
Nelson: Seagull - you must type BYE to end
Seagull: BYE
Try again
Nelson: Try again
Seagull: BYE
Chatter: Seagull has left the discussion.
BYE
Nelson: BYE
Chatter: Nelson has left the discussion.
Connection closed by foreign host.
```

When running the chat server using telnet, some oddities may emerge when trying to say goodbye, or with the echoing or non-echoing of lines locally. It is worth experimenting to find out how your computers react.

SUMMARY

Java programs can fetch files and images identified by their URL names. A file can be fetched in one go, or line by line via streams set up between the program and the resource. In order to handle networks and user interaction better, Java provides for multi-threading. Classes can be turned into threads which run independently via their own `run` methods. Communication between threads is via method and variable access. If there is a chance that threads might interfere with each other, the methods they call are declared as synchronized. Java then guarantees that a thread in a synchronized method will finish before another is allowed into any synchronized method in the same object. To control threads so that one can wait for another, there are two thread calls, `wait` and `notify`.

At the lowest level Java provides for programming sockets. Clients and servers can be set up in different machines and connect in via Internet addresses assigned to sockets via ports. Multiple clients can access the same server, each with its own client socket.

11.1 If `elephant.jpg` is an image file in the same directory as an applet which is currently running, give Java statements to access and display it.

11.2 In the statement

```
a.b = a.createImage((ImageProducer) imagename.getContent());
```

identify the class of each of the following objects:

a   b ImageProducer imagename

11.3 Give a statement to create a new thread called `x` of class `T`.

11.4 In multi-threaded programs, does `start` call `run` or the other way round?

11.5 Do all methods in a monitor class have to be synchronized? Explain your answer.

11.6 Look at the output from the Walkman program in Example 11.6. Which group had to wait a very long time to get their Walkmen?

11.7 Can `getInputStream` and `getOutputStream` be used by both clients and servers?

11.8 In Example 11.7, the handler thread can call

```
server.closeDown()
```

if a special message is received. When will the server react to the message?

11.9 The following class is being turned into a thread:

```
class picture extends Canvas {
    public void paint (Graphics g) {
        g.drawImage (i,50,50,this);
    }
}
```

Complete the transformation.

11.10 Suppose some Walkmen are being mended, and during the day a Curator thread is started up in the Museum program (Example 11.6) which will add in a number of Walkmen to the pool. Is this possible in the given system, and what method(s) would such a Curator thread call?

11.1 **Listing via HTML**. Experiment with the Lister program (Example 11.3) as an applet, with the name of the file coming in from a text field added to the applet's interface. Put the applet in an html page and have the html give a list of suggested files that can be fetched.

11.2 **Traffic lights duration**. Complete the traffic lights simulation (Example 11.5) by letting the user set the time that each of the lights in a set must be on for. For example, red and green should be on for much longer than yellow.

11.3 **British traffic lights**. In Great Britain, there is a fourth phase on every set of traffic lights. Between red and green, both the red and yellow lights come on. Alter the program in Example 11.4 to take this into account.

11.4   **Visible Walkmen**. The Walkman program (Example 11.6) could really do with a user interface which (a) shows how the Walkmen come and go; and (b) has a control panel so that the arrival of parties can be under the user's control, rather than generated automatically. Create such a user interface to run as an additional thread in the system.

11.5   **Broken Walkmen**. It could well happen that visitors find Walkmen that are no longer working when they finish. Instead of handing them back directly, we ask them to go back to the counter and hand them in specially. How would the class diagram have to change if we did this, and what methods would be needed? Implement this change and also add a Curator class which comes round periodically and collects broken Walkmen, returning them later.

11.6   **VIP visitors**. Some visitors are VIPs and should not have to queue long for Walkmen. Add another function to the Curator class to bring in such VIP groups occasionally and let them get Walkmen with a higher priority. Show on comparative sample outputs the effect that they would have.

11.7   **Chatting clients**. The Chatter program (Example 11.7) provides a server only. Using the Ports program in Section 11.4 as a basis, create a Java program which can be started up on the client side and provide similar facilities to telnet.

11.8   **Chatting on the web**. Even after Problem 11.7, the user interface to the Chatter is pretty basic. Try making the server into an applet and embody it in an html page which provides instructions, displays the output, and has a separate line for typing in input.

11.9   **Working watch**. In Problem 9.6, we designed the face of a digital watch. Now, using a thread, make it actually work, with the digits clicking over and the buttons for resetting and displaying being active at the same time.

CHAPTER 12

Algorithms and data structures

12.1   About data structures

We conclude our study of Java by looking ahead to a more advanced computer science course, and the study of data structures.

> A **data structure** is a collection of **nodes** of the same class or type which is organized and accessed in a defined way.

A node would usually be an object, but could be as simple as an integer. The fact that the definition states that the nodes must be of the same class or type means that we can refer to a structure of that type, for example a list of coffees or a hash table of strings.

The linked list data structure that we built up in Section 7.3 was an *ad hoc* one, designed for the purpose. Another problem might require a very different data structure. In

Table 12.1 *Table of data structures.*

Data structure	Java class (if any)	*Java Gently* section
Array	*built-in*	6.1, 6.2
Extensible array	`java.util.Vector`	6.5
Linked list		7.3, 12.5
Stack	`java.util.Stack`	12.4
Queue		12.4
Tree		
Hash table	`java.util.Hashtable`	6.5
Set	`java.util.BitSet`	12.6
Dictionary	`java.util.Dictionary`	
Sequential file	`java.io.File…Stream`	4.3
Random file	`java.io.RandomAccessFile`	

computer science, though, there are several recognized data structures that crop up again and again in solutions to problems. They have names and defined properties, and in a sense can be regarded as an extension of the basic data types of a language.

Java has recognized the importance of data structures and has supplied classes in its standard packages for a good number of them. Just to provide a check list, Table 12.1 gives a canonical list of data structures, indicating those that are in Java and those that are covered in this edition of the book.

In this chapter we revisit linked lists in order to add some more features and give another example of their use. We also cover two more Java data structures classes – `Stack` and `BitSet` – and look at how queues can be implemented based on arrays or linked lists.

Properties

Each data structure has properties relating to the following:

- relationship to other nodes;
- composition of a header node;
- point of addition of nodes – front, back or anywhere;
- point of deletion of nodes – front, back or anywhere;
- direction of scanning – none, forwards, backwards or other.

As we get to each data structure, we shall address these issues.

Representation

Data structures can be represented as either **arrays** of objects or as nodes **linked** by their references, as already shown in Section 7.3. The decision as to which method to employ depends on two factors. A linked representation has the advantage that the number of nodes in the structure can be completely flexible: with an array representation, the maximum number would have to be fixed. On the other hand, linked-based structures require space for the links, and these increase the overall size of the structure.

There is no inherent complexity related to the programming in either case, and we shall present both representations, endeavouring to show the underlying algorithms as independent of the representation. In so doing, we create **abstract data types** which have recognizable forms and properties, and can be used only as specified.

Algorithms

Two of the operations we will often need for a data structure as a whole are sorting and searching. Before we start on looking at the inner details of data structures, therefore, we complete our study of the basic algorithms that should be part of a computer scientist's toolkit. The list includes:

- a linear search and a faster one;

- a straight sort and a faster one.

A linear search was shown in Section 7.3 for linked lists, but we reiterate it here for arrays, and straight sorting was covered in Section 6.4. Both the faster algorithms make use of a basic computing technique – **recursion** – without which no textbook on programming would be complete.

12.2 Linear and binary searching

We can define a **sequence** as a data structure which has the property that each element is reachable after the previous one. In other words, the structure can be accessed in sequence. Examples of such structures would be an array, a list or a file stream. A hash table is not a sequence, however, although a Java hash table can be accessed sequentially via an enumerator.

If we have a sequence of values then we can search for a particular value by starting at the beginning of the sequence and comparing each element in turn. This is called **linear** searching, because we scan the sequence in a linear way.

The linear searching algorithm is an example of a double-exit loop: either the value is found in the sequence, or the end of the sequence is reached before the value is found. These kinds of loop were examined extensively in Section 5.3, where the sequence was the input data stream, and again in Section 7.3 for a linked list. Let us now translate that logic to searching an array.

The advantage of searching an array is that we know its length. We can therefore use a for-loop, together with the extra control it provides for stopping if not found. A first attempt at the linear search is:

```
int i;
for (i = 0; i< a.length; i++)
  if (a[i] == x) break;
```

Though simple and neat, this loop has an unfortunate defect: at the end we do not know if we exited the loop because we found the item or not. Now, if we are certain of finding the item, this is fine. But in the general case, we cannot be so sure. Notice also that we deliberately declared i outside the loop so that we could access a[i] afterwards.

That means that the algorithm returns two values: a yes/no indicator (or Boolean, say) and an index. This makes it very difficult to parcel the search up into a method, since we can return only one value from a method (unless we return a multi-valued object).

A possible technique is to return the index, but to set it to some out-of-range value if the item was not found. Possible values could be –1 or length. Instinctively this smacks of bad practice. An altogether better approach is to use a user-defined exception. Consider the following proposal:

```
class ItemNotFoundException extends Exception { }

item a [] = new a[n];

static int LinearSearch (item a [], item x)
                        throws ItemNotFoundException {
  for (int i = 0; i< a.length; i++)
    if (x.equals(a[i])) return i;
  // item not found: no normal return
  throw new ItemNotFoundException();
}

//Test the method
try {
  int found = LinearSearch (a, x);
  // do what ever is necessary with a[found]
    …
}
catch (ItemNotFoundException e ) {
  // react to x not being there
    …
}
```

The method is passed the array and the item being sought after. It loops through the array, using the array's own length as a stopping condition (which makes the method nicely general), comparing each item with x. The comparison is done via a call to equals, since we are assuming here that the items are objects. If the item is found, we return immediately. If the loop eventually ends, we throw the exception.

The calling method has a try–catch pair. If the search is successful, the next statement is executed, whatever it is. If not, control transfers to the handler in the catch-part and alternative arrangements must be made. There is a test program on the web site which shows this method in action. We do not include it here, because we want to press on to the next search algorithm – the binary search.

Binary searching

If the data to be searched is ordered, that is, sorted, then there are more efficient searching methods than linear search. The archetypal one is called **binary search**. It involves splitting the sequence in half, and searching only that part where the value must lie. One can be certain about which half the value is in, because the sequence is assumed to be sorted.

For example, suppose we have the sorted sequence:

```
23  45  61  65  67  70  82  89  90  99
```

and are searching for the value 90. Informally, we could divide the sequence in two between 67 and 70 and see that 90 must be in the right-hand side:

```
23  45  61  65  67     70  82  89  90  99
```

We divide this subsequence in two between 89 and 90 and move to the right again:

```
70  82  89     90  99
```

The sequence we are interested in is now two long, but we still divide and move to the left, where we find 90:

```
90     99
```

This took four divides and compares, compared with nine with a linear search.

Clearly, binary search is faster *on average*, but not every time. If the value being sought was 23 (the first in the sequence), binary search would still start in the centre and move gradually to the left to find it.

The best way to formulate such a binary search is by using a technique called **recursion**:

> **Recursion** allows us to describe an operation in terms of itself, based on modified data and with a stopping condition.

Using this idea, an algorithm for binary search is:

Binary search a sequence for x
  If the sequence has one element,
      compare x with it and return found or not found.
  Otherwise consider the element in the middle of the sequence.
      If $x <$ middle element, then **binary search** left subsequence for x
      else **binary search** the right subsequence for x.

In many cases, the sequence or subsequence to be split will not have an even number of elements and so we adopt the convention that the extra element goes to the left subsequence. Looking at the algorithm, one can see that an improvement would be to add an additional condition in the second part, to consider whether the value being sought is in fact the middle element at the time.

Conditions for binary search

Binary searching relies on the values being ordered, but it also relies on being able to index the sequence. Thus, binary searching is not possible on files or lists. It works on arrays only.

EXAMPLE 12.1   Animated binary search

Problem In order to illustrate binary search, we will develop a Java program to implement the algorithm above, and will show the stages of the search as it develops.

Solution We start off with a sequence of numbers, and every time we split the sequence, we shall print out only those numbers left in the sequence. This begs the question of how we 'split a sequence'. The answer is that we do not! What we do is we keep only one sequence and indicate the left and right limits each time.

Algorithm There is a slightly difficult part in splitting a sequence. If the sequence starts at 0, the midpoint is at $n/2$, where n is the last index. For example, for an array going from 0 to 9, $9/2 = 4$ is the midpoint. However, if a subsequence runs from j to k in a larger sequence, then the midpoint of the subsequence is at position $(j + k)/2$. You should verify that you understand why this is so.

Program The program to animate the binary search follows. We have chosen to use character data stored as objects, and to read it in. Remember to keep the data sorted, or the program will not function correctly. (Alternatively, slot in a sort procedure and sort the data first, just to make sure.)

The important part of the binary search method is its use of recursion, and we therefore list it separately first, with line numbers.

```
1.   static int BinarySearch (item a [], item x, int left, int right)
2.        throws ItemNotFoundException {
3.     display(a,left,right);
4.     if (left==right)
5.       if (x.equals(a[left])) return left;
6.       else throw new ItemNotFoundException ();
7.     else {
8.       int mid = (int) ((left+right) / 2);
9.       if (x.equals(a[mid]))
10.        return mid;
11.      else
12.      if (x.less(a[mid]))
13.       return BinarySearch (a, x, left, mid);
14.      else
15.        return BinarySearch (a, x, mid+1, right);
16.   }
17. }
```

BinarySearch will call itself with the left or right subsequence (lines 13 and 15) until the subsequence is of length one (detected on line 4). Then it either exits with an exception (line 6), or returns the index of this subsequence (line 5). The point of call was line 13 or 15, so the return comes back to one of these. Both result in the method reaching a natural end (line 17) and so a return to the previous point of call is made again. Once again, this could be line 13 or 15. Eventually, the very first call of BinarySearch, which was made with the full sequence, will reach its natural end, and control will go back to the main program. All along, the index value that was detected as holding the required item *x* is being passed back as the return value of the method.

The main program and associated classes look like this:

```
import javagently.Text;
import java.io.*;

class binary {

    /* The animated binary search program      by J M Bishop  Jan 1997
       searches a sorted sequence for a given value
       and shows the workings of binary sort.

       Illustrates recursion.
    */

    static int BinarySearch (item a [], item x, int left, int right) {
    … etc. as above
    }

    public static void main (String args [])
        throws IOException {

      DataInputStream in = new DataInputStream(System.in);
      System.out.println("**** Testing the binary search ****");
      System.out.println("Type in 10 characters separated by spaces");
      for (int i=0; i<a.length;i++)
        a[i] = new item (Text.readChar(in));

      // Loop to try several searches
      while (true)
        try {
          counter = 0;
          Text.prompt("Find what value?");
          item x = new item(Text.readChar(in));
          System.out.println("The array is:");
          System.out.println("0 1 2 3 4 5 6 7 8 9");

          try {
          int found = BinarySearch (a, x, 0, a.length-1);
          // do whatever is necessary with a[found]
          System.out.println((char) x.data+
            " was found at position "+found
           +" in "+counter+" probes.");
          }
          catch (ItemNotFoundException e ) {
```

```
            // react to x not being there
               System.out.println((char) x.data+" was not found in "
                  +counter+" probes.");
            }
         }
       catch (EOFException e) {break;}
    }

    static item a [] = new item [10];
    static int counter;

    static void display (item [] a, int left, int right) {
      for (int j = 0; j < left; j++)
        System.out.print(" ");
      for (int j = left; j <= right; j++)
        System.out.print((char) a[j].data+" ");
      System.out.println();
      counter++;
    }
  }

class ItemNotFoundException extends Exception { }

class item {
  item (char i) {
    data = i;
  }

  boolean equals (item x) {
    return data==x.data;
  }

  boolean less (item x) {
    return data < x.data;
  }
  int data;
}
```

Testing   Several tests are shown, including one when the number was found, and one when it was not. Note that e and j were found in fewer probes than with a linear search, but that finding b took slightly more. A real advantage of the binary search is that it can always establish that an item is not there in far fewer probes than a linear sort can. The exact number of probes is given by a formula which we shall discuss in the next section.

```
**** Testing the binary search ****
Type in 10 characters separated by spaces
a b c d e f g h i j
Find what value? e
The array is:
0 1 2 3 4 5 6 7 8 9
a b c d e f g h i j
```

```
e was found at position 4 in 1 probes.
Find what value? b
The array is:
0 1 2 3 4 5 6 7 8 9
a b c d e f g h i j
a b c d e
a b c
b was found at position 1 in 3 probes.
Find what value? j
The array is:
0 1 2 3 4 5 6 7 8 9
a b c d e f g h i j
          f g h i j
                i j
                  j
j was found at position 9 in 4 probes.
Find what value? x
The array is:
0 1 2 3 4 5 6 7 8 9
a b c d e f g h i j
          f g h i j
                i j
                  j
x was not found in 4 probes.
```

12.3   Quicksort and performance

There are many different algorithms for sorting, but one that is a classic because of its overall good performance is known as **Quicksort**. Sorting is based on the twin operations of comparing and exchanging; Quicksort is based on the principle that any exchange must take place over the greatest distance possible. Thus, instead of exchanging adjacent elements, we select elements that are at virtually opposite ends of the sequence. To do this, we adopt the split-in-half idea used in binary search. Basically, we split the sequence at a certain point and move all the bigger items to the right and the smaller items to the left, using 'long exchanges'. This done, we concentrate on each subsequence in turn, doing the same until only one item remains in each. Quicksort does not split each subsequence exactly in half, as binary search did, but divides on the position around which the last exchange was made.

Put in algorithmic terms, Quicksort is:

Quicksort
    Provided the sequence has more than one item
        Choose an item as a pivot (e.g. the midpoint)
        Move all items less than it to the left
        Move all items more than it to the right
        Quicksort the left subsequence
        Quicksort the right subsequence

where the algorithm for the Move is given in Figure 12.1.

Quicksort is quite complicated, and strangely enough, animating it, or performing an example in detail does not make it clearer. It is one of those algorithms that one has to understand in theory, and then accept as correct. It is, however, possible to program it quite concretely in Java.

In Java, a recursive Quicksort is:

```
1. static item [] Quicksort (item [] a, int l, int r) {
2.    if (l < r) {
3.       display(a,l,r);
4.       int i = l;
5.       int j = r;
6.       int k = (int) ((l+r) / 2);
7.       item pivot = a[k];
8.       do {
9.          while (a[i].less(pivot)) i++;
10.         while (pivot.less(a[j])) j--;
11.          if (i<=j) {
12.             item t = (item) a[i].clone();
13.             a[i] = a[j];
14.             a[j] = t;
15.             i++; j--;
16.          }
17.       } while (i<j);
18.       a=Quicksort (a, l, j);
19.       a=Quicksort (a, i, r);
20.    }
21.    return a;
22.}
```

Note some points about the programming. On line 7 we set up the pivot as a reference to the middle element using assignment, but on line 12, we use `clone` to make a copy of a[i]. Why the difference? The reason is that lines 12–14 are performing a swop of the two elements, a[i] and a[j]. Before we wipe out a[i] on line 13, we need to copy its contents.

Like `BinarySearch`, `Quicksort` is a typed method returning an array. Therefore when it is called, it takes a as a parameter and returns the new version as its result.

Move

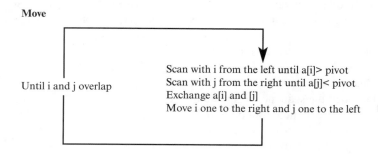

Until i and j overlap

Scan with i from the left until a[i]> pivot
Scan with j from the right until a[j]< pivot
Exchange a[i] and [j]
Move i one to the right and j one to the left

Figure 12.1

There is a test program for `Quicksort` on the web. Here is some typical output:

```
**** Testing Quicksort ****
27 91 42 23 40 74 96 28 31 59
27 31 28 23
27 23 28
   27 28
      28 31
                  74 96 42 91 59
                  42 96
                     96 74 91 59
                        91 96
   23 27 28 31 40 42 59 74 91 96
```

On each line, the method displays the subsequence it has been given to sort. The initial pivot, 40, is not considered after the first line, because we had shifted everything greater than it to the right and everything less than it to its left. That means that 91 and 42, which were originally on its left, would have swapped with 31 and 28 respectively. You can see the result on lines 2 and 6, which show the first two subsequences.

A look at performance

The need to look for different algorithms to solve the same problem stems from a desire for speed: newer algorithms may be faster and therefore, in everyone's eyes, better. What differences in speed are found? With searching and sorting algorithms, they can be quite considerable. Moreover, the speed of the algorithms is proportional to the number of items involved, and therefore can become quite significant once there are thousands or millions of items.

There are two ways of comparing performance: theoretical and experimental. Let us look first at the theoretical performance. We calculate the speed of an algorithm based on the number of 'basic operations' it has to perform. These basic operations are rationalized to include only comparisons and exchanges, and assessing the performance boils down to counting the occurrence of these inside loops.

Comparison of sorts

Consider selection sort which we dealt with in Section 6.4. The outer loop goes for $n-1$, and includes $n-1$ exchanges. The inner loop runs from *leftmost* to $n - 1$ and so reduces by one at each iteration. The number of comparisons is therefore:

$$(n - 1) + (n - 2) + (n - 3) + \ldots + 1 = n\,(n - 1) / 2$$
$$= (n^2 - n) / 2$$

To simplify matters, we ignore the coefficients in the number of exchanges and simply say that they are of the order n^2. If we add in the number of exchanges, the whole process is still dominated by the n^2 term.

Quicksort, on the other hand, uses a partitioning algorithm, which in rough terms involves $\log_2$ iterations. On each iteration, n comparisons are done, and roughly $n/6$

exchanges. Quicksort is therefore considered to operate at a speed proportional to $n \log_2 n$. In real terms, how does this compare with the order of performance of selection sort? Table 12.2 evaluates both formulae for various values of n. The difference is phenomenal. Suppose the unit of time for one iteration is 1 microsecond (10^{-6} s). Then for a million items, Quicksort will take 20 seconds, whereas selection sort will take around $11\frac{1}{2}$ days! It is interesting, though, that at this rate of 1 μs, the difference between the two sorts would not really be noticeable until n exceeds 1000. At this point, selection sort will take a full second, whereas Quicksort will take only 1/100 of a second. In an interactive environment, the difference may not even be noticed.

So why don't we use Quicksort all the time? The answer is provided by the other performance indicator we have: space. Java methods occupy space in memory for their instructions, as well as for their data. Both the algorithms have roughly the same number of statements, so there is not much to choose on the instruction side. However, there is a big difference in data space used. Selection sort declares four local variables and uses them throughout. Quicksort declares eight local variables and parameters for each recursive call. Since recursive calls are stacked up, it may be in the worst case that for a million items, there are 160 items stacked up by Quicksort.

Yet even this is not a lot, and therefore we can probably conclude that the slight wariness with which ordinary programmers regard Quicksort is probably due to an unfamiliarity with recursion. Of course, Quicksort does not have to be programmed recursively, but the non-recursive version is even more awkward.

Comparison of searches

The two searches we looked at can easily be seen to have performances related to n (linear) and $\log_2 n$ (binary). Here, the difference in speed is even more dramatic than sorting (Table 12.3). Put in real terms, this means that to search a telephone directory of a million entries by means of binary search, we should be able find any entry in no more than 20 goes. Very much better than an entry-by-entry linear slog!

Where is this leading?

The study of algorithms, and their analysis of performance, is a cornerstone of computer science, and a major part of a second computer science course. In addition to the two sort-

Table 12.2   *Comparison of the speed of selection sort and Quicksort.*

n	Selection sort order n^2	Quicksort order $n \log_2 n$
10	100	30
50	2 500	300
100	10 000	700
1 000	1 000 000	10 000
10 000	100 000 000	130 000
100 000	10 000 000 000	1 600 000
1 000 000	1 000 000 000 000	20 000 000

Table 12.3 *Comparison of the speed of linear and binary search.*

n	Linear search order n	Binary search order $\log_2 n$
10	10	3
50	50	6
100	100	7
1 000	1 000	10
10 000	10 000	13
100 000	100 000	16
1 000 000	1 000 000	20

ing algorithms mentioned here, you will learn other sorts such as bubble sort (very slow), merge sort and tree sort (very fast), and pigeonhole sort (extremely fast, but fussy). You will learn how to choose an algorithm for a given solution, and look at the limits of algorithms: how fast can they really get? It is a fascinating study, and we have merely touched on it here.

12.4   Stacks and queues

We now start on the first of our data structures – the humble **stack**. Informally, a stack is defined as its name suggests: it is a pile of items which gets added to and removed from its top. A stack is often drawn upright, as in Figure 12.2(a), although it can be drawn on its side as in Figure 12.2(b).

Stack properties

Formally, we can detail the properties of a stack according to the criteria stated in Section 12. 1 as:

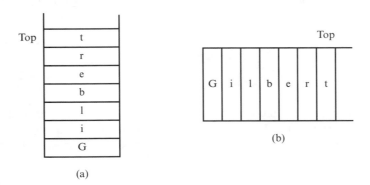

(a)

(b)

Figure 12.2 *Diagrams of stacks.*

- Nodes are arranged in sequence.

- There is one end, the **top**.

- Nodes are added to the **top**.

- Nodes are removed from the **top**.

- The stack cannot be scanned: only the **top** node is visible.[1]

A stack can also be known as a LIFO or Last-In First-Out list.

The Stack Class

We are now in a position to define the stack as a class. Fortunately, Java provides such a class in its util package, with the following methods:

```
Stack
public class Stack extends Vector {
    public Object push (Object item);
    public Object pop () throws EmptyStackException;
    public Object peek () throws EmptyStackException;
    public boolean empty ();
```

The Push method takes the item and pushes it on to the top of the stack. The Pop method returns the top item, 'popping' the stack at the same time, while the Peek procedure returns just the top item, without popping the stack. The Empty method determines whether there are any items on the stack. The Stack class is based on Vector, which means that a stack would be efficiently implemented as an array, but would not be restricted to a specific size.

The stack methods are defined for the superclass Object, so that we can put any other class's objects onto a stack, and remove them, provided we provide the correct type cast. Although Java will not enforce it, we should restrict each stack to items of the same class.

The next example is a simple one, but serves to illustrate the effect of using a stack.

EXAMPLE 12.2   Reversing a sentence

Problem   Reverse a sentence of any length, word by word.

Solution   Stacks have the property that they can be used to reverse a sequence. Each word is put on the stack as it is read. Eventually when the sentence ends, the words will be stacked up, one on top of each other. We can then go through the stack again, popping the words off.

---

[1]Actually Java cheats: it provides a method for seaching through a stack (called search), but we shall ignore it here.

Program

```
import java.io.*;
import javagently.*;
import java.util.Stack;

class Stacker {

  /* Testing the stack class      by J M Bishop  Jan 1997
     Reads a sentence and reverses it using a stack.

     Illustrates push, pop and empty in Java's Stack class.
  */

  public static void main (String args [])
    throws IOException {

    DataInputStream in = new DataInputStream (System.in);

    Stack S = new Stack();
    System.out.println("**** Testing the Stack class ****");
    System.out.println("Type in a sentence and end the input "+
      "(cntrl-D or cntrl-Z)");
    System.out.println("The original sentence is: ");

    while (true) {
      try {
        String word = Text.readString(in);
        S.push(word);
      }
      catch (EOFException e) {break;}
    }

    System.out.println("The reversed sentence is:");
    while (!S.empty())
      System.out.print (S.pop()+" ");
    System.out.println();
  }
}
```

Testing Expected input and output would be:

```
**** Testing the Stack class ****
Type in a sentence and end the input (cntrl-D or cntrl-Z)
The original sentence is:
The curfew tolls the knell of parting day,
The reversed sentence is:
day, parting of knell the tolls curfew The
```

Uses of stacks

Stacks are useful for recording the state of a computation as it unfolds. A typical example is the evaluation of expressions which involve precedence and nesting. A stack is also the data structure that implements recursion. In a language such as Java, it is usually possible to use recursion with its implicit stack rather than an explicit stack. The next data structure is probably more useful in practice.

Queues

Although stacks are the simplest structures we have, their property of reversibility is not always useful. A more common data structure is one where the items can be removed in the same order in which they were inserted. Such a structure is known as a **queue** or FIFO list (First-In First-Out).

In order to implement this property, a queue has to have two ends, indicating the front and back. New items are added on to the back, and items are removed from the front. Queues are usually drawn sideways, as in Figure 12.3(a). However, an innate property of queues is that they move forward: as an item is removed from the front, so all the other items behind it move up one. We can see immediately that such moving in an array implementation would be inefficient, and so we can already consider an alternative depiction of a queue as a circle. Here there is a fixed number of slots in the circle and the queue moves around it, as in Figure 12.3(b).

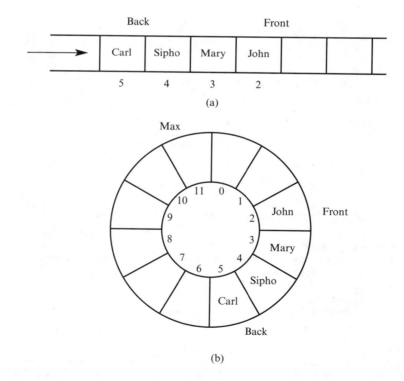

Figure 12.3 *Diagrams of queues.*

Queue properties

Formally, we can detail the properties of a queue as:

1.   Nodes are arranged in sequence.

2.   There are two ends, the **front** and **back**.

3.   Nodes are added to the **front**.

4.   Nodes are removed from the **back**.

5.   The queue can be scanned from the front to the back.

The queue abstract data type

We are now in a position to define the queue as a data type. As for stacks, we define it in terms of the superclass Object. However, Java does not have a predefined queue class, so we need to implement one. On what should it be based? The choices are an array, the Vector class or the List class. The last two will allow the queue to be of variable size. The List is probably more powerful than we need, since we do not need to remove elements anywhere in it, only at the front. Vector provides complete extensibility, but we actually want to control the queue by reusing elements that have been vacated, in a circular manner, as in Figure 12.3(b). In fact, a simple array is a good choice.

What should we do if the queue gets full or if an attempt is made to remove an element when it is empty? The correct response is to throw an exception. This we do, using one exception with a parameter for full or empty. As was done with the Java Stack class, we define Queue based on the Object superclass.

```
Bounded Queue

class Queue {
  Queue(int n);
  void      add (Object x);
  Object    remove ();
  boolean   empty ();
  boolean   full ();

  void      reset ();
  void      succ ();
  boolean   eol ();
  Object    current ();
}
```

A property of a circular queue is that it is bounded, and we can specify the bound in the constructor. In an array implementation, any bound specified would have to be less than the maximum size of the array declared within the queue class itself. The Add method (sometimes known as enqueue) adds an item to the back. Remove takes the item off the front (providing such an item exists). This is sometimes known as dequeue. Empty checks for an empty queue, and full checks if all the spaces allocated to the queue have been used up.

Property 5 above indicated that we should be able to scan the queue, perhaps doing something to each item. For example, we may wish to print the queue out, or search for a particular item. Without more sophisticated language features, it is difficult to generalize the scanning operation. We therefore have to allow the user access to the queue itself. This can be done in a controlled way by insisting that all scanning operations use the four iterator methods, which are the familiar ones defined before for the `List` class.

We now consider an example of the use of the above defnition of a queue, *before* looking at how the queue itself is implemented.

EXAMPLE 12.3 Doctor's waiting room

Problem A doctor has a small waiting room with a small number of chairs – say seven or so. Patients can come in and wait there, but once the seats are full, they tend to go away and come back later. Simulate this behaviour, so that the doctor can decide if it is essential to build a bigger waiting room.

Solution We can set up a queue with a maximum size and randomly let patients arrive and be seen by the doctor. The state of the queue can be continuously displayed and when it is full, a signal can be made, and arrivals ignored until there is space again.

Algorithm We can simulate what is happening with the algorithm of Figure 12.4. There is a 50% chance at each iteration that a patient will arrive (signified by checking whether the dice throw is even) and there is a 30% chance that the doctor will be ready to see another patient (dice is 1 or 2). There is also a 30% chance that nothing will happen (dice is 3 or 5). We run the simulation for a set number of times and watch what happens.

Program The contents of the queue are the same simple integer items we used for the `Stack` example. The class item is taken from that example (12.2), and not repeated here.

Simulation

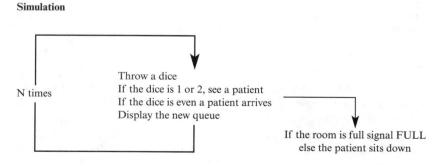

N times

Throw a dice
If the dice is 1 or 2, see a patient
If the dice is even a patient arrives
Display the new queue

If the room is full signal FULL
else the patient sits down

Figure 12.4

```
class WaitingRoom {

  /* Simulation the Waiting Room by      J M Bishop  Jan 1997
     Shows a queue growing and shrinking in response to
     random events.

     Illustrates queues and queue iterators.
  */

  public static void main (String args []) throws QueueException {

    Queue chairs = new Queue (7);
    item patient;
    int choice;

    System.out.println("*** Doctor's Waiting Room Simulation ***");
    System.out.println("There are 7 chairs");
    System.out.println("Arrivals on 2,4,6; patients seen on 1,2");
    System.out.println();
    System.out.println("Time\tChoice\tPatient numbers");

    for (int i = 2; i<30; i++) {
      choice = (int) (Math.random()*6+1);
      System.out.print(i+"\t"+choice+"\t");
      display(chairs);
      try {
        if (choice == 1 || choice == 2)
          if (!chairs.empty())
            patient = (item) chairs.remove();
        if (choice == 2 || choice == 4 || choice == 6)
          chairs.add(new item(i));
      }
      catch (QueueException e) {
        System.out.println("\t\t\tWaiting room "+e.getMessage());
      }
    }
  }

  static void display (Queue q) {
    if (q.empty()) System.out.print("Empty"); else
    for (q.reset(); !q.eol(); q.succ())
      System.out.print(((item)q.current()).data+" ");
    System.out.println();
  }
}
```

Testing   A run could look like this:

```
*** Doctor's Waiting Room Simulation ***
There are 7 chairs
Arrivals on 2,4,6; patients seen on 1,2

Time    Choice    Patient numbers
2       4         Empty
3       3         2
```

4	5	2					
5	3	2					
6	4	2					
7	3	2	6				
8	3	2	6				
9	4	2	6				
10	2	2	6	9			
11	5	6	9	10			
12	6	6	9	10			
13	1	6	9	10	12		
14	4	9	10	12			
15	5	9	10	12	14		
16	4	9	10	12	14		
17	4	9	10	12	14	16	
18	5	9	10	12	14	16	17
19	1	9	10	12	14	16	17
20	5	10	12	14	16	17	
21	1	10	12	14	16	17	
22	5	12	14	16	17		
23	3	12	14	16	17		
24	6	12	14	16	17		
25	4	12	14	16	17	24	
26	6	12	14	16	17	24	25
27	4	12	14	16	17	24	25	26
				Waiting	room	Full	
28	3	12	14	16	17	24	25	26
29	3	12	14	16	17	24	25	26

The room got full only once in this short run, but given the random nature of the 'dice' throwing, completely different runs could be obtained. Notice that when we have a 2, the queue is both added to and removed from in one iteration. This circumstance occurs on lines 10–11.

Queues using arrays

The best array implementation for a queue is a circular one. The back of the queue starts at 0, and gradually moves up to the maximum size. Once there, the next position considered for adding is 0 again, provided a remove has taken place and there is no live data there. Because of this, the conditions for full and empty are not based on whether the indicators are 0 or max, but on a count of the number of live items. The full class definition for a queue is:

```
class Queue {

  /* Queue abstract data type      by J M Bishop  Jan 1997
     Implements a queue as a bounded circular array.
     Has a set maximum of 100 elements. */

  Queue (int m) {
    if (m <= maxQueue) size = m; else size = maxQueue;
    front = 0;
```

```
      back = - 1;
      live = 0;
      reset();
   }


   void add (item x) throws QueueException {
     // throws an exception if the queue is full
     if (live < size) {
       back = (back + 1) % maxQueue;
       Q[back] = x;
       live++;
     }
     else throw new QueueException("Full");
   }

Object remove () throws QueueException {
  // throws an exception if the queue is empty
  if (live >=1) {
    Object x = Q[front];
    front = (front + 1) % maxQueue;
    live--;
    return x;
  }
  else throw new QueueException("Empty");
}

boolean empty () {return live == 0;}
boolean full () {return live == size;}

// Iterator methods
void reset () {now = front;}
void succ () {now = (now+1) % maxQueue;}
boolean eol () {if (back==maxQueue)
                    return now == 0;
                else return now > back;}
Object current () {return Q[now];}

private
int size,          // total vector capactity;
    front, back,   // indicators
    live,          // number of used spaces in the circular queue
    now;           // position for displaying the queue
private Object Q [] = new Object [maxQueue];
static private int maxQueue = 100;


}

class QueueException extends Exception {
  QueueException (String s) {super(s);}
}
```

Notice that all the data items are declared private in the queue, and are instance variables, to be replicated for each object.

Queues using lists

As with stacks, queues cannot be altered except at the ends, so the only advantage of using a list as a base for the queue is to obtain complete flexibility of the size. Notice that we would still provide a border facility, so that a queue can stop growing. The above class definition can be very simply translated into a version based on lists and is left as an exercise for the reader. The `WaitingRoom` program should run without change if the one class is replaced by the other.

12.5   Linked lists again

The list discussed in Chapter 7 was very simple, and had the odd property that by adding new items to the front, it stored data backwards. What we were really creating was a stack – a very neat data structure because it has only one indicator. If we would prefer to store the data in the correct order, then we need two indicators – one for the front and one for the back, as in a queue.

In fact, linked lists can be more general than either a stack or queue and can permit operations to occur not just at the ends, but anywhere in between.

Linked list properties

Formally, we can define the properties of a list as:

- Nodes are linked together linearly in both directions, forwards and backwards.

- There are two ends to the list – the front and the back.

- Nodes can be added anywhere in the list.

- Nodes can be deleted anywhere in the list.

- The list can be scanned forwards or backwards.

The new `List` class

The formal definition of the full-blown `List` class is given below. It gives more control to the programmer, and makes the `Node` class and two indicators visible so that positions within the list can be discovered, retained and used later.

```
List

void      addBefore (Object x, Node pos);
void      addAfter (Object x, Node pos);
Object    remove (Node pos);
Node      search (Comparable x, int comp);
boolean   isempty ();
```

```
Object    current ();
void      reset ();
boolean   eol ();
void      succ ();

Node front, back;
int size;
```

The add method is replaced by addBefore and addAfter. Remove is augmented by a parameter, indicating which node should be removed. A search method based on the linear search of Section 11.2 has been added. It has the option to search either for equality, in which case the constant SAME must be supplied as a second parameter, or for ascending or descending order (LESS and MORE). That is why the item that is being searched for is not an Object, but is of the interface class Comparable. Comparable is defined as follows:

Comparable interface

```
interface Comparable {
   boolean less (Object x);
   boolean same (Object x);
   booelan more (Object x);

   final static int LESS = 0;
   final static int SAME = 1;
   final static int MORE = 2;
}
```

By using Comparable in the List class, we can leave the actual implementation of the comparison methods to the data types themselves. For example, a typical type that could be stored in a list would be:

```
class Student implements Comparable {

   double height;
   String name;

   Student(double h, String s) {
      height = h;
      name = s;
   }

   public boolean same (Object x) {
      return (name == ((Student) x).name);
    }

   public boolean less (Object x) {
      return (height < ((Student) x).height);
   }

   public String toString () {
      return ("\t"+height+"\t"+name);
   }
}
```

The constants are there so that users can select which order they require. If they select SAME and the item is not found, then an ItemNotFoundException is thrown.

A call to List's constructor will initialize the list, setting the front and back indicators to null, and the size to zero. Unlike the other data structures, we allow the user of the object to have access to the list indicators. If we really wanted to protect them, we could make them private and provide equivalent access methods. The class Node is used to indicate a single node in the list. We do not, however, reveal exactly what class this is, and so maintain a degree of protection.

The following example makes excellent use of the new facilities of the List class. It is followed by a look at the implementation of the class.

EXAMPLE 12.4   Photograph line-up

Problem   A photographer is going to photograph a class of students, and wants them neatly arranged by height. The idea is to have the taller people in the back rows, and for each row to slope downward from the centre. Given a class of students and their heights, we would like a plan of where each should stand.

Example   Each row should be lined up as shown in Figure 12.5.

Solution   We start by creating a single line of everyone in height order. Then, starting at the tallest, we peel off however many we want per row, and create a new list starting in the middle and adding alternately to the right and left. Suppose we label the people A, B, ... where A is the tallest. Then a row of seven people would be arranged thus:

    G E C A B D F

Algorithm   The algorithms make very good use of the list methods defined above. First, we consider how to create a list in height order (Figure 12.6). The result will be a list with the front pointing to the tallest person.

Now we consider how to peel off a row and create the left–right effect (Figure 12.7). For ease of computation, we assume that the row will have an odd number of people.

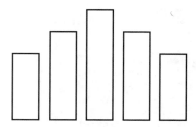

Figure 12.5

Create an ordered list

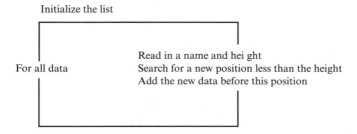

Initialize the list

For all data
                    Read in a name and hei ght
                    Search for a new position less than the height
                    Add the new data before this position

Figure 12.6

Create a left–right sorted list

Initialize the line
Remove the front of the main list
Add it to the line

N/2 times
                    Remove the front of the main list
                    Add it to the back of the line
                    Remove the front of the main list
                    Add it to the front of the line

Figure 12.7

Adding to the back equates to `addAfter(back)` and adding to the front becomes `addBefore(front)`. We can print out or display the line, by calling the iterator methods. Then, we can erase the line and start with a new one. Erasing a list in Java is as simple as setting it to null, as then all the nodes that were associated with it will be garbage collected in a short while.

Program As before, the program is surprisingly clean and short, since all the work is done in the well-defined list methods.

```
import java.io.*;
import javagently.*;
class Photo {

    /* Photo Line Up program      by J M Bishop  Jan 1997
       creates a plan for a photo line up with each
       row of students high-low from the centre.

       Illustrates full featured linked lists. */

    static List studentList = new List();
```

```
static void lineUp () throws IOException, ItemNotFoundException {

    /* create the initial sorted line from the data
       as it is read in from a file */

    DataInputStream in = new DataInputStream (
        new FileInputStream("students.dat"));
    System.out.println("The students as read in are:");
    while (true) {
      try {
        double h = Text.readDouble(in);
        String n = Text.readString(in);
        Student s = new Student (h,n);
        System.out.println(s);
        Node higher = studentList.search(s,Comparable.MORE);
        studentList.addBefore(s,higher);
      }
      catch (EOFException e) {break;}
    }
    System.out.println("The students in height order are:");

    for (studentList.reset(); !studentList.eol();
         studentList.succ())
      System.out.println(studentList.current());
}

public static void pickOff (int row) {
  /* For each row, pick off 7 students and add
     them alternately to the left and right of
     a new list. Print the list, then destroy it. */

  System.out.println("Row "+row+"\t");
  List line = new List ();
  Student s;
  s = (Student) studentList.remove(studentList.front);
  line.addAfter(s,line.back);
  for (int i = 0; i<rowSize/2; i++) {
    s = (Student) studentList.remove(studentList.front);
    line.addAfter(s, line.back);
    s = (Student) studentList.remove(studentList.front);
    line.addBefore(s, line.front);
  }
  for (line.reset(); !line.eol(); line.succ())
    System.out.println(line.current());
  line = null;
}

public static void main (String args [])
        throws IOException, ItemNotFoundException {
  System.out.println("**** The Class Photo ****");
  lineUp();
  for (int row = 1; studentList.size > 0; row++)
    pickOff (row);
}

static final int rowSize = 7;
}
```

Testing   The program would process this and produce the following arrangement:

```
**** The Class Photo ****
The students as read in are:
        1.8     Danie
        1.58    Petra
        1.9     John
        1.55    Harry
        1.81    Mary
        1.75    Craig
        1.71    Sipho
        1.77    Diamond
        1.4     Tiny
        1.79    Michael
        1.76    Robert
        1.69    Elizabeth
        1.68    Lucy
        1.5     Sarah
The students in height order are:
        1.9     John
        1.81    Mary
        1.8     Danie
        1.79    Michael
        1.77    Diamond
        1.76    Robert
        1.75    Craig
        1.71    Sipho
        1.69    Elizabeth
        1.68    Lucy
        1.58    Petra
        1.55    Harry
        1.5     Sarah
        1.4     Tiny
Row 1
        1.75    Craig
        1.77    Diamond
        1.8     Danie
        1.9     John
        1.81    Mary
        1.79    Michael
        1.76    Robert
Row 2
        1.4     Tiny
        1.55    Harry
        1.68    Lucy
        1.71    Sipho
        1.69    Elizabeth
        1.58    Petra
        1.5     Sarah
```

The program has the restriction that the number of students must be a multiple of the row size, but this is a minor detail.

Implementing linked lists

We have assumed that the lists will be implemented using references and the Node class. Since insertion and deletion are allowed anywhere, it would be messy to use an array. We have also committed ourselves to supplying a front and back indicator, and to maintaining the size of the list.

There are still, however, several choices to be made in the implementation. The first issue is whether we go for a **singly-linked list** or a **doubly-linked list**. A singly-linked list will have links going from the front indicator to the last node, where the link will be null. The list's back indicator will refer to the last node. This is shown graphically in Figure 12.8.

The advantage of this implementation is that it uses up the minimum of extra space (one reference per node). However, it is not so easy to insert nodes before another node, and scanning the list backwards will require recursion.

An alternative is to spend an extra reference per node and to link the list in both directions. This gives us Figure 12.9. Doubly-linking a list is the most flexible arrangement, and is not all that difficult to maintain. First of all, we need to augment the Node class with the extra reference:

```
class Node {
  /* The Node class version 2      by J M Bishop  Jan 1997
     for storing objects in doubly linked lists
  */

  Node (Object d, Node f, Node b) {
    data = d;
    forward = f;
    backward = b;
  }

  Node forward, backward;
  Object data;
}
```

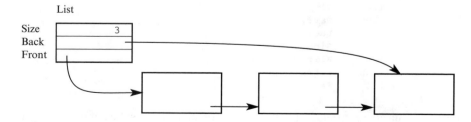

Figure 12.8 *A singly-linked list.*

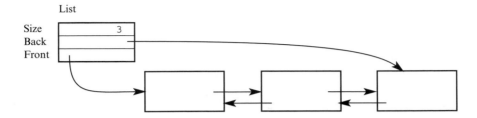

Figure 12.9 *A doubly-linked list.*

The implementation of such a `List` class is:

```
class List {

  /* The List data structure      by J M Bishop  Jan 1997
     Implements a doubly-linked list with
     add, remove, search and iterator facilities. */

  List () {now=null; front=null; back=null; size = 0;}

  void addBefore (Object x, Node pos) {
    if (size == 0) {
      // add to front (special)
      front = new Node (x,null,null);
      back = front;
    }
    else if (pos==null) {
      // add to front
      Node T = new Node (x,null,back);
      back.forward = T;;
      back = T;
    }
    else if (pos==front) {
      // add before front
      Node T = new Node (x,front,null);
      front.backward = T;
      front = T;
    }
    else {
      // add in the middle
      Node T = new Node (x,pos,pos.backward);
      pos.backward.forward = T;
      pos.backward = T;
    }
    size ++;
  }

  void addAfter (Object x, Node pos) {
    if (size == 0) {
      // add to front (special)
      front = new Node (x,null,null);
      back = front;
    }
```

```
    else if ((pos==null)||(pos==back)) {
      // add to back
      Node T = new Node (x,null,back);
      back.forward = T;
      back = T;
    }
     else {
      // add in the middle
      Node T = new Node (x,pos.forward,pos);
      pos.forward.backward = T;
      pos.forward = T;
    }
    size ++;
  }


Object remove (Node pos) {
  Object T = pos.data;
  if (front == back) {
    front = null;
    back = null;
  } else
  if (pos == front) {
    front.forward.backward = null;
    front = front.forward;
  } else
  if (pos == back) {
    back.backward.forward = null;
    back = back.backward;
  } else {
    pos.backward.forward = pos.forward;
    pos.forward.backward = pos.backward;
  }
  size--;
  return T;
}


Node search (Comparable x, int comp) throws ItemNotFoundException {
  if (front == null) return front;
  for (reset(); !eol(); succ())
    switch (comp) {
    case Comparable.LESS :
      if (x.less((Comparable) current())) return now;
      break;
    case Comparable.SAME :
      if (x.same((Comparable) current())) return now;
      break;
    case Comparable.MORE :
      if (!x.less((Comparable) current())) return now;
      break;
    }
  if (comp == Comparable.LESS) return null; else
  if (comp == Comparable.MORE) return null;
  else throw new ItemNotFoundException();
}
```

```
boolean isempty () {return front == null;}

Object current () {return now.data; }
void reset () {now = front;}
boolean eol () {return now == null;}
void succ () {now = now.forward;}

  Node front, back;
  int size;
  private Node now;
}


class ItemNotFoundException extends Exception { }
```

In the `add` and `remove` procedures, we consider four different cases, depending on whether the list is empty or we are dealing with an end, whereupon the front and back pointers need special attention. In the general case, the insertion of a new node before another one, referred to by `pos`, follows the symmetric pattern:

```
newnode.backward = pos.backward;
newnode.forward = pos;
pos.backward.forward = newnode;
pos.backward = newnode;
```

and removal is done by:

```
pos.backward.forward = pos.forward;
pos.forward.backward = pos.backward;
```

12.6   Bit sets

The last data structure that we shall consider in this edition of *Java Gently* is the bit set. As we know from mathematics, a set is an unordered collection of items of the same type on which operations such as union, intersection and membership are defined. A bit set is different in that it is envisaged as a sequence of bits, each of which is known by number and can be turned on and off. Sets and bit sets are very similar in effect, but differ in the way they are used. In a set of integers, one could check whether it contained 8; in a bit set, one would check whether the 8th bit was on.

Some of the methods provided for Java's bit sets are given in the following form:

Bit sets

`BitSet ();`
`BitSet (int n);`
 	
`public boolean` `get (int b);`
`public void` `set (int b);`
`public void` `clear (int b);`

```
public void and (BitSet s);
public void or  (BitSet s);
public void xor (BitSet s);
```

After having created a bit set with a given size or by using the default, we can set, get and clear individual bits. Then we can also combine two sets using the three operations shown. For an explanation of the results of bit operations, go back to Section 3.2 on Booleans.

Bit sets are fairly restrictive in that they can record only integer numbers. That is, we cannot have sets of characters, for example. We can now consider an example of the use of sets, in fact of arrays of bit sets in this case.

EXAMPLE 12.5 Training schedules

Problem   Employees at Savanna Inc. attend training courses, and a record of each course attended or planned to attend is kept on a file. We wish to discover which employees are signed up for which courses, and which courses overall have been used. We would also like to know which employees need computer user codes, given a list of courses that will be using the computer.

Solution   One could construct arrays with the name of each employee who has done a course. Alternatively, if both the employees and courses are identified by number, then sets can be used.

Algorithm   Assume that the data has employee numbers followed by a list of course numbers. A typical file would look like this:

```
50      1 2 3
44      3 8 7
99      1
61      1 7
```

meaning that employee 50 is meant to attend courses 1, 2 and 3; employee 99 is meant to attend 1 only, and so on. We need to keep a set of employee numbers for each course, and a set of all courses taken. This is done with the data structures:

```
static BitSet courses [];
static BitSet schedules [];
```

The algorithm then consists of reading in a number followed by its courses. For each course, we add the employee number to the set in the `courses` array indexed by that course. Then we also add the course to the employee's record in the `schedules` array. The important statements are:

```
// Put employee n on course c
   courses[c].set(n);
```

```
// Put course c in employee n's schedule
    schedules [n].set(c);
```

Before we can set bits in a bit set, though, we must take care that the object has been created. For example, creating a new course set would be done like this:

```
// Create course c if not yet started
    if (courses[c] == null)
        courses[c] = new BitSet (employeeMax);
```

Program   The program is arranged in three sections, each its own method, namely: readIn, display and userCodes. One aspect of this program, unrelated to bit sets, is how to read data which has a terminator such as the end of a line. The Text class will not work in this case because it is oblivious to ends of line. Never mind: by now we are able to write our own input routines, picking off numbers from a StringTokenizer as we want them.

Reading in starts by getting a whole line, then tokenizing it and counting the number of tokens (using a predefined method). After getting the employee number, a for-loop can be used to process each course as described above.

```
static void readIn () throws IOException {
    // Uses its own StringTokenizer since data is read a line
    // at a time. A blank line signifies zero tokens and
    // ends the reading of data.

    String s;
    StringTokenizer T;
    int n, c, ntokens;

    while(true) {
      s = in.readLine();
      T = new StringTokenizer (s);
      ntokens = T.countTokens ();
      if (ntokens == 0) break; // no more employees
      n = getInt(T);

      //Create a schedule for employee n
      schedules [n] = new BitSet (courseMax);
      for (int i=0; i<ntokens-1; i++) {
        c = getInt(T);

        // Create course c if not yet started
        if (courses[c] == null)
          courses[c] = new BitSet (employeeMax);

        // Put employee n on course c
        courses[c].set(n);

        // Put course c in employee n's schedule
        schedules [n].set(c);
      }
```

```
      }
      System.out.println("Data read in successfully.");
   }
```

Getting in the list of courses that use the computer follows a similar pattern, and the students enrolled for that course are added into another bit set as follows:

```
codesNeeded.or(courses[c]);
```

The rest of the program is concerned with printing out the sets neatly.

```
import java.util.*;
import java.io.*;
import javagently.*;

class Training {

   /* Training schedules program        by J M Bishop Jan 1997

      Creates class lists and schedules for employees,
      including a list of those who are taking special courses.

      Uses bit sets and its own StringTokenizers rather than
      javagently's Text class.
   */

   static BitSet courses [];
   static BitSet schedules [];
   static DataInputStream in = new DataInputStream (System.in);
   static int employeeMax, courseMax;

   public static void main (String arg []) throws IOException {

      // The main program declares two arrays of sets and then
      // calls the three static methods to read and print out
      // the data.

      System.out.println ("*** Training Schedules ****");
      Text.prompt("What is the highest course number?");
      courseMax = Text.readInt(in);
      Text.prompt("What is the highest employee number?");
      employeeMax = Text.readInt(in);

      // Create an array of sets, one for each course
      // Each set will be EmployeeMax big
      // but is created later as the data is read in
      courses = new BitSet [courseMax];

      // Create an array of sets, one for each employee
      // Each set will be CourseMax big
      // but is created later as the data is read in
      schedules = new BitSet [employeeMax];
```

```
        System.out.println("Enter each employee's schedule as follows:");
        System.out.println("Employee number course numbers");
        System.out.println("Example 100 12 7 4 15");
        System.out.println("End with a blank line");

        readIn();
        display();
        userCodes();
    }

static void readIn () throws IOException {
  … as shown above
}

static void display () {
  // prints each of the set arrays slightly differently.
  // calls printSet for printing a single set

  System.out.println("The course lists");
  System.out.println("================");
  for (int c =0; c<courseMax; c++) {
    System.out.print(c+": ");
    if (courses[c]==null) System.out.println("No students");
    else
      printSet(courses[c]);
  }
  System.out.println("The schedules");
  System.out.println("=============");
  for (int n = 0; n < employeeMax; n++) {
    if (schedules[n] != null) {
      System.out.print(n+": ");
      printSet(schedules[n]);
    }
  }
}

static void userCodes () throws IOException {
  // A method to illustrate a bit set operation.
  // given a subset of the course numbers,
  // create the union (or) of all the employees
  // signed up for them and print that set.

  Text.prompt("Which are the computer-related courses?");
  BitSet codesNeeded = new BitSet(employeeMax);

  String s;
  StringTokenizer T;
  int c, ntokens;

  s = in.readLine();
  T = new StringTokenizer (s);
  ntokens = T.countTokens ();
  for (int i=0; i<ntokens; i++) {
    c = getInt(T);
    codesNeeded.or(courses[c]);
  }
```

```
    System.out.println("Employees needing usercodes");
    System.out.println("============================");
    printSet(codesNeeded);
    }

    static void printSet (BitSet b) {
      // Prints the members of a single bit set

      for (int i = 0; i < b.size(); i++)
        if (b.get(i)) System.out.print(i+" ");
      System.out.println();
    }

    static int getInt (StringTokenizer T) {
      String item = T.nextToken();
      return Integer.valueOf (item.trim()).intValue();
    }
  }
```

Testing

A sample run would give:

```
*** Training Schedules ****
What is the highest course number? 10
What is the highest employee number? 100
Enter each employee's schedule as follows:
Employee number course numbers
Example 100 12 7 4 15
End with a blank line
50 1 2 3
44 3 8 7
99 1
61 1 7

Data read in successfully.
The course lists
================
0: No students
1: 50 61 99
2: 50
3: 44 50
4: No students
5: No students
6: No students
7: 44 61
8: 44
9: No students
The schedules
=============
44: 3 7 8
50: 1 2 3
61: 1 7
99: 1
```

Which are the computer-related courses? 2 3
Employees needing usercodes
============================
44 50

SUMMARY

This quick tour through algorithms and data structures emphasized that there is always more than one way of approaching the solution to a problem. In sorting and searching, we had linear or binary methods (with vastly differing performances). Recursion was also introduced as a means of expressing solutions in a simple and elegant way.

In data structures, we can implement via arrays or linked lists, with different effects. However, what we did manage to achieve is a defined set of properties for each data structure, which are adhered to no matter what the implementation chosen.

Four data structures were discussed – stacks, queues, linked lists and bit sets. The two Java-implemented ones – stacks and bit sets – served as guides for the definition of the other two. In the examples associated with illustrating the data structures, some of the lesser-used Java features cropped up again: interfaces, tokenizers and user-defined exceptions.

QUIZ

12.1 If the linear search in Section 12.2 was to be used to search an array of integers, what line would you change?

12.2 Give the phases that would be printed by the animated binary search looking for 35 in the following list of numbers:

8 17 25 35 41 52 60 75

If 86 was added as the last number, how many comparisons would it take to find 35?

12.3 Under what condition is binary search always faster than linear search?

12.4 If we pushed the numbers one to ten onto two stacks, S1 and S2 alternately, and then took all of S1 followed by all of S2 off, what would be printed out? The code is:

```
Stack S1 = new Stack(5);
Stack S2 = new Stack(6);

for (int i = 1; i<=10; i+=2) {
  S1.push(i);
  S2.push(i+1);
}
while (!S1.empty())
  System.out.print(S1.pop()+" ");

while (!S2.empty())
  System.out.print(S2.pop()+" ");
```

12.5 In the doctor's waiting room example (12.3), assume that each time period is 15 minutes. In the run shown here, how long has the first patient in the queue been waiting when the simulation ends?

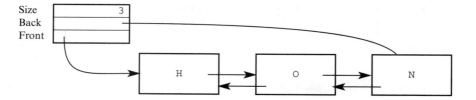

Figure 12.10

12.6   Given a list defined as

```
List L = new List ();
```

write a call to the search method of the `List` class to check whether the object C is in the list or not, and to print out the result.

12.7   Given the doubly linked list shown in Figure 12.10, show all the statements that would be executed to add a node containing W after the O, making HOWN.

12.8   Show the steps to then add a node containing S before the front of the list, making SHOWN.

12.9   Give a definition of a new bit set that will keep track of all courses taken by anyone in the Training Schedules Example 12.5.

12.10 Write the statement that can be added to the `readIn` method to update the set of all courses each time a student's particulars have been processed.

PROBLEMS

12.1   **Speedier concordance**. How could the concordance of Problem 6.7 be speeded up with faster sorting and searching?

12.2   **Stack spy**. Suppose we wanted to print out the contents of a stack, without destroying them, and without using anything other than push and pop operations. Write a program to do this.

12.3   **Waiting statistics**. It is clear that some patients in Example 12.3 could wait a long time before being seen by the doctor. At each display, compute the total time waited by all the patients in the queue and print this out on the right hand side.

12.4   **Queues with lists**. Implement a queue class based on linked lists. Could it be done by inheriting from the new `List` class?

12.5   **Palindrome with a stack**. Solve the palindrome problem (6.6) using a stack rather than an array.

12.6   **Winning a raffle**. At a party, everyone is given a numbered raffle ticket. After supper, a number is drawn and the person with the number wins the prize, and so does that person's family. Write a program to read in people in families into lists, to organize a draw, and to print out the winning person and his/her family.

12.7   **Sorting lists**. Linked lists can be sorted as follows: Create a new list of the same kind. Add each element into it with a LESS or MORE comparison as required. Then the new list is a sorted version of the old. Add such a sort method to the `List` class and test that it works.

12.8 **Electronic diary**. Students at Savanna University have to undertake a group project in their third year. The number of groups and the number of students in a group varies from year to year. One of the difficult tasks at the beginning of the year is establishing when members of a particular group can meet and discuss their project, since they may be taking different courses and have different timetables. They would like to get computer assistance in arranging meetings. Making use of bit sets and linked lists to set up such an electronic diary program.

Answers to quizzes

Chapter 1

1.1 A compiler translates a program written in a human-readable computer language into a computer-executable machine language.

1.2 A compilation error occurs if the language is used incorrectly, e.g. with incorrect spelling or grammar. A logic error results from a program that is asked to perform an invalid action, such as division by zero, or to take a sequence of steps that do not produce the desired result.

1.3 Clock speeds are going up all the time, but you could have a 150 megaHertz processor.

1.4 Computers running Java would start at 24 megabytes.

1.5 Removable diskettes are fairly standard at 1.44 Mbytes. Hard disk drives start from 1 gigabyte upwards.

1.6 This textbook certainly fits on a 1.44 Mbyte diskette on my computer.

Chapter 2

2.1 The call for a completely symmetrically placed circle may need slightly different pixel coordinates on different computers. The following works on a Sun:

```
g.setColor (Color.blue);
g.drawOval (20,30,260,260);
```

2.2 `Tree marula = new Tree ();`

2.3 Instance variables, because we need a name for each instance of a tree.

2.4

```
System.out.println
("————————————\n" +
"|    Jane Bramley    |\n" +
"| 104 Cane Street |\n" +
"|      Freetown      |\n" +
"————————————");

System.out.println ("-------------------");
System.out.println ("|   Jane Bramley   |");
System.out.println ("| 104 Cane Street |");
System.out.println ("|     Freetown     |");
System.out.println ("-------------------");
```

In the first example, the five lines of the address would not fit on one program line, and so will need to be split into separate strings, concatenated together.

2.5   2
900009
64
3
100
1

2.6   x = Math.sqrt ((b*b–4*a*c)/(2*a))

2.7   1908 April 12

2.8

```
int distance;
double flour;
int age;
int minutes;
double balance;
```

2.9
main	method
final	keyword
System	class
newArrive	variable
NewFleet	class
out	object
Math	class
class	keyword
println	method
round	method
100	constant
arrive	variable

2.10

```
quiz2.java:3: Identifier expected.
max = 10;
    ^
```

```
quiz2.java:5: Identifier expected.
   double K =1,1000;
                ^

quiz2.java:7: Identifier expected.
  static int 2ndPrize = G25;
               ^

quiz2.java:7: Invalid character in number.
  static int 2ndPrize = G25;
                    ^

quiz2.java:9: Duplicate variable declaration: double x was double x
  static double x = 6;
                 ^

5 errors
```

Line 2 did not have a type. Line 4 used a comma instead of a full stop in a number. Two reasons for rejecting an identifier starting with a digit caused line 6 to fail. Line 8 redefined the variable x.

Chapter 3

3.1   None.

3.2   The output from the loops as given would be:

```
1
2
3
4
1
2
3
4
+
        for (int number=1; number < 6; number++) {
          System.out.print(number);
          for (int sign = 0; sign < number; sign++)
            System.out.print("=");
          System.out.println('+');
        }
1=+
2==+
3===+
4====+
5=====+
```

3.3   First of all, calculate the number of characters in your name. Subtract from 80, divide by 2, and print that many spaces before the name, using a loop.

```
String name = "John Smith";
int chars = 10;
for (int i = 0; i < (80-chars)/2; i++)
  System.out.print(" ");
System.out.println(name);
```

Later on we shall cover how to find out the length of a string without counting it ourselves.

3.4

```
for (int century = 1900; century < 2000; century +=10)
  System.out.print(century+" ");
System.out.println();
```

3.5

```
boolean scoreok, mathsok, csok, qualified;
scoreok = score >= 20;
mathsok = maths >= 'C';
csok = cs >= 'D'
mathsok = mathsok or (maths >= 'D' and csok);
qualified = scoreok and mathsok;
```

3.6

```
Tickets blank ('=', '|', 7, 15);
varyBox (' ');
```

3.7 The reason for declaring `price` as a character is quite convoluted. Start at the last method called, namely `aLine`. It has three parameters, and the middle one is called `centre`. When `aLine` is called for the top and bottom lines of a ticket, the character in `hori` is supplied as the actual parameter. `hori` is initialized in the constructor, and is usually '=' or '-'. Thus if `hori` is a character, so must `centre` be, and therefore so must `price` be a character. In terms of what is printed out, it would not matter whether `price` is character or integer, but the former makes more sense, as well as being compatible with the rest of the class.

3.8

```
taxrate -= 0.5;
```

3.9

```
mountain (0, 0)      invalid because second parameter must be char
mountain (8,'8')     fine
mountain (6)         invalid because only one parameter
```

3.10 No, because `aLine` has been declared as private.

Chapter 4

4.1 Firstly, there are no braces around the three statements involved in the swap, so that copying x into `temp` is the only statement that depends on the `if`. The others are

done in either case. Secondly, once x has been changed via x=y, it is no use to say
y=x if we want the old value of x. The corrected version is:

```
if (x > y) {
  int temp = x;
  x = y;
  y = temp;
}
```

4.2

```
DataInputStream marksIn = new DataInputStream
    (new FileInputStream ("marks"));
```

4.3 It will print out

Error in number. Try again.

4.4 4 10 9 8   7 or
    4   7 8 9 10

4.5 EOFException could occur while reading (it will get thrown on by the Text
class) and DivideByZeroException could occur during the division.

4.6 The readString method of the Text class expects words to end with white
space, i.e. a blank or end of line or tab. Therefore a call to read a country name will
only give United, unless we fool readString by joining the two words some-
how.

4.7 Unix uses control-D. Windows uses control-Z.

4.8

569833

Ha! Remember to put explicit strings of a couple of spaces, or a string containing
a tab escape character, between numbers when they are written in one println
call. Thus the following would be better:

```
System.out.println(i+"  "+j+"  "+k);
```

4.9 pre can have only one of the values listed. So once it has been established which
it is, checking for the others can be skipped. The answer is to put in else-parts or
even better to use a switch-statement as discussed in the next chapter.

```
if      (pre == 'm') System.out.print("milli");
else if (pre == 'c') System.out.print("centi");
else if (pre == 'K') System.out.print("kilo");
System.out.println("metre");
```

4.10 We would have to separate the numbers and the units, as in 65 kg and 7 and then
read the number followed by the string. readString will read everything after

the number, including the space. If we do not want the space, we can trim the string as follows:

```
n = Text.readInt (in);
unit = Text.readString(in).trim();
```

Chapter 5

5.1 The last one looks like it may be different but in fact it relies on the default value of ch to get it going. Thereafter it works the same as the others.

5.2

```
switch (i) {
  case 0: System.out.println("Sunday"); break;
  case 1: System.out.println("Monday"); break;
  case 2: System.out.println("Tuesday"); break;
  case 3: System.out.println("Wednesday"); break;
  case 4: System.out.println("Thursday"); break;
  case 5: System.out.println("Friday"); break;
  case 6: System.out.println("Saturday"); break;
}
```

5.3 In every case we need an impossible value. For ages, maybe 999 or −1. For air temperatures in celsius, 999 would also work. For years, we really cannot predict a finishing year, so −1 would be best.

5.4 Over to you!

5.5 If the value is not specified, none of the cases is executed, and the switch 'drops through' to the next statement.

5.6

```
while (true)
```

5.7 The do-try will enable an exception to the operation to be caught and handled, and then the loop can repeat again.

5.8

```
int n = 0;
while (n<=20) {
  System.out.print(n+" ");
  n+=2;
}
```

5.9

5.10 The calling statement would become:

```
if (mygame.getYourChoice(in)) break;
```

Chapter 6

6.1

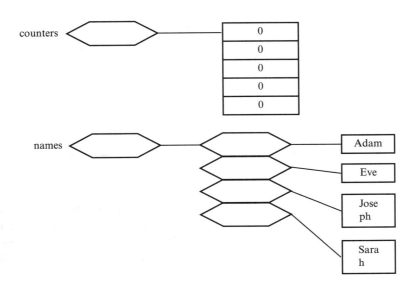

6.2

```
for (int i = 0; i<3; i++)
  System.out.println(names[i]+" e at "+names[i].indexOf('e'));
```

6.3 Its own class, which is `Judge`, gives it a length in the constructor, i.e.

```
score = new int [noofJudges];
```

6.4 The declaration of A should include an array indication, i.e.

```
int A [] = new A[10];
```

Then `A.length` returns 10, but the last index for A is 9, so `A[A.length]` does not exist.

6.5 Yes.

```
monthlyAverage (B, 100);
```

6.6

```
exchangeRates.put ("yen", new Double (167.9));
Double rate = (Double) exchangeRates.get("yen");
System.out.println(rate.doubleValue());
```

6.7 1.

6.8 `java.util`

6.9 The last line returns an `Object` which has to be converted into a `Date` before it can be assigned. The correct line is:

```
Dates d = (Dates) holidays.get ("Foundation Day");
```

6.10 pop

Chapter 7

7.1 name is declared as private.

7.2 Yes. In the `CoffeeShop` method, a new object is created for each new coffee, referred to by an array item `C[blend]`. If we pass this reference to a class method `prepareToStock` in the `Coffee` class, then its data items can be accessed and updated, even though the reference itself will not be changed. The `prepareToStock` method would become:

```
static void prepareToStock (DataInputStream in, Coffee c)
  throws IOException {
  c.name = Text.readString(in);
  // and so on, using c. to access each member
c.newBatchIn(in);
```

7.3   The reference to `display` inside `sell` refers to the `display` method visible at the time, i.e. `Coffee`'s one. b is a batch, so that inside `display` itself, the reference to `b.display()` is to the `display` method of the `Batch` class.

7.4

```
public Object clone () {
  // clones a Coffee object
  Coffee c = new Coffee ( );
  c.name = new String (name);
  c.price = price;
  c.stock = stock;
  c.reorder = reorder;
  c.BatchStock = BatchStock.clone ();
  return c;
}
```

Of course, the `List` class does not have a clone method, and so one will have to be created before the above will compile.

7.5

```
public Object clone () {
  // clones a Date object via its string representation
  String s = new String (this.toString());
  Date d = new Date (Date.parse(s));
  return d;
}
```

7.6

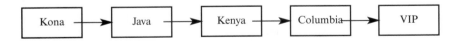

7.7   The 90 kg of the Thu Jan 16 1997 batch would be sold first, then 10 kg from the Feb 05 batch to complete the sale. 2 kg would be left.

7.8   Comparing s to `null` with == does not tell us whether s is an empty string or not. It tells us whether s is a null object or not.

7.9   To find out if s is the empty string, we must use

```
System.out.println("s is an empty string is " + s.equals(""));
```

7.10 The class diagram for the Coffee class is

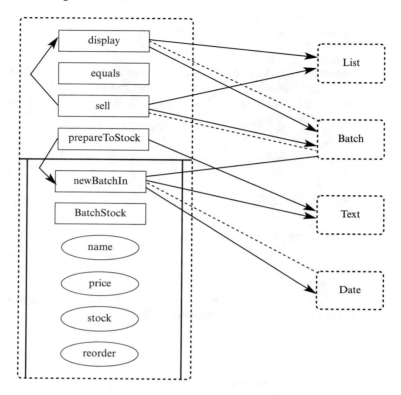

Chapter 8

8.1

```
class Giraffe extends Herbivores {
   Giraffe (String n, int w, double k) {
      name = n;
      grassneeded = w;
      neck = k;
   }
   private double neck; // its length
   // and more about giraffes
}
```

8.2 car must implement at least the five methods defined in the Movable interface.

8.3 Sortable

8.4
```
public boolean lessThan (Sortable a) {
  Giraffe g = (Giraffe) a;
  return (neck < g.neck);
}
```

8.5   No. There is only one constructor for Elephant and it needs three parameters.

8.6

8.7   In the XTags class, the previous version of toString, defined in the inherited class Tags, is overridden.

8.8   Depending on whether the object stored in register[i] is a Tag or an XTag, different versions of toString (as explained in 8.7 above) will be called. The one returns a string made up of two values, the other a string made up of three values.

8.9   checkTag is a static method in the main Vet2 class. The whole method is bracketed by a try-catch pair. In the try-part, a lost pet's name is read in. If instead a control-D or control-Z (signalling end of data) is typed, the catch-part is executed. It throws the EOFException back at the caller, which is the main method.

8.10   a = n; cannot assign an object of a superclass without a cast. Needs

        a = (Animals) n

e = r; e and r are not related by inheritance.

Chapter 9

9.1   Component is an abstract class and therefore cannot be directly instantiated as an object.

9.2
```
p.add (new Label ("Name"));
Textfield name = new TextField("", 40);
```

9.3   BorderLayout

9.4
```
Choice c = new Choice ();
c.addItem ("Monday");
c.addItem ("Tuesday");
```

```
c.addItem ("Wednesday");
c.addItem ("Thursday");
c.addItem ("Friday");
c.addItem ("Saturday");
c.addItem ("Sunday");
```

9.5 It will colour the field in on the screen (from white to light grey usually) and data cannot be entered into it until a `setEditable(true)` is called.

9.6

```
double getDouble (Textfield t) {
  return (double) Integer.valueOf
    (t.getText().trim()).intValue();
}

// called by

kg = getDouble (weighfield);
```

9.7 Adding three more products is simple: there are three gaps at the end of the `items` and corresponding `unitcosts` arrays. If we add more than three more items to these arrays (which can be done without formality) these will not be displayed unless we increase the arrangement of the grid of buttons as well. This is set up in Till's constructor, which at the moment refers to 12 buttons precisely. It could be altered to refer to `items.length` as the ending for the for-loop. We may then also need to increase the height of the frame, as set out in the main program.

9.8 The way to do this is to use `fillOval` for each ring, rather than `drawOval`. This produces a solid circle of a particular colour. Follow such a call with one in the background colour which starts say three pixels in from the original, and has a correspondingly smaller size. Experiment yourself to get the right calls.

9.9 The sequence which handles the pressing of the WEIGH button would become:

```
if (arg.equals ("WEIGH")) {
  weightField.setText("");
    if chosen
      weighField.setEditable(true);
}
```

9.10 `p` is a panel declared as part of the frame that `ButtonTest` extends. We add the `Reboot` button to this panel, then add the panel to the `South` of the frame. The second `add` refers to the current object which is the frame itself.

Chapter 10

10.1 `drawString`

10.2 The applet takes over the function of setting up the program and its size.

10.3 A constructor.

10.4

```
<APPLET code="Orange.class" width=200 height=200>
</APPLET>
```

10.5   `getCodeBase` finds out where the applet came from so that it can fetch other information from the same source.

10.6   .gif and .jpg

10.7   `getAppletContext` finds out where the applet is running so that the applet can perform operations on that machine. An example is writing in the status bar.

10.8

```
String s = getParameter ("yenexchange");
double yen = Double.parseDouble(s);
```

10.9   The `paint` method is called. It has new coordinates for the duke, who therefore seems to have moved.

10.10   images

Chapter 11

11.1

```
Image e = getImage(getCodeBase(), "elephant.jpg");
g.drawImage (e,0,0,this);
```

11.2

```
a                       any classextended from Frame and Component
b                       class Image
ImageProducer           is an interface
imagename               class URL
```

11.3

```
T x = new T();
```

11.4   `start` does indeed call `run`.

11.5   No, only those methods that access data items at potentially the same time as other methods must be declared as synchronized.

11.6   Counter 1 asked for four Walkmen at time 7. It only got them at time 26.

11.7   Yes.

11.8   A handler that detects a SHUTDOWN message, calls the `closeDown` method in the server. This causes the Boolean `done` to be set to true. However, the server will not detect that `done` is true until it comes around the loop to start a new client. So it needs another new client to start up before it can shut down! It is, however, polite enough to keep going with this new client until they both close together.

11.9

```
class picture extends Thread {

  private Canvas a;

  picture (Canvas a) {
    area = a;
  }

  public void paint (Canvas a) {
    Graphics g = area.getGraphics ();
    g.drawImage (i, 50, 50, this);
  }
}
```

11.10 The Curator could call the `replace` method in the Museum class. This would
have the effect of adding more Walkmen, but it would also take money out of the
till, which is not what would be intended. A version of replace is needed which adds
Walkmen but does not affect the deposits.

Chapter 12

12.1   The if-return statement would become

```
if (x == a[i]) return i;
```

12.2

2	5	7	8	10	13	16	20
					10	13	16	20
					10	13
					10

12.3   If the item being sought is not present, binary search will detect this fact in $\log_2 n$
probes, whereas linear search will require the full n.

12.4   The stacks after the pushing part look like this:

```
S1    1 3 5 7 9
S2    2 4 6 8 10
```

The resulting printout is:

9 7 5 3 1 10 8 6 4 2

12.5   Patient numbered 12 was added to the queue at time 12. At time 29 he or she had
been in the waiting room for (29–12+1)*2 minutes, i.e. 36 minutes.

12.6

```
try {
  // X will be the place in the list where C is found
  Object X = L.search(C,Comparable.SAME);
  System.out.println("C is in the list");
```

```
  }
catch (ItemNotFoundException) {
  System.out.println("C is not in the list");
}
```

12.7   The question is not well specified. First of all, we assume that `Wobj`, `Oobj` and so on are the names of objects with the corresponding data (separate to the copies in the list). Then we have to find the position of O. This can be done with:

```
try {
  // Opos will be the place in the list where O is found
  Object Opos = L.search(Oobj,Comparable.SAME);
}
catch (ItemNotFoundException) {
  System.out.println("O is not in the list");
}
```

Now we call

```
L.addAfter (Wobj, Opos);
```

Inside `addAfter` the following statements are executed:

```
if (size == 0)
else if ((Opos==null)
else {
Node T = new Node (W,Opos.forward,Opos)
Opos.forward.backward = T
Opos.forward = T
```

12.8   The call would be

```
L.addBefore (Sobj, Hobj);
```

Inside `addBefore` the following statements would be executed:

```
if (size == 0)
else if (Hpos == null)
else if (Hpos == front)
Node T = new Node (Sobj, front, null)
front.backward = T
front = T;
```

12.9

```
allcourses = new BitSet (courseMax);
```

12.10

```
allcourses.set(c);
```

Index